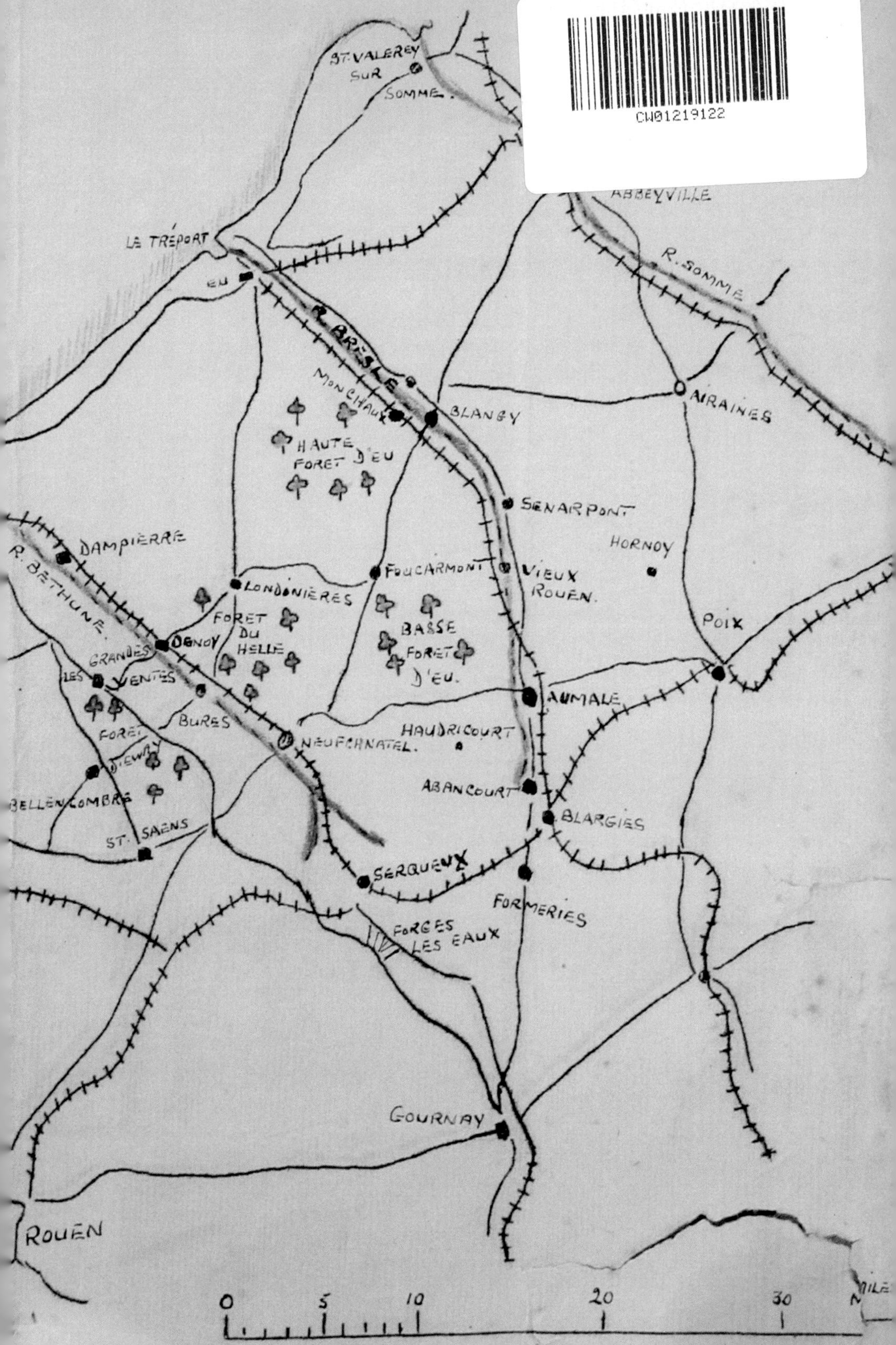

ST. VALEREY SUR SOMME.
LE TRÉPORT
EU
R. BRESLE
MONCHAUX
BLANGY
ABBEVILLE
R. SOMME
AIRAINES
HAUTE FORET D'EU
SENARPONT
HORNOY
DAMPIERRE
R. BETHUNE
LONDONIÈRES
FOUCARMONT
VIEUX ROUEN.
FORET DU HELLE
BASSE FORET D'EU.
POIX
GRANDES
LES VENTES
DENOY
AUMALE
BURES
HAUDRICOURT
NEUFCHATEL.
FORET D'EWAY
BELLENCOMBRE
ABANCOURT
BLARGIES
ST. SAENS
SERQUEUX
FORMERIES
FORGES LES EAUX
GOURNAY
ROUEN
0
5
10
20
30
MILES

FROM A HARD PLACE TO A ROCK

FROM A HARD PLACE TO A ROCK

FIRST-HAND ACCOUNTS OF SOLDIERS
OF THE BRITISH EXPEDITIONARY FORCE
ON THE RUN IN WORLD WAR TWO

TIMANDRA SLADE

Copyright © 2022 Timandra Slade

The moral right of the author has been asserted.

Apart from any fair dealing for the purposes of research or private study, or criticism or review, as permitted under the Copyright, Designs and Patents Act 1988, this publication may only be reproduced, stored or transmitted, in any form or by any means, with the prior permission in writing of the publishers, or in the case of reprographic reproduction in accordance with the terms of licences issued by the Copyright Licensing Agency. Enquiries concerning reproduction outside those terms should be sent to the publishers.

Matador
Unit E2 Airfield Business Park,
Harrison Road, Market Harborough,
Leicestershire. LE16 7UL
Tel: 0116 2792299
Email: books@troubador.co.uk
Web: www.troubador.co.uk/matador
Twitter: @matadorbooks

ISBN 978 1803131 924

British Library Cataloguing in Publication Data.
A catalogue record for this book is available from the British Library.

Printed and bound by CPI Group (UK) Ltd, Croydon, CR0 4YY
Typeset in 11pt Minion Pro by Troubador Publishing Ltd, Leicester, UK

Matador is an imprint of Troubador Publishing Ltd

Dedicated to the memory of

Lieutenant Colonel C D Waters MA OBE
Royal Engineers

Major J D Lennon MC CBE ARIBA
Royal Engineers

Colonel J R Johnson DSO OBE MC
Royal Welch Fusiliers

Captain H R Trythall MC
Royal Regiment of Artillery

Also

to all the other escapees and evaders mentioned within these pages and to those who offered them food and shelter en route.

Nor must we forget those who were less fortunate in finding an opportunity to escape spending the remainder of the war in captivity.

I remember Jimmy Johnson in later life, bowed but never broken. In 1997 he came with other veterans to the dedication of the memorial at St-Venant, where he had been wounded and captured in 1940. I thought then that whenever I and my generation considered we had had a tough time on operations, even in Iraq and Afghanistan, we had seen nothing compared to what Jimmy and his contemporaries went through. This book is a vivid and at times humbling reminder of just what those men did – it was courage like theirs that brought our country through the war and to the defeat of Germany and Japan.

Lieutenant-General Jonathon Riley CB DSO
Late Colonel, The Royal Welch Fusiliers

In this tale of courage and determination, four remarkable soldiers of the British Expeditionary Force escape their German captors. Running the gauntlet of French and Spanish authorities who are treading a thin line of neutrality, they make their way across war-torn Europe to Gibraltar and so to England. The men's first-hand accounts provide the reader with rich personal insights into wartime conditions. Told with good humour and in a spirit of old-fashioned British ingenuity, the escapees ultimately prevail against extraordinary dangers as they blaze a path to freedom, but not until events throw them one last cruel twist of fate.

The story of brave men and remarkable World War Two 'home runs'. And a decade later, one of these chaps was to become my commanding officer in Jamaica.

William 'Bill' Roache OBE
Actor, Captain (retired) RWF

Jimmy Johnson's daughter Sara was a chum of mine. We shared a flat in London. On our visits to the family home in Tingewick for weekends, Jimmy was invariably hospitable, funny and unflappable but underneath you could detect the steel will that had barred him from settling for life in a PoW camp. Nothing would stop him getting home to his beloved wife Diana and to his regiment so he could get back into the war. Sara was immensely proud of her father's epic escape, accomplished in spite of his near-fatal injuries.

This book is an affectionate and thoroughly researched tribute to a small band of brave and determined men. It's important for their story to be told.

Chris Serle
Writer-broadcaster and family friend

A sparkling but detailed account of four brave soldiers of the BEF and those who helped and travelled with them through war-torn France and Spain, demonstrating the courage, determination and ingenuity of men anxious to return home.

This will be of interest to the general reader as well as the military historian and add a further chapter to the distinguished history of the Corps of Royal Engineers, a regiment in which I was proud to serve.

The Right Hon the Lord Lancaster of Kimbolton TD PC

Stepping out with my father Chris c1960 [Author's collection]

MY INSPIRATIONS

My father, Chris Waters, died when I was barely a teenager. Like many soldiers he spoke very little about his experiences in World War Two, although he did share a few snippets if we found ourselves passing through a town or village in which he had been billeted. Following his death, my mother either could not or would not answer my questions. Hence I knew very little about him. Uncle Jimmy, his first cousin, had been appointed my guardian. I would spend Christmas and summer holidays at the Johnson family home in the Buckinghamshire village of Tingewick listening to Jimmy's own experiences. He had led an extraordinary life giving him a wealth of stories, including dancing with Ava Gardner, which he would bring to life after family meals round the lovely large ex-army mess table. He would tell me as much as he could about Dad, with one of my favourite stories being the visit my beaming father, carrying a paper bag full of grapes, had paid to Jimmy whilst the latter was temporarily incarcerated in a prison in Figueras, southern Spain. It was not until after my mother's death in 2016 that I began to piece together more of my father's military life and learn about the events that led to the prison visit.

Clearing out Mum's house I found hidden at the back of a wardrobe a briefcase containing Dad's papers and photographs. It included a roadmap of France and Spain marking a journey my parents had made by caravan over the winter of 1968/69 and a manuscript detailing Dad's wartime escape. Looking at the two I realised they had been retracing his escape route. Although I joined them in Spain over the school Christmas holidays, the only reference I recall being made to my father's escape was when Figueras in Spain was again unkind to him, issuing a traffic ticket for some driving offence. However I was soon to uncover the full story and the background to an extraordinary family coincidence that occurred after the fall of France in 1940.

The briefcase also had Dad's address book which included an address for his escape partner, Dennis Lennon. By good fortune two of his sons were still living at the same property: Chris, who had been named after Dad, and Peter. They too had a manuscript. Only on exchanging copies did we discover the works to be a collaboration by our fathers. As I was in possession of a typed manuscript it is my father's copy which is reproduced here.

Their grandfather had kept a scrapbook of his son's army career. This included sketches, maps, train ticket stubs and other papers that Dennis had safely pocketed and brought back to England when he scored his home run – an escape from Nazi-occupied Europe. I realised that by combining all these documents an interesting story could be brought to life.

Uncle Jimmy could not be left out though. He too had fought in the Second World War, been captured and escaped back to England. He had written an article covering his capture and escape and the family still had a file of correspondence that covered the events of 1940.

The time had come to collect together all this carefully stored information, to follow the routes that had been taken, attempt to find family members of anyone they had come across and hopefully, strand by strand, allow the story of these remarkable men to make its escape once more.

Readers should be aware that the narrative in the manuscript and the letters written to family members back in England were written in August and September 1940 and contain attitudes and language of the time. I trust this will not detract from the overall enjoyment of the book.

CONTENTS

Index of Maps		xv
Introduction		xvii
One:	The Principal Escapees	1
Two:	A Bullet at Robecq: 24 May–16 June	12
Three:	Surrender at St-Valéry: 4–12 June	24

ACTING CAPTAIN CHRIS WATERS AND SECOND LIEUTENANT DENNIS LENNON

Four:	A Morning Escape: 12–24 June	31
Five:	South to Paris: 25–30 June	39
Six:	Disquieting Events on the Home Front	46
Seven:	Wading the Cher: 1–4 July	52
Eight:	A Change in Fortune: 4–7 July	57
Nine:	Stuck in Vichy: 7–19 July	59
Ten:	Five Days in Marseilles: 19–24 July	68
Eleven:	A Night in the Pyrenees: 24–27 July	75
Twelve:	Spain – At the Border: 27–28 July	81
Thirteen:	Figueras: 28 July–22 August	86
Fourteen:	News for the Home Front	93
Fifteen:	Four Weeks in Gerona 22 August–19 September	97
Sixteen:	Oiling the Negotiations	102

CAPTAIN JIMMY JOHNSON AND CAPTAIN TOMMY TRYTHALL

Seventeen:	An Afternoon Escape: 17–27 June 1940	107
Eighteen:	Turning South: 28 June–29 July	114
Nineteen:	Internment: 30 July–23 September	122
Twenty:	Back on British Soil: 19–23 September	142

FROM A ROCK TO HOME

Twenty One:	Unfriendly Fire: 23–25 September	149
Twenty Two:	A Letter from Sir Samuel Hoare	155
Twenty Three:	Homeward Bound: 26 September–28 October	157
Twenty Four:	Dakar	166
Twenty Five:	The Not So Lonely Roads	170

Timeline	187
Postscript	189
Historical Report of 1st Field Squadron RE Sept 1939 – Jun 1940	207
Final Thoughts and Acknowledgements	219
Illustrations	223
Further Reading	227
Endnotes	229
Index	231

MAPS

The route taken by Chris Waters and Dennis Lennon

The map taken from the estaminet	35
Map 1 – St-Valéry-en-Caux to Paris	37
Map 2 – Paris to Vichy	54
Map 3 – Route over the Pyrenees	77
Map 4 – Marseilles to Gerona	83
Map 5 – The complete route	101

The route taken by Jimmy Johnson and Tommy Trythall

Map 6 – Camiers to Liomer	115
Map 7 – Ronchois to La Trinité-des-Laitiers	117
Map 8 – Tourgéville to Châteauroux	120
Map 9 – Route over the Pyrenees	138
Map 10 – The complete route	139

INTRODUCTION

On 10 May 1940 Nazi Germany began its invasion of Belgium, France, Luxembourg and the Netherlands. Pushing their way through the Ardennes Forest with the help of the Luftwaffe the German divisions headed for the English Channel, forcing the Allies back to the coast. On hearing the news of the invasion Neville Chamberlain resigned from his position as Prime Minister.

Wanting to avoid another war, Chamberlain had previously sought appeasement with Hitler, believing the 1938 Munich agreement of ceding the Czech industrial region of Sudetenland to Germany would provide 'peace for our time'. Without consulting his Cabinet or Parliament Chamberlain had persuaded the democratic Czechoslovakia and France, which had a military treaty with the Czechs, that Britain was not ready to fight a major war at that time. However neither was Germany, and Hitler used the following months to accelerate his country's rearmament; Chamberlain defied pleas from members of his government to do likewise. Despite declaring war when Hitler invaded Poland in September 1939, Chamberlain still believed a peaceful solution could be found and even encouraged the British press to follow the government's lead on appeasement.

Britain had treaty obligations to help France defend itself against a possible German attack. Both governments were bound by their mutual treaty with Poland and in consequence a British Expeditionary Force (BEF) came into being, despatched to France to support the left wing of the French armies. It was deployed in readiness east of Lille on the Franco/Belgium border on what *was known as the Maginot extension, a part of the frontier defences still under construction.*

A growing unease amongst the British public came to a head when Hitler's Germany invaded Norway and Denmark in response to Anglo/French moves in Scandinavia. Badly armed and equipped British forces had been despatched to Norway, but were just as quickly routed by the invaders and had to be evacuated. Anti-appeasement Tory rebels were now able to use this embarrassing defeat and the mood of the country to begin a concerted effort to oust Chamberlain, leading to a debate in the House of Commons on the PM's conduct of the war. With a huge majority in the Commons Chamberlain won the vote of confidence, but eighty MPs deserted him. Finally recognising the mood in Parliament and the country, and realising the importance of a government supported by all parties, Chamberlain resigned. He knew that neither the Labour party nor the Liberals would join a government headed by him.

When Hitler came to power in 1933, Winston Churchill, who did not at the time hold a ministerial position, warned the British government of the dangers of the Nazi regime. He later raised concerns over the development of the Luftwaffe and was against Chamberlain's plan for appeasement. Instead he called for action to deter German aggression as their army and air force continued to expand. At the outbreak of war Churchill was finally appointed to the War Cabinet as First Lord of the Admiralty and immediately began to prepare the Royal Navy for war against Germany. It was Churchill who had argued for an aggressive strategy and proposed the Allies occupy Norway recognising, just as Hitler did, the strategic importance of the Norwegian coastline; however this turned out to be a miscalculation and diversion of scarce war resources. Churchill was lucky to escape censure. Following Chamberlain's resignation the King, with the support of the public, approached Winston Churchill, asking him to form a coalition government at the head of a five man War Cabinet.

This is the story of four officers from the British Expeditionary Force. Their three different regiments had arrived in France at different times before and after the commencement of the German Blitzkrieg. All were tasked either to man defensive positions or harass and slow down the advancing enemy to allow the main body of the BEF to escape from the beaches of Dunkirk, or the port of Le Havre, before hopefully getting away themselves. All four were captured but were determined to escape at the earliest opportunity. Two had been shot in the upper body and met in a convalescence hospital from which they made their escape; the other two were brother officers supporting the 51st Highland Division that surrendered at St-Valéry-en-Caux. They later escaped from the line of march. Following two different routes, all four met up in Spain and together made their final journey to freedom, but an act of war was to deliver one final tragedy.

Acting Captain Chris Waters Royal Engineers (RE) and Second Lieutenant Dennis Lennon RE wrote about their escape in Figueras whilst interned in Spain awaiting release to the British authorities.

Captain Jimmy Johnson Royal Welch Fusiliers (RWF) recounted his escape many years later using notes he and Captain Harold Trythall Royal Artillery (RA) had made en route, together with those written shortly after his return to England.

CHAPTER ONE
THE PRINCIPAL ESCAPEES

The character of these men and their ability to deal with stressful and at times horrific situations has been partly forged by their backgrounds. Together with brief biographies I have therefore given some details of their immediate families.

CHRIS WATERS

My father was born in Marlow in 1915. At the outbreak of the Second World War 24-year-old Chris was a Lieutenant in the Royal Engineers.

His father Major Robert Sidney Waters OBE had served with the 40th Pathans in India having first been in South Africa with the 2nd Manchester Regiment. In May 1904 the 40th Pathans were tasked to provide reinforcements to the Tibet Mission Force when Colonel Younghusband and his garrison found themselves under siege by the Tibetans. The reinforcements were able to quell the opposing forces allowing Younghusband to continue his Mission to Lhasa. Although Waters was not with the Lhasa column, he remained in Tibet until the autumn of 1905 to garrison various posts in both Tibet and Sikkim, a neighbouring British protectorate. In 1909 he married his Australian bride, elder sister to Jimmy Johnson's father, in Rangoon.

After a brief spell in Hong Kong, Captain Waters, as he then was, sailed to France with his regiment in March 1915, arriving in Marseilles early April. By train and marching column they reached Ypres on the 24th, in time for the second German offensive on the salient. On 25 April the 40th Pathans were tasked with an assault on a ridge held by the Germans. Attempting to ford a brook they were bombarded with machine gun fire and shells, killing or wounding two-thirds of their number, including Waters who suffered a bullet wound to the head. Chris, born three months later, was named after two fellow captains who had been killed outright, Captains Leonard de Lona Christopher and John Francis Cecil Dalmahoy.

Unable to fully recover from his wounds, Major Waters retired in 1920 and turned to writing. He started with *Simple Tactical Schemes with Solutions* used as an army training manual for many years, followed by *The History of the 40th Pathans*, a book used as a source of reference for scholars and novelists to this day.

Chris riding Pot Luck *at the Aldershot Show 1939 [Author's collection]*

Like his father before him Chris was educated at Charterhouse. On leaving he entered the Royal Military Academy, Woolwich, and was then commissioned into the Royal Engineers in 1935. After obtaining an Honours degree in Engineering at Cambridge University he was posted to 1st Field Squadron RE in Aldershot. He was a keen and successful sportsman winning the regimental boxing competition in the Lightweight division in 1938 and the Subalterns Point to Point Cup in 1939. Chris was popular with the officers and men of his Squadron and proved to be a natural leader. By the time the 1st Field Squadron was sent to France he was appointed Acting Captain and second in command in spite of his youth and junior rank.

DENNIS LENNON

Three years Chris's junior, Dennis Lennon was in his final year at university at the outbreak of war. He was born in Chile in 1918, his parents having eloped from Ireland to South America to start a new life. Dennis's father John had joined a geological company looking for minerals and would spend weeks on end on horseback searching for treasure in the rocks of the Andes. Working his way up the ranks to become a manager in the Shell-Mex mining company, he transferred to London in the 1930s to work in Shell Mex House which had recently been built on the Embankment.

When Dennis was thirteen he was enrolled at the newly built Merchant Taylors' School in Moor Park. He was a keen cross country runner and also joined their military cadet training corps. Wishing to have a career as an architect, he followed this by studying at the Bartlett College of the University of London. He was elected to become a member of the Royal Institute of British Architects in January 1941 having passed his final examination the previous year.

Dennis sketching on a river bank 1938 [Lennon family]

In 1939 he was serving as a volunteer in the Artists Rifles, a volunteer battalion attracting recruits with interests in the arts, including architecture, from public schools and universities. Called for active service on declaration of war in September 1939, Dennis was sent to Fontmell Magna near Blandford Forum in Dorset for divisional training, where he first met the Royal Engineers. The Artists Rifles were not deployed during the war, functioning instead as an Officer Cadet Training Unit (OCTU). An application for a commission in the Royal Engineers, which was open only to professional engineers and architects, was successful resulting in Dennis joining the 1st Field Squadron RE in April 1940.

After inspection by His Majesty King George VI accompanied by Queen Elizabeth on 14 May, the 1st Field Squadron including Chris and Dennis embarked for France. They arrived in the early hours of 17 May 1940, the day the Germans entered Brussels. On 12 June, whilst waiting for re-embarkation in separate areas on the beaches of St-Valéry, they were forced to surrender to the Germans. Details of the actions taken by the Squadron can be read in the Historical Report at the end of this book.

JIMMY JOHNSON

Jimmy Johnson of the Royal Welch Fusiliers was Chris's first cousin. His parents and siblings were Australian; Jimmy was to be the only 'Pom' in the family having been born in England in 1910. He too attended Charterhouse and then Sandhurst, and was commissioned in his father's regiment, the Royal Welch Fusiliers, in 1930. Initially with the 1st Battalion at Tidworth, two years later he joined the 2nd Battalion in Gibraltar. Jimmy was a successful point-to-point rider and keen polo player. He met his future wife Diana, daughter of Sir Roger and Lady Keyes, in Gibraltar at a polo match.

Lord Keyes had known Jimmy's father Robert [or Robin as he was known] since 1900. They were both enthusiastic polo players and amateur jockeys in Hong Kong, Johnson being particularly successful as a jockey. Both men were involved in the relief of Peking during the Boxer Rebellion. Keyes had commanded the destroyer which took men from the Royal Welch Fusiliers, including Johnson, to the railhead at Tung-chau. Keyes was then given permission to join in the assault, becoming the first of the relief party to enter the besieged legation.

*2nd Battalion Polo Team
Lt W S A Clough-Taylor, Captain W P Kenyon,
Lt J R Johnson, Lt E C Parker-Jervis [RWF Museum Trust]*

Keyes was to have a distinguished naval career. Having commanded numerous destroyers, he was appointed Inspecting Captain of Submarines in 1910 then Commodore Submarine Service from 1912-15, though would prefer to go to sea in destroyers due to the primitive visibility from the early submarines. Being prone to seasickness would not have helped either. In February 1915 he was appointed Chief of Staff to the Commander of the Royal Navy squadron off the Dardanelles where he took charge of an operation to clear a minefield at the entrance to the Straits. Unfortunately this was unsuccessful due to heavy bombardment by Turkish artillery which unnerved the civilian sailors manning the minesweepers. With a naval attempt to force the Straits abandoned, Keyes returned to home waters to take command of the battleship HMS *Centurion* in the Grand Fleet under Admiral Jellico and then Admiral Beatty.

In January 1918 he became Commander-in-Chief, Dover and Commander of Dover Patrol. By altering the Patrol's tactics five U-boats were sunk in the first month, compared to two in the previous two years. In April Keyes planned and led the raid on the German submarine pens in the ports of Zeebrugge and Ostend. Hailed as a great British victory at the time Keyes was knighted, but the Germans were able to get both ports operational within a few days. Post war Sir Roger Keyes was promoted to Admiral of the Fleet in 1930 and elected as Conservative MP for Portsmouth North in 1934, retiring from the navy the following year. Like Churchill – the two were close friends and regular correspondents – he had been opposed to the Munich Agreement with Adolf Hitler in 1938 and had been anxious to be given active service at the outbreak of war. In May 1940 Churchill first appointed Keyes as Liaison Officer to Leopold III, King of the Belgians. In June 1940, after Belgium surrendered, Keyes became the first director of Combined Operations implementing plans for the training of commandos and raids on enemy coasts.

One of Lady Keyes's brothers had served with a cavalry regiment, the Royal Scots Greys. With all five of her children being brought up in the hunting field and therefore keen equestrians, it was a foregone conclusion that her eldest son Geoffrey would follow suit and join the regiment. He served in Palestine and volunteered for special operations in Finland and Norway. In June 1940 he put his name down for the Commandos, unaware his father would be his ultimate boss. After training he was sent to the Middle East where he won the Military Cross. At the end of 1941 a plan was formed to attack Axis installations behind their front lines. One of the targets was the rest quarters used by Erwin Rommel and officers of the Afrika Korps in Libya. Geoffrey chose this hazardous task for himself and was shot and killed shortly after entering the building. His actions are portrayed in the opening sequence of the film *The Desert Fox*. Under Rommel's orders Geoffrey was buried with full military honours and posthumously awarded the Victoria Cross by the British.

Jimmy too had a posting to Hong Kong with his regiment, before returning to England to marry Diana in June 1936. Pathé News covered their wedding in the Henry VII Chapel, Westminster Abbey. Two months later he was appointed aide-de-camp (ADC) to the Governor of Tasmania. This had been arranged by his father as at that time the RWF did not encourage junior officers to marry. It was here in 1938 that their first child, Robin, was born.

In August 1939 Jimmy returned to England joining the 1st Battalion of the Royal Welch Fusiliers at Blackdown. From there he embarked for France with the British Expeditionary Force on 24 September as Captain, Officer Commanding B Company. There are no family records of the first months of the war, apart from a letter home in January that talked of plans for a joint birthday party of champagne and oysters with a fellow officer, though being unsure of whether they would be able to obtain any oysters! By the end of January home leave had been suspended.

Jimmy's battalion spent the months of the Phoney War in the Gort Line – an extension of the Maginot Line running across the northern frontier of France. When the Germans invaded Belgium they went with the rest of the BEF to meet them. Once it was realised the German main effort was through the Ardennes and therefore threatened to encircle the BEF the battalion, along with the BEF, withdrew. With the 2nd Division of which it formed part, Jimmy's battalion was tasked to delay the Germans at St Venant, beyond the outer ring of the Dunkirk defences, thus enabling so many of the BEF to be evacuated at the end of May 1940. On 25 May he was wounded and taken prisoner, having been shot by a sniper through the neck and shoulder, at Robecq, 25 km south-east of St Omer. Of the more than 700 men with 1 RWF at the start of the campaign, only about 200 made it back to Britain.

HAROLD 'TOMMY' TRYTHALL

Born in 1895, Harold was the oldest of the four officers. He had also served in the First World War, initially in the Western Desert with the Surrey Yeomanry [a territorial force unit], followed by the Mounted Military Police. He had remained with the Territorial Army (TA) after his unit had been disbanded at the end of the war, rising to the rank of Captain. He was the youngest of seven children. His identical twin brother Arthur had also served in WWI, enlisting with the New Zealand Field Artillery when in Auckland for reasons no longer clearly remembered by the family. Initially landing at Suez the NZ Field Artillery saw action at Gallipoli before moving to the Western Front. Arthur later died from wounds received in the Somme campaign in October 1916 and was buried at Étaples Military Cemetery.

Harold and his bride Lucy in 1922 [Trythall family]

At the outbreak of the Second World War the TA was mobilised for service and the distinction in unit titles was removed. Now in his early 40s, married with two young children, Harold's peacetime role as the assistant manager of Barclays Bank in Bognor Regis came to an abrupt end when he was ordered to join a Searchlight Regiment of the Royal Artillery. This was a unit made up of regular soldiers but all the officers came from the TA. There were not enough regular officers in the army at this time which meant it became necessary to use TA officers wherever possible, often as seconds-in-command. Jimmy was to recall that although they would be less fit, the TA officers' abilities in war were just as good as those of the regular officers, whilst the latter were very fit but had spent less time training until war was a certainty.

In January 1940, during the Phoney War when there was little in the way of military activity, Harold's unit was sent to France. Expecting periods of inactivity soldiers would often take personal items with which to occupy themselves when off duty. Harold was no exception, taking a set of golf clubs which were later abandoned. It is not uncommon for popular and well respected men to be given a nickname by their regiment. Harold was known as 'Tommy' by military comrades.*

By mid-May the German infantry divisions were advancing rapidly through Belgium as the Panzers cut across the rear of the BEF in France; the BEF and its French allies had no option but to fall back towards the coast. The port of Dunkirk offered the best option for evacuation across the Channel but the German advance needed to be slowed. Brigadier Nicholson, Commander of the Calais Garrison, was asked by Churchill to hold off the German advance as long as possible, drawing German troops away and thus buying time for a defensive perimeter to be established around Dunkirk. *'Every hour you continue to exist is of the greatest help to the BEF. The government has therefore decided you must continue to fight. Have the greatest admiration for your splendid stand.'* Anthony Eden, Secretary of State for War to Brig. Nicholson, Commander of the Calais Garrison. In spite of heavy losses, Nicholson and his troops were able to hold out for four days.

On 22 May Trythall's 2nd Searchlight Battery was deployed to guard crossroads outside Arras as an enemy attack was anticipated.[1] The following day the German attack intensified and it became necessary to abandon most of their searchlights and, along with the 1st Battery and Regimental Headquarters, withdraw to Calais. Here it was to defend the outer perimeter of the city in an anti-aircraft role as well as providing defence from land attack. Withdrawal had been slow as the roads were crowded with refugees, some with horses and carts, but many pushing barrows or prams, loaded with their belongings. Abandoned cars and lorries were strewn by the roadside with hundreds of Belgian soldiers lying about, not knowing what to do. During this move one of the convoys was bombed as a result of which the Second-in-Command of the regiment, Major Heywood, received wounds from which he subsequently died. Reaching the outskirts of Calais the battery found

---

* In the late Eighteenth Century a satirical character called Tommy Trifle appeared in print. It is possible that someone from the regiment had come across him in a magazine and chose this alliterative nickname. Jimmy was known as Johnny by his regiment.

themselves acting as infantry in hasty defensive positions using some of their equipment as roadblocks. At night, any remaining searchlights were used in pairs to illuminate enemy tanks which retired once lit up. Second Lieutenant Oliver was injured after borrowing his captain's car and driving into a bomb crater on the unlit roads.

By the morning of the 25th three more officers, Major Deighton and Second Lieutenants Neave and Anderson were wounded and Tommy found himself as the sole officer in charge of the battery. In the afternoon he was shot and wounded in the left shoulder but refused medical help as this would leave his men, amongst whom he was well liked and respected, leaderless. Wearing a sling he continued to stand alongside them and help load any that

> Second Lieutenant Neave was to become well known as Colonel Airey Neave DSO OBE MC TD. On leaving university he had transferred his territorial commission to the Royal Engineers, was mobilised at the outbreak of war and sent to France with the 1st Searchlight Regiment. Wounded and captured at Calais he eventually found himself at Oflag IV-C, known better as Colditz Castle. At his second attempt he made a successful escape, becoming the first British officer to make a 'home run' from the Castle.
>
> He was recruited as an intelligence agent for MI9. Through his work with underground escape organisations including the Pat O'Leary Line, he assisted downed Allied airmen and military personnel to evade and escape capture by the Germans. After D-day he went to France and Belgium where, with the help of the resistance, he rescued more than 300 Allied airmen who had been shot down and were hiding in the forests.
>
> He entered politics as a Conservative MP in 1953, at his third attempt to gain a seat. In December 1974 he suggested to Edward Heath that he stood down for the good of the party. Neave became Margaret Thatcher's campaign manager and helped her to become the first female leader of the Conservative Party in February the following year. She appointed him head of her private office and later Shadow Secretary of State for Northern Ireland.
>
> In 1979, two months before Thatcher became Prime Minister, Airey Neave was critically injured when a car bomb exploded as he drove out of the car park under Abbey Green, opposite the Palace of Westminster. The Irish National Liberation Army claimed responsibility. Neave died shortly after of his wounds.

were injured into ambulances. This included his own driver Sam Wingrove who was eventually evacuated back to England. Three months later, from internment camp in southern France, Tommy wrote to Wingrove's mother enquiring after him.

The German attack continued to intensify and the following day, weak and delirious, Tommy was captured and sent to a French hospital at Le Touquet. When the defence of Calais finally collapsed on the afternoon of 26 May, it is estimated that over 3,500 Allied troops surrendered to spend the next five years in captivity.

Almost one month later, on 23 June, Tommy was well enough to be transferred to the British hospital at Camiers where Jimmy was now recuperating.

Three months later all four men were brought together in Spain. A Timeline following the progress of each pair can be found later in this book.

CHAPTER TWO

A BULLET AT ROBECQ
24 MAY-16 JUNE

To capture my uncle Jimmy's voice and style of writing many of the details of his story have been compiled directly from reports written by him and a tape recording he made later in life.

When the Germans began their invasion on 10 May, the 1st Battalion Royal Welch Fusiliers (1 RWF), which formed part of 6 Infantry Brigade, was in training.* Captain Jimmy Johnson was on a few days' leave in Lille. One day he

Digging in at Ottenburg [RWF Museum]

---

* Brigades have cardinal numbers, divisions have ordinals. The sequence in staff duties is: 1st Battalion, 2 Brigade, 3rd Division, IV Corps, Fifth Army, 6th Army Group.

heard a loud bang and looked out the window to see three shells bursting in a field nearby. It had to mean the war had started in earnest. He rushed back to his regiment which was immediately ordered to Belgium to take up a position in the front line on the river below Ottenburg.

Four days later, after a battle on the river line, they were in retreat, initially on foot, with transport trucks not arriving until the 19th. They were taken to the Escaut River, holding this line under intense bombardment for the next two days. Extremely tired, the battalion was moved to an area just north of Béthune to rest. The BEF were under threat of being outflanked or encircled. Forces were being moved to defend a line of rivers and canals which run through Gravelines, Aire, Béthune, La Bassée, etc, following a line of old fortified towns. This unbroken line of waterways formed a natural barrier.

After only two hours the men were sent back into action with orders to recapture four bridges over a three mile length of the Bourre Canal south of St Venant in an attempt to establish a new defensive line. Three battalions of the SS Germania Regiment had crossed the canal at Robecq and were heading for St Venant. BEF troops were withdrawing or being wiped out.

German tank at St Venant [RWF Museum]

Battle weary and under strength 1 RWF made its advance, C Company to the north-west, D Company to the east, and B Company to the two bridges at Robecq. This was the first time during the war that SS troops had been pushed off a position. At the first attempt on the evening of the 24th D Company under Lt Boyle was *ambushed. After a sharp firefight the troops managed to disengage and withdraw, but not before Boyle was killed. The remaining companies withdrew for the night.*

On the morning of the 25th the advance resumed and St Venant was taken by A and C Companies before being held up. B Company, under command of Jimmy Johnson fought its way into Robecq but heavy machine gun fire prevented the men from reaching either bridge. Intent on holding their position Jimmy's fusiliers began fortifying their positions, discovering too late that they were surrounded. All they could do that evening was strengthen their defences around the brewery at the intersection of the Calonne and St Venant roads.

When the Royal Welch Fusiliers formed up in England after the evacuation they learnt that twenty-five officers and 490 other ranks had either been killed, wounded or were missing.

Despite being told they were probably going into Reserve, very early in the morning of 24 May, the Royal Welch Fusiliers under command of 6 Infantry Brigade and part of the 2nd Infantry Division received orders to take up a position on the general line of the La Bassée/Aire Canal. The Battalion advanced, meeting some resistance that night. Jimmy's orders were to outflank the opposition with B Company and go to the bridgehead at Robecq.

Germans crossing the bridge at St Venant – a similar construction to the bridges at Robecq [RWF Museum]

The village was captured at about 7am on 25 May but B Company were unable to take either bridge. Repeated attempts were made throughout the day but all exits from the village were covered by the enemy. At some time during the afternoon it became apparent that they were surrounded and cut off. Owing to the general situation they decided to stay put and send a message requesting help.

They had taken shelter in a farmhouse. At around 7pm a lookout called 'Watch out, there's a sniper'. 'Cock' exclaimed Jimmy. Rising cautiously to take a bearing he was thrown backwards by the force of a shot through his body. The sniper's bullet entered his chest above the heart and exited just below the shoulder blade. Incredibly neither the carotid artery nor spinal column were ruptured. A quick thinking Sergeant Major applied first aid which, contrary to medical theory, comprised a tourniquet to the throat. It saved his life. Unable to take part in any activities during the night, the Company was taken over by Second Lieutenant Mike Edwards. The following morning, 26 May, Jimmy gave orders that they should stay where they were for the day and withdraw that night.

> Lieutenant Michael Edwards was captured a few hours after Jimmy had been and was sent to Laufen in Bavaria. He quickly gained a reputation as a determined lock-picker and escaper, starting with the prison Commandant's wine cellar, enabling him and his companions to enjoy wine with their evening meals. He was transferred to Oflag VII-D in Tittmoning where he and another officer attempted an escape with helmets made of custard powder, only to be discovered by a vigilant sentry as the helmets were the wrong shape. Three prisons and further escape attempts finally led to a transfer to Colditz where he joined the team making the famous Colditz glider which was approaching completion when the American Army liberated the prisoners in April 1945.

At about 10am the Germans attacked, surrounded and took Robecq. A few able-bodied men did manage to get away while the wounded stayed where they were in a crowded dirty cellar. The first intimation that Jimmy had that the Germans had taken their area was two German soldiers standing at the door of the Aid Station cellar ordering a guttural 'Raus', *[i.e. everyone out]*. Gone was all the familiar khaki and in its place was field grey.

Captured Aid Station at St Venant [RWF Museum]

On the roads the British military transport and carriers were replaced by sinister tanks.

With his battledress removed and his upper body wrapped in bandages it was obvious there was no need to search Jimmy, but he was annoyed at not being allowed to collect his tin hat. Some ten minutes later the German CO arrived and in a broad American accent gave a brief speech to all who were there saying it had been a fair fight. They were placed under guard and the wounded looked after by a German stretcher bearer who gave some of his dressings to his British counterpart. A half hour later another German officer arrived who also made a short speech in English. The impression given was this man was in command of all the units that were mopping up areas, whilst the first officer had been in command of the unit who had actually made the attack. After meeting up with some forty officers and orderlies, Jimmy was taken off in a motor cycle, together with Second Lieutenant Desmond Llewelyn who had been captured, to what appeared to be a Divisional HQ for food and a drink, and then interrogation. The HQ was filled with officers saying 'Heil Hitler' and the noise of clicking heels. Some hours later Jimmy was taken to another HQ and finally seen by a doctor. The night was spent in an outhouse with a sergeant's overcoat to keep him warm as he was still without any kit.

> Desmond Llewelyn's acting career was interrupted by World War II. Captured at St Venant he spent the next five years at Oflag VII-C [Laufen Castle] then Colditz. After the war he returned to his chosen career, appearing in a wide variety of television dramas and series. In 1963 he was cast as Q, the quartermaster of the M16 gadget lab, in the James Bond films. He first appeared in *From Russia With Love*, the second of the series, and went on to become the only actor to work alongside five different Bond actors, reprising his role in a further sixteen films.

The following morning, after a breakfast of coffee, bread and a sausage, Jimmy was sent off to a prisoners' collecting centre where he found about thirty of his own company including his acting Company Sergeant Major G Davies 49, Platoon Sergeant Major Turvey and Lance Corporal Gilchrist.

After examination by another doctor Jimmy was sent to St Pol in a motor car. Here a French emergency hospital was being organised, under the orders of the Germans, in a workhouse. Jimmy called it 'a ghastly place' with the only latrine being in the middle of the town square. The arrangements were

PoW Arrival March [Water colour by WSA Clough-Taylor, RWF Museum]

very haphazard. An Englishman named Crawford worked there, serving his time as a Poilu *[i.e. an infantryman]* having taken his doctor's degree in Paris preparatory to having a practice in France. Without his presence many of the English there would not have been so well treated. Jimmy ran into a great friend of his from the regiment, Captain W S A [Clough] Clough-Taylor, who had been very badly wounded in the knee.

> Captain Walter Clough-Taylor was wounded by three bullets while trying to defend the bridge at St Venant. Having had half his calf shot off by an anti-tank bullet on reaching the bridge, he managed to crawl across and was then shot in the hip and arm on the far side. Staggering to reach the shelter of some houses he was soon captured. His water colour of the PoW Arrival March is on the previous page.

It was at St Pol, while drinking a cup of coffee and eating what appeared to be a dog biscuit, that Jimmy met Second Lieutenant Colin D Yarrow of the Queen's Own Royal West Kent Regiment. The coffee must have had a good effect on them both because, for the first time, they started to discuss the future. Two things were immediately apparent. It was clear that medical attention would take some time coming as it was rightly being reserved for the worst cases. Also they should take the first suitable opportunity to go home before they were taken to the depths of Germany from where it would be difficult to escape.

Three days later they were evacuated to Doullens. Although this was a better organised hospital with a rudimentary annex in some sort of outhouse, patient care was still not good. Nobody paid any attention to the patients, letting them wander about unchallenged. That first evening, whilst looking for other members of their regiments, Jimmy and Colin noticed a lot of field ambulances, including German and French, being lined up. They realised this could be an opportunity to get somewhere else where they might receive better care. A rumour circulated that some patients were being sent to Le Touquet, a base hospital area captured by the Germans, with a method of selection that was somewhat haphazard. Using a combination of efficient queuing and a little bribery with their remaining cigarettes, Jimmy and Colin jumped into a German controlled French ambulance containing empty stretchers and hid under the sheets. Four hours later they were in the Hotel des Anglais, converted to a temporary hospital by the British, in the holiday resort of Le Touquet.

This hospital was considerably better organised although there was still a great shortage of material. The hotel had been converted into a temporary hospital by the British, but was now in the control of the Germans, although the doctors were all French. The hospital had lots of beds and bedding but was otherwise badly equipped, except for a good modern X-ray set. The majority of this shortage, particularly of the food, was due to the Germans having commandeered it. Also the hospital authorities had been relying on getting many of their requirements from Paris when they were needed, which of course they were now unable to do. Jimmy and Colin were placed in a small ward with another officer and a Frenchman from the Swiss frontier, whom they could not understand at all, such was his accent. No doubt the Frenchman could not understand theirs!

It was now 31 May and the first proper rest for Jimmy since the Germans started their attack. It was glorious waking up in the morning in a real bed. Breakfast that first morning consisted of a bar of chocolate, some roasted grain coffee and four biscuits. Typical other meals were; Lunch – soup composed of hot water with what tasted like one onion per gallon to flavour it, a small piece of meat, a small helping of beans or lentils and sometimes potatoes, then a little tinned fruit or jam with either biscuits or a piece of bread 'of very genteel size': Tea – almost identical, except weak tea instead of soup. At night they were given 'tisane', a herbal tea, generally made of lime leaves.

During the course of the first morning several doctors and sisters asked about their wounds but did nothing as they were only attending to the more severe cases. The sisters returned in the afternoon to dress wounds. They had to do all the dressings for the whole floor, about ninety people. It was not until the following morning Jimmy was finally examined in the operating theatre where the wound was X-rayed and again dressed.

Jimmy was permitted to send postcards to his wife. On 3 June he wrote:

> I hope you got a postcard from me sent a few days ago saying I was all right. I do hope you have not been too worried about me. I am alright, in hospital now. Being well looked after. The wound is healing up well although I fear it will be some time before I get back the full strength of my left shoulder and arm. I cannot give you an address to

write to but believe it is through the Red Cross. Do try and find out and write. I have lost all my kit and belongings, perhaps later you will be able to send me things. I shall not be writing to anyone else but you, so will you explain my non writing to my family and friends.

Stamped with the German Gepruft XI this was received on 29 August.

There was very little surveillance by the Germans, just a French sentry on the front door. With nothing to stop patients going into the garden which was separated from the road by an ornamental hedge and fence, as soon as he was able Jimmy went into the garden. He had not been there long before he saw a well-dressed woman cycling along the street. As she started offering cigarettes to French soldiers Jimmy heard her asking if there were any English in the hospital. 'I shall be coming around again – give a shout' she said, and sure enough she did. Jimmy and Colin promptly introduced themselves and were delighted to be given two Players cigarettes each. They were a great luxury and almost unobtainable. Apparently her husband was an officer in Indo-China and her sister was married to an RAF sergeant pilot. Jimmy had visited Le Touquet just prior to the war and therefore had a number of acquaintances in the area. During the course of a hasty conversation it transpired she knew one of these, Jacqueline Grant, who had been a great friend of one of his comrades in the regiment, Ned Parker-Jervis.

> Jacqueline Grant was the daughter of a Scottish professional golf player. She had been secretary to P G Wodehouse who lived and worked in Le Touquet from 1934 until being interned by the Germans.

The following day the woman returned with Jacqueline. The two women proved to be very kind and extremely helpful, lending them some money as well as producing a few books, as there were no English ones in the hospital. They also brought a railway timetable with accompanying rail map in lieu of a road map, and a

> Captain Edward Parker-Jervis, Officer Commanding C Company 1 RWF, was killed in action on 27 May 1940 defending a house which had been surrounded.

child's charm compass. Both women visited every day until Jimmy and Colin were moved to the next hospital. It seemed very unwarlike sitting chatting in the bright sun, in spite of the gunfire which could often be heard far away to the south. *[N.B. This could have been gunfire from the direction of the Somme where the 51st Division was being pushed back upon Le Havre and St-Valéry action in which his cousin Chris was involved.]*

By another extraordinary coincidence, on the evening they all first met, an escapee from Belgium had arrived at the first woman's house asking for food and somewhere to sleep. It turned out he was Anthony Taylor, a friend of Jimmy's wife, Diana. Anthony was looking for someone to escape with him to England. Neither Jimmy, who still had no use of his arm, nor Colin whose injuries were just as debilitating, could manage this at the time, so both had to decline. However they did ask the women to tell Anthony to let their families know that they were all right. Jimmy later learnt the escape was successful. Diana heard about her husband on 11 June which saved her a great deal of anxiety for, as we have seen, Jimmy's first letter did not arrive until some three months later.

Goudhurst, Kent
9.vi.40

My dear Diana,

I don't know what news you have had of your husband or what you know of his present fate. In case you know nothing I can tell you that he is in hospital at Le Touquet and I think is quite comfortable and well and being well looked after. He is wounded, I believe not badly in an arm, and I think is nearly recovered now. He is of course a prisoner at the same time and when recovered will presumably be taken off to some prisoner of war place in Germany.

From my recent experience I can say that the Germans are treating and caring for their prisoners extremely well and you have no cause for any anxiety about him though of course it is miserable for both of you being separated for so long.

I was a prisoner for eight days in Belgium but managed to escape close to Maastricht when we were being marched into Germany and after walking a great many miles through Belgium and France and, amongst other adventures, being recaptured once in Belgium and once on the Somme when trying to get through the German lines and re-escaping again both times, finally fetched up at Le Touquet from where I set sail to England in a little rowing boat on Thursday night and was picked up by the Navy in the Channel. I heard about Jimmy from Jacqueline Grant an extremely nice English girl whom I met at Le Touquet when I got there.

Please give my love to all your family.

Yours ever

Anthony Taylor[2]

Captain Anthony D Taylor, Adjutant 15th/19th The King's Royal Hussars was captured on 18 May.

Whilst returning to cross the river Dendre in Belgium, the leading tank in his column was knocked out at close range by anti-tank guns. Ordered to lead the column to another bridge Taylor met three enemy armoured cars. Opening fire he forced them to retire and pursued them down the road. However, rounding a corner the steering mechanism of his tank failed causing his vehicle to run off the road and break a track leading to Taylor's capture.

It has been estimated he covered 220 'great many miles of walking', often up to forty-five per day. Taylor was awarded the Military Cross in September 1940.

On 8 June Jimmy and Colin were moved to the Royal Picardy which was an enormous hotel nearby for 'petits blessés' or minor injuries, into which category they were now admitted. Here too the food was scanty but much better cooked and served than before. They were able to go into the garden for stated periods, but were not allowed within fifteen yards of the road. Restrictions on the activities of patients had become more severe owing to the escape of a number of French officers. They only saw the women once more, and that was when they boldly marched into the Picardy and asked for the men by name. They were now doing a bit of nursing in the hospital in Le Touquet; knowing they would be unable to visit the Picardy again they said their goodbyes.

The Royal Picardy hospital was very comfortable. They slept in a ward with four French Officers, all getting on well. The French did not like the Armistice talk at all. Here it was much easier to get books to read and a few extras like eggs, if you had the money.

The doctor looking after them was a heart specialist and lectured at the Faculty of Medicine in Lille. He knew nothing whatsoever about wounds or bandaging but insisted on doing them himself, in spite of his able assistant who often had to go round afterwards redoing them. After being at the Picardy for about a week the word went around that, because of the Armistice, the Germans were separating the French, English and Belgians.

War Office, Casualty Branch
13 June 1940

Madam,

In confirmation of the War Office telegram dated 12th June 1940 I regret to have to inform you that a report has been received that Captain J R Johnson, The Royal Welch Fusiliers, is believed missing.

No further information is available at present, but you will be immediately informed as soon as any definite news is received. In the meantime, should you receive any further information regarding your husband from any source it would be appreciated if you would communicate immediately with the Department.

I am, Madam,
Your obedient Servant

CHAPTER THREE

SURRENDER AT ST-VALÉRY
4-12 JUNE

An ill-equipped second British Expeditionary Force comprising the 1st Armoured Division was despatched to France in May 1940 under the command of Major-General Roger Evans. Two units of Royal Engineers, the 1st Field Squadron, which included Captain Chris Waters and Second Lieutenant Dennis Lennon, and the 1st Field Park Troop, were sent as part of the Division's Support Group arriving in stages by the middle of the month. The main body of the BEF was trapped north of the Somme therefore the 1st Armoured Division had landed at Cherbourg and Le Havre. The smaller landing areas made it impossible to land all the brigades at the same time which resulted in the Division crossing the Channel in two waves.

Almost on arrival, infantry battalions of the Division were sent to the defence of Calais. While still waiting for the arrival of the second wave, which included the heavy armoured brigade, General Evans with his light brigade was given orders to capture and hold key bridgeheads on the river Somme, which had been taken by the rapidly advancing German forces. Despite capturing four key bridgeheads near Abbeville (see Map 1) with the aim of linking up with the retreating BEF, the Germans held their ground. Unable to consolidate his forces Evans was forced to retreat.

The 1st Armoured Division now came under command of the French 7th Army with orders to spearhead a joint attack with the French. The assault began on 27 May but with little support from French infantry any gains made were soon given up. The remaining battered and exhausted Brigades of the Division joined up with the 51st Highland Division to regroup.

On 4 June the evacuation of Dunkirk was completed allowing the German Panzer divisions to turn their attention to the remaining Allied forces. By 8

June it was apparent French forces had collapsed and orders were given for the remaining Allies to retreat across the Seine and back to Cherbourg in Normandy and Brest in Brittany for evacuation on 17 June.

The 51st Highland Division remained in support of those Divisions of the French army still offering resistance. The Support Group including the Royal Engineers remained with the 51st to fall back on Le Havre and then St-Valéry.

The days leading to the surrender of the 51st at St-Valéry-en-Caux were confusing and chaotic as they were pushed back by the advancing German army.

On 6 June 1 Troop led by Captain Chris Waters blew a demolition in the face of the advancing Germans in the area of the River Bresle. On 8 June Lieutenant Dennis Lennon of 3 Troop, with a handful of men, was busy demolishing 'everything' at Aumale, withdrawing when the Germans arrived. By the 10th he was back with the rest of his Troop who were waiting with their lorries. He crammed the back of his truck with anti-tank mines plus the Troop Sergeant, his Batman and a Scottish Corporal. Staying briefly to lay mines on the road, Dennis reported back to Squadron HQ near Dieppe as he had been selected as Liaison Officer between the Field Squadron and other units of the Armoured Division.

From here on it was retreat, going back in slow stages hoping to re-embark at Le Havre. Having reached the town first, the Germans completely encircled the 51st and the French 9th Corps and gradually drove them back to the sea near St-Valéry.

For all those in retreat it was very hectic. No food, no sleep, fighting, continual driving.

During the day of 10 June the 1st Field Squadron was under continual fire and at 6pm was pushed back from St Geneviève in the direction of St-Valéry-en-Caux. A large proportion of the unit collected in the wood at the north-east of the town.

About noon the next day, Tuesday 11th, they were heavily shelled and the officers and men scattered in different directions. As Liaison Officer with Divisional HQ, at 2pm Dennis went down to St-Valéry and found the town under constant bombardment.

Things got gradually worse. He learnt that the Navy were not sure where everyone was as the liaison naval commander had been captured. On Tuesday night Dennis returned to Support Group to fetch it down to St-Valéry, as there was some hope of getting away. They stayed on the outskirts as the whole town was on fire and there were heavy casualties, as there had been all afternoon.

As Dennis wrote later: 'You wouldn't imagine the noise. However no ships came and the Germans had complete control of the cliffs by then and were just firing down into the town. It was a dreadful sight. People were split up all over the town. Most of the Field Squadron were on the other side hiding in some caves and I was with the support group.'

At 9pm on the 11th Major David Cleeve, Chris Waters and some of the HQ troop were seen at the edge of the wood. At dawn the next morning, 12th, David saw Lieutenant George Fenney [who managed to return to England], and told him that Chris was 'wounded but not seriously' and had gone on to see the Medical Officer at the Regimental Aid Post. *[N.B. Fenney along with three other officers and around fifty men from the squadron, had managed to embark at Veules-les-Roses – see Historical Report.]**

St-Valéry-en-Caux – late 1930s? Veules-les-Roses is located in the distance at the far end of the cliffs [Author's collection]

---

* A naval flotilla had been sent to rescue the men of the 51st Division. Whilst waiting for orders to evacuate air attacks kept the boats offshore, then heavy fog descended obscuring the coast. Finally enemy gunfire from clifftop positions made evacuation impossible. However a small number of boats were able to reach Veules-les-Roses approximately seven kilometres to the east and lift off some of the British soldiers from that beach.

Towards 2 or 3am on Wednesday morning Acting Captain Raikes, Adjutant to Commander RE (CRE) 1 Armoured Brigade, told the support group that no boats were coming and they would have to surrender. He suggested to Dennis they make a break for it. Taking Sergeant Major Cloke, Sergeant Harness and Private Bonella they made their way to the beaches on the west side of St-Valéry. It was clear there were no boats so they tried to get away down the beach in the direction of Le Havre. As they walked along the beach under the lee of the cliffs they were joined by a Captain from the Gordons and a party of other ranks.[3] Dennis recorded 'As the Jerrys could not reach us with rifle fire they threw down big boulders, which luckily did not hit anyone. After walking about five miles on the shingle, the beach suddenly narrowed with great cliffs one side and sea on the other and Germans in the middle.' Dennis and his group surrendered, by now there were about twenty to thirty of them.

Chris meantime was with other members of the 1st Field Squadron who were ordered to proceed to the front ready for embarkation. He later reported 'the boats were inadequate and we received orders to surrender whilst actually on the beach. This was at about midday on 12 June. The Unit was at that time very scattered owing to disorganisation when proceeding to St-Valéry and prisoners were taken in various parts of the country.'

200 of the 290 members of the squadron were taken prisoner. Chris and Dennis were to make a successful escape. Three months later, whilst imprisoned in Spain, they recorded their story.

ACTING CAPTAIN
CHRIS WATERS

AND

SECOND LIEUTENANT
DENNIS LENNON

CHAPTER FOUR

A MORNING ESCAPE
12-24 JUNE

With the exception of Chapters Six and Fourteen, this section comprises the unedited original account written by Chris and Dennis. Explanatory notes in the body of the text are in italics.

On capture we were taken to a temporary camp outside St-Valéry where we spent the night. We had thrown our arms into the sea before being captured.

From there we were taken, by stages in lorries, to the neighbourhood of Doullens, three-quarters of a day's journey. Afterwards we marched down to near Rouen then up towards Belgium *[N.B. possibly via Domart and St Pol]*, doing about twenty miles a day. They didn't treat us badly though rations were very inadequate. The column of prisoners extended for two to three miles. Inhabitants of villages through which we passed were extremely kind and gave food to all who asked for it.

On the second night Chris and Dennis met two fellow Royal Engineer officers, Lieutenant H S M Hogg of the 26th Field Company and Acting Captain P P Raikes whom Dennis had last seen on the beach. Hogg described the first temporary camp in his MI9 report.*

---

* All servicemen who had escaped and managed to return to England were required to report to Military Intelligence Section 9, a department of the War Office that operated from 1939-1945. Details were taken of the routes that had been followed, as well as any additional information of note that might help anyone else trying to escape through the same territory. The information supplied was used to build up networks to assist Allied airmen who were shot down over Europe to return to England.

> "The first night of capture was spent at a farm where around 4,000 prisoners, French and British, were billeted; officers in the main farm building and surrounding garden, troops elsewhere. We were given a meal of captured French and British rations, but drinking water was in short supply. The following morning we were woken at 0500 and at 0600, without breakfast, were loaded into lorries and transferred to a place near Rouen. This was a temporary camp for prisoners with an orchard divided into two – troops very overcrowded on one side, but a reasonable amount of room for officers on the other. Everyone was out in the open with ablution facilities consisting of a pond in the middle of the orchard shared by troops and officers. The surrounding ground soon became a quagmire.
>
> "Fresh water was scarce and a German lorry water carrier fetched water twice daily. We were fed on arrival with a loaf of black bread and a tin of British meatloaf shared between six men. At 1600 hours cold coffee arrived, and at 1900 hours two loaves of bread and sufficient salted fish between twenty-five to provide each man with one fish. Unsurprisingly ill feeling began to rise between the British and French due to the inadequate provisions."

Although we had been considering escape ever since the day of our capture on June 12th at St-Valéry, it was not until June 20th that we decided that this particular form of existence would have to cease. We had been subjected to a particularly unpleasant march of 35 kilometres in a broiling sun and on arrival at Béthune were herded into an especially unpleasant camp, a disused sports stadium. There was no grass or shade and two enormous latrines at each end.

That evening we resolved to escape from the column at the first opportunity on the following morning. Thinking that some form of disguise might help, we canvassed round the prisoners for suitable clothes, but could only get one beret, for which we had to pay a French officer fifty francs. Having made a few preparations in the way of provisions, shaving kit, etc, and having told our

> Major David Cleeve took the decision to stay with his men and remained in captivity until freed by the Americans in 1945. In August 1941 he was transferred to Oflag IV-C, Colditz Castle. Records show he made an attempt to escape from there in 1943 but was captured the following day.

O.C. *[Officer in Charge Major Cleeve]* that we proposed to depart at the first opportunity, we settled down to sleep.

The prospect did not seem so easy in the cold light of the morning. The column marched out of the camp at 6am with no food and another thirty-five kilometre march to look forward to. However, as we came to the outskirts of the town, the column became disorderly and the "fusil mitrailleuse" *[i.e. a machine-gun]* mounted on the lorry in front passed completely out of sight. For a few seconds there was not a guard to be seen and, seizing our opportunity, albeit with great trepidation, we jumped through a gap in the hedge into a back garden, crawled under a bush and waited until the column had passed. We made certain that the column had got well away before we came out from our hiding place, and must have been there at least an hour when the owner of the house, an old peasant woman, came out and found us. She entreated us to go away immediately, otherwise she and all her family would be shot. Threats followed pleas and it was clear that we should have to comply. She did, however, give us a sandwich each and some advice as to the best way out. Having digested both of these, we discarded our service jackets and crawled out along the edge of the neighbouring wheat field. It did not take us more than an hour or two to discover that this was a hopeless method of progression. So I put on the beret and went for a walk across the fields to try to find some clothes while Dennis hid in the wheat. Fortunately the very first man I met was very helpful, and within an hour had returned with two sets of old clothes. He was a splendid man whom I hope understood our gratitude. An hour later we set out in the direction of the coast, two passable gamins.

Whatever the risks of dressing as a civilian with the danger of being shot as a spy, it had not taken us long to discover that it was essential if we were to make any reasonable progress. The only alternative, of course, was to lie up all day and march across the country by night – an impossibly slow and difficult process. [We subsequently met escaped prisoners who had done this for the first two or three days, but who had soon found it impracticable.] So with our newly acquired clothes – Dennis's were very ragged but mine fairly respectable – and a "sac-des-provisions" containing the bare minimum of belongings and a little food, we set forth in what we hoped was the right direction. Having neither map nor compass we could only steer a rather erratic course by the sun, and after a few hours we began to suspect an error somewhere. Fortunately we had been told that all French calendars in estaminets *[i.e. small cafés selling alcohol]* had maps concealed behind them, and it didn't take long to acquire one of these, after which we had few difficulties in navigating.

Our plan at this time was to head for the coast in the neighbourhood of Calais to see if we could get a small boat and cross the channel by night. If this failed, we would turn off south and make for unoccupied France. Although discussions took place every night, this plan never altered substantially.

It soon became evident that, at our present rate of progress, it would take us several weeks to reach the coast and at least six months to reach unoccupied France. Besides this we were tired of marching as prisoners, and it was about time we began to live more comfortably. So we began to look about for bicycles and, after trying a selection, we "acquired" two; one was very serviceable, but the other never ceased to give trouble with at least one puncture a day. That night we congratulated ourselves on a good day's work, and opened the map of Europe; this soon became a regular proceeding, and caused endless discussion, usually without reaching any useful or definite conclusion. One thing, however, we were certain of, and that was that we could tear off Spain from the map as being quite unnecessary.

We slept in an isolated barn under piles of hay, and were alarmed at the slightest noise. One's imagination always works at full throttle on these occasions, and even a British aeroplane overhead might have been looking for us. Actually we had nothing to fear, as the Germans had no record of the number or names of the thousands of prisoners, and our only danger was that of running into him unexpectedly, or of being given away by the French. This latter was, I think, unlikely, although we did not think so at the time.

We left Hazebrouck early next morning, and after a rather unpleasant day, mostly on a flat tyre, we arrived at the little village of Dohem. It became more and more evident, as we progressed, that it was simply a waste of time trying to dodge the Germans. The first one we saw of course terrified us and we immediately dashed into somebody's back garden until he passed, but we soon got tired of that and realized how unlikely we were to be questioned. After a few days we found ourselves bicycling through literally thousands of them without turning a hair. We even said "Bonjour" occasionally, but first making quite sure we were not addressing an officer. Only twice were we spoken to by Germans, on both occasions to be asked the way. Of course we too hadn't the slightest idea, and anyway we didn't want to say more than we could help in case we betrayed ourselves by our English accent, so we used to point in the first direction we could think, hopefully the wrong one, and say "la-bas" *[i.e. that way]* in a fatuous way. And they gaily set off without any suspicion at all. If we had not been so anxious to get back to England quickly, we could have spread a considerable amount of disorganisation throughout the area; particularly by sabotage of telephone wires etc. However, the Hun had given this consideration and stuck up numerous notices to say that the penalty was death, and in our present state we were more keen on getting away.

It became increasingly clear that if we really wanted to, we could make this escape quite a comfortable affair, in fact almost a tour of France. But if we were to stay in farms every night it was essential to concoct some story to hide our identity. The French peasants were terrified of harbouring escaped prisoners, and we soon discovered that it was hopeless, if not dangerous, to admit one's identity. They immediately begged us to leave, otherwise "they and all their family would be shot".

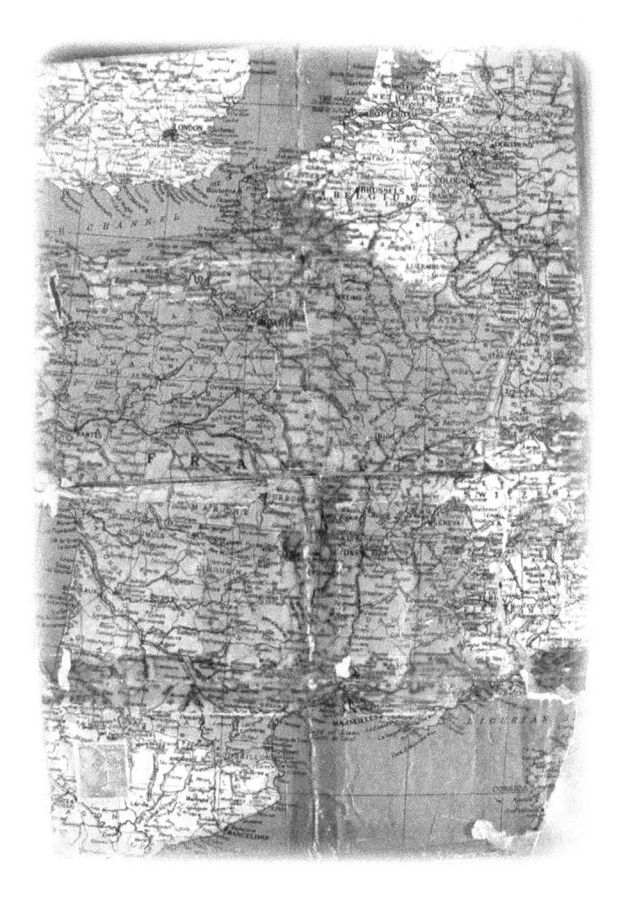

The map taken from the estaminet – with Spain torn off

The story was easy, as there were already thousands of refugees on the roads. We were simply "refugees belges", but Flemish speaking of course, to account for our rather feeble French. Thank heaven we were never asked to speak Flemish – it was the only thing we feared. A few days later we were about to enter a farm when we heard that there were already Flemish refugees there. As we had already told our story, we made a hurried excuse and beat it for the next village.

Arriving at Dohem that evening we tried our story out, and found that it worked like a charm. We found an empty house at the end of the village and asked the owner, a very garrulous old man, if we could sleep in it. He was all over us and took us along to "la grande ferme" where we were given an excellent meal and spent a really comfortable night in a barn. The people at Dohem were very kind and we looked back on this as one of the best nights we spent.

I was very tempted to spend the next day resting here, but Dennis was all for pushing on. The garrulous – and very loud voiced – old man took us down to the river to bathe and suggested that we should stop and find some work on a farm. Fortunately we didn't take his advice, otherwise we should probably still be there.

As we didn't leave Dohem till about four in the afternoon we didn't get very far that day – some village on the main road to Boulogne. We had some difficulty in finding a farm here, but this was a thing we soon got used to. Although we think most people believed our story they were usually unfriendly, and we always had to allow an hour every evening trying four or five farms before we found anyone willing to let us "dormir dans leur grange". Once we were in they nearly always thawed out and sold us milk and eggs, and often made us an omelette. *[N.B. Presumably any search by their captors had been limited to weapons, maps and compasses with prisoners being allowed to retain money and personal belongings.]*

The particular farm we stayed at this evening had a wireless and we were trying to think how we could listen to the English news without arousing suspicion. Eventually Dennis said he could understand a "little English" and switched the wireless on; but either there was a Gestapo agent behind the door or the lights fused – anyway – that was the end of hearing the news. It was the day of the Armistice *[N.B. The Armistice was signed on 22 June 1940 and went into effect three days later]* and we were particularly anxious to hear about it.

Map 1

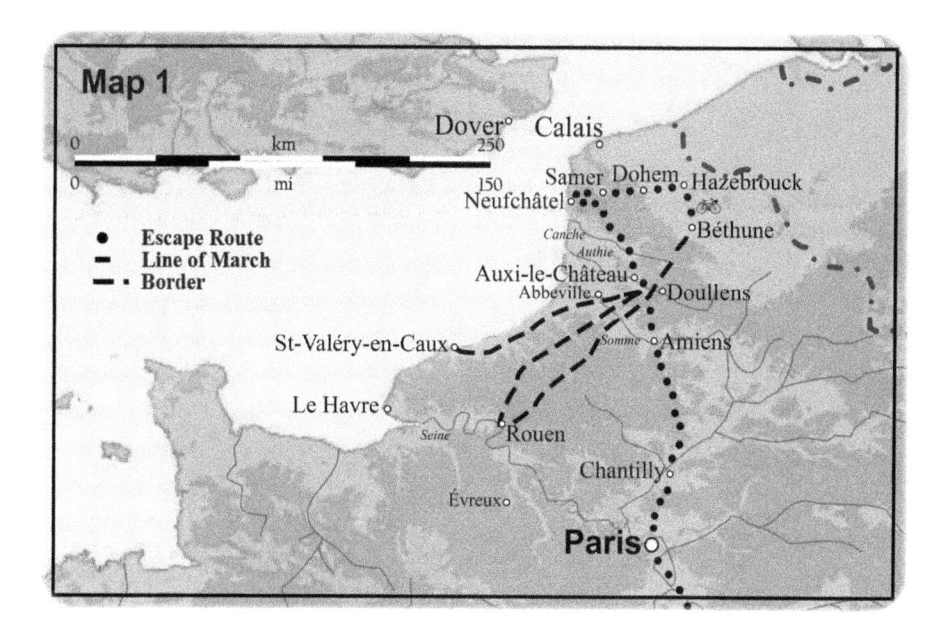

The following day we expected to reach the Coast but were delayed by the inevitable punctures; there is <u>no</u> rubber solution in France. We spent some time getting through Samer owing to the possibility of guards at entrances to the town, and did not reach the small town of Neufchâtel *[Hardelot]* until late in the afternoon. Here I walked through the village until I came across a German guard who was holding up everyone going towards the coast. After pretending to go into a house for a few minutes I returned to Dennis and the bicycles, and it occurred to us for the first time that we should be very lucky if we even saw the coast. As it was getting late we returned towards Samer, where I went to buy some bread and Dennis looked for a farm.

Our story did not work quite so well this time. Dennis picked on a likely looking farm and started off with the usual formula "Avez-vous une grange ou nous pouvons dormir pendant la nuit? Nous sommes refugees belges..." *[i.e. Have you a barn where we can spend the night? We are Belgian refugees]*. "Oh, no you're not" replied the man. "You're English – there's no doubt about that." After the first shock Dennis could hardly deny it. The man turned out to be a Dutch refugee* who had fled with his wife from Holland at the German invasion. He was very friendly, gave us an excellent meal and some new clothes and told us all the local gossip. Apparently the Germans had already

---

*   After VE day, on 21 June 1945, F van Ruyssevelt, the Dutch refugee, wrote to Chris's father from Antwerp, anxious to know what had happened to Chris and Dennis after they had left him, hoping they had safely reached home.

ordered the departure of all refugees from this neighbourhood, and he and his wife were leaving by train the following morning. Of course we had heard nothing about this, and he even suggested that we should go back with him to Holland. After some discussion we decided not to do this, as there was little or no chance of getting a boat from there, Holland being in German hands. But one thing was evident from this; namely that we should have to get away from the coast, otherwise we should be arrested for not having complied with the German order. So that night we decided to give up the idea of the coast altogether and head southwards towards Paris, now in German hands, to see if we could get any help there. We have often thought since then that we were too easily deterred from our visit to the coast, but from the stories of other escaped prisoners we have since met, the chances of finding a boat were very small.

We were very sorry to say goodbye to the Dutchman, as he and his wife had been the soul of kindness. The latter mended our clothes and gave us all kinds of useful things.

CHAPTER FIVE

SOUTH TO PARIS
25-30 JUNE

The Germans entered Paris on 14 June 1940 and Hitler visited on 23 June.

On the morning of the 25th we set forth for Paris and after a comparatively uneventful day reached a small village buried in the hills. I managed to fall off my bicycle, although it scarcely deserved that name by now as it was decaying rapidly; in fact it became obvious that we should very soon have to "acquire" a new one.

We had now settled down to the routine of each day's journey, and we could hardly have done it more comfortably even in peacetime, on so little money. We carried a loaf or two of bread, plenty of fresh butter and milk, and often a few eggs. Whenever we were hungry we stopped in the shade and ate. We existed on this diet for days on end, and neither of us have ever felt better. At the moment, writing this in August in Spain, it doesn't look as if we shall ever see any butter or decent bread again.

We arrived rather late at our village and did not meet with much success at first, but found a friendly farmer after a search. We were always compelled to waste valuable daylight in the evening as the Hun had issued an order that everyone was to be indoors by 8pm. It was only by good luck that we happened to hear of this on our first day of escape, otherwise we might have been badly caught out.

The farmer was kind but uninteresting and next morning we set forth through villages which became more and more occupied by Germans. We assumed this to be a massing of troops in connection with the proposed invasion of England. If we had been able to get back to England soon enough we could have provided the R.A.F. with a lot of useful information, but by now that was a forlorn hope.

Towards evening an opportunity arose to collect another bicycle, but this very nearly led to complete disaster and only by the greatest luck did we escape undetected. After a rather feverish retreat we managed to find a pleasant farm in a village already almost entirely occupied by Germans, near Auxi-le-Château. Naturally we always made a point of avoiding them as far as possible in case of awkward questions, and when one of them came into the farm and spent an hour milking the cow and making butter, we were compelled to hide in the cowshed, fearing that he would come in. The owners of this farm, quite a well-to-do family, had fled southwards at the German invasion, and chose this particular evening to return. However, they welcomed us and gave us food to take away the following morning. The father was comparatively well-educated and I think suspected our identity, particularly as we were only a few miles from the big prison camp at Doullens. When I asked why he thought England would lose the war, he replied:-

> "Austria didn't fight
> Czechoslovakia didn't fight
> Poland didn't fight
> <u>You</u> didn't fight" [meaning the Belgians of course. We resented having to feel responsible for Leopold, but one can't have everything.]
> "France didn't fight
> So why should England fight?"

On the following day, June 27th, we set out early just in case there were to be any repercussions from the bicycle incident. The moment we left the farm we were horrified to see my old bicycle outside a shop, and all kinds of fearful thoughts assailed us. There was only one thing to do, flee, which we did in a state of complete panic. Fortunately both the bicycles behaved themselves and by lunch time we had covered a good 30 kilometres without being asked any questions. But everyone we passed seemed to look at my bicycle in a most enquiring sort of way.*

---

*   To help fund road building, France was one of many European countries that imposed a road tax on bicycles. Proof of payment was by way of attaching a brass plaque to the frame. It may be that this plaque, or possibly lack of plaque, was drawing the attention of the local inhabitants.

Up to now we had been keeping to side roads, had spoken to very few people and had seen very few signs of damage left by the German advance. But as there seemed to be so many refugees about we decided that from now on we could take to the main roads, and thereby cover about twice the distance we had been doing. For the next few days also the wind was in our favour, and we bowled along at a rate of knots for miles and miles. Besides this it was far more interesting as one saw more people, and in particular the results of the German advance towards Paris a fortnight previously.

That afternoon we reached Amiens. We had some discussion as to whether we would go round it or through it, but Dennis had by now determined to make this a sightseeing tour, so we went through it. And he was quite right, as nobody was being stopped. Large parts of the town were in ruins, in particular all the houses round the Cathedral. But the Cathedral itself was untouched except some broken glass; fortunately this had been taken out and replaced at the beginning of the war. Most of the bridges were blown, and we had to make a detour to find one which wasn't. At the exit of the town, on the Paris road, there were several Huns looking as if they might be stopping traffic, so here we invented our little "charade" which soon became automatic. One of us would stop and pretend his tyre was flat and while we were pumping it up and generally adjusting the bicycle, the other would have a good look at the Huns and see if they were stopping people. Usually it was perfectly alright and we were merely wasting our time, but sometimes we did have to turn back and make a detour.

I shall never forget the road from Amiens to Paris – about 120 kilometres. Every few yards there was some sort of vehicle, either tank, truck or civilian car, overturned in the ditch, all along the road. Most of them were upside down. The Hun must have advanced at phenomenal speed and simply pushed anything that was in the way into the ditch. Most of the vehicles had their wheels removed; of course the rubber tyres were extremely valuable to the Germans. They must have had a very efficient salvage company following directly behind their fighting troops. All other useful parts of the vehicles were also removed, but may have been pillaged by neighbouring garages.

Every village was a shambles and showed the desperate fighting of the French as they retired back to Paris. The Hun had obviously concentrated his full force along this road and didn't worry much about the surrounding country, and every village on this road must have received the full force of his bombers. Between the villages there were rather pathetic signs of rearguard actions by the French, and the smell of all kinds of decaying and burning matter was appalling. Graves of dead soldiers were dotted on each side of the road; what the ratio of German-French casualties was we had no means of telling as the Hun had probably taken more trouble over their graves than those of the French, and what we saw may have had little relation to actual casualties. But in any case we did not think they could have been very great as there was not sufficient scope for fighting on a big scale.

As we rode past all this it made one think how efficient and ruthless the German advance had been. It was a completely new idea, and nobody would have thought it possible before. Its success was amazing, and the effects must have been too rapid for the French to have had time to think. It was mostly due to air superiority but the Hun must have been prepared for any losses. All the standard obstacles such as craters, felled trees, demolished houses, and bridges blown, did not seem to have held up his advance at all. His engineers must have been trained to the highest pitch of efficiency.

Refugees were streaming back from Paris and we, of course, were going the wrong way for "refugees". However, we saw several other bicycles going in our direction and it didn't worry us at all that our story didn't quite fit the facts; we were becoming hardened by now. We invented a story about going to see some friends in Paris, just in case we were asked anything.

That evening we stopped at a small village just off the road, but soon found that there was scarcely a house left standing and only about one inhabitant. So we decided to try further into the country and stopped at a large farm. The woman was hospitable, gave us a good meal and said we could stay the night. I spent a happy half-hour helping a Polish refugee to drive in the cows, while Dennis sketched the farm. Just as he was about to present the sketch to the woman, a foal the tamest either of us had ever seen, calmly sauntered up, took it off the seat and ate it. Just after this the "patron" arrived and asked who we were. He was drunk and staggered out of his car in a most sinister way. He looked even more sinister when we told him our story, and we felt like the "Babes in the Wood" or very naughty children. We then, rather foolishly, decided to tell him the truth, upon which he looked even more sinister, instead of being helpful as we had hoped. Our imagination was working at full pitch by now. Thinking all kinds of fearful things would befall us, we took our leave and fled back to the ruined village. Actually we suspected that he was Mayor of the village and might have Nazi tendencies and report us to the Hun. But it was probably mere imagination.

We spent an uncomfortable night in a barn wondering whether he would send gendarmes out to look for us. Two people came past during the night and we distinctly heard them say "On m'avait dit qu'il-y-a deux prisonniers echapes ici" *[i.e. I was told there are two escaped prisoners here]* so he had evidently been talking. And two others found our bicycles so there must have been something afoot. In view of this we decided to beat it at dawn next morning.

As we rode out we met a large column of German horse-drawn transport – the German army still has a very large proportion of horses. The day proved uneventful and we rode on, with a following wind, along miles of dead straight road, through scenes of desolation and ruined villages. Approaching Paris this became less pronounced, and at Chantilly there were no signs of fighting at all. The French had evidently decided to give up the struggle on this road and retire behind Paris, rather than face such appalling damage and destruction as would have followed. Near Chantilly we found a deserted house close to the main road and spent a very comfortable night with mattresses and blankets. The house evidently belonged to some quite well-to-do Paris people, but had been pillaged and turned upside down by refugees. This was perhaps one of the worst aspects of the War. Of the thousands of refugees we saw, probably not more than 10% need have left their homes – but of course they could not be expected to know this. All the remainder suffered far more damage from pillaging than they ever would have done from bombing. We saw many châteaux and houses completely sacked and looted of everything; the wine cellars were usually the first object and were invariably the scene of indescribable chaos. This looting was done almost entirely by passing refugees. It was very instructive to see how quickly man would return to the animal stage as soon as law was suspended.

We woke the following day with high hopes, as we were now only ten miles from Paris, and the next few days might hold all kinds of excitements, and possibly assistance for our return to England. We entered the City without any difficulty at all and headed straight for Montparnasse where we found a very cheap hotel hidden away in a side street, just suitable for our purpose. We trotted out the same old story to the proprietor, but were quite unprepared for the form we had to complete. We hadn't even prepared our names beforehand, but after a lot of stuttering and hesitation we managed to concoct a few ridiculous details which seemed to satisfy him. When he asked us for our papers we had to admit that we just hadn't got any "of course we had lost them all when our house in Ghent was bombed" and he didn't ask any more questions.

There was only one man we knew in Paris, a M. Pourtabourde, father of the French liaison officer of our unit. Dennis professed to know of a few high-sounding millionaires but wasn't quite sure after all if they were in Paris. So he went off to find the only man we were quite sure about, and I did a round of the principal stations to see if we could get a train south. This proved to be impossible. Dennis failed to return until the evening, and just as I was getting really anxious and wondering if he had fallen into the Seine or been arrested, Dennis appeared beaming all over his face and describing the five-course lunch he had been given at the best hotel in Paris. I was disgusted, but decided Dennis had earned his living when he produced 750 Fr., very kindly given to us by M. Pourtabourde. He had also furnished us with maps and some very useful information about the boundary of German-occupied territory – this subsequently proved invaluable and made our visit well worthwhile. The following day was Sunday and we decided that by now it was time we had a well-earned rest; so we spent the day, in real tourist fashion, rubber-necking round Paris.

It was already full of Germans, both in and out of uniform, and all were clicking away with their cameras as fast as they could go. Cinemas had been opened especially for the German soldiers. German money had to be accepted at a ridiculous rate of exchange, but the shopkeepers beamed all over their faces and thought they were doing a good deal over it. The Germans bought up everything they could see, whether they wanted it or not.

All the important public services were by now entirely controlled by them – the curfew also applied here and everyone had to be indoors and lights out by 10pm. Newspapers were, of course, an excellent opportunity for propaganda, and one could already detect the beginning of Anti-British feeling. The sensible and educated people realised they were being fooled, but propaganda is a powerful weapon. It is very difficult not to be influenced by the paper if it says the same thing day after day, particularly if it was a paper you could trust a few weeks previously. The less educated were more easily impressed and could even eventually be persuaded that Germany was its ally and England their enemy. We only saw the very first signs of this feeling in Paris and it wasn't until we reached unoccupied France that it began to have any significance.

After a visit to Notre-Dame and a tour of the City we finished up at the Champs Elysées and the Place de l'Etoile. The latter so impressed us that we cycled round and round it, thinking how appalling it would have been if this city had been destroyed. The Germans all seemed as impressed as we were. It was a memorable Sunday afternoon, the first on which the Germans had really taken possession of Paris. Food was scarce, and for the first time since our escape we had to do without butter! We ate in a second-rate restaurant near Les Invalides, but were slightly perturbed by two German officers who sat at the table opposite, and looked suspiciously at us when we walked out. As we returned to our hotel we found several Germans in the bar.

That evening we decided we had spent long enough in Paris, and it was not till then that we had to come to any big decision as to our future plans. We were all for catching a train south as soon as possible, but could not do this until we reached the unoccupied area. After that there were two alternatives, either Spain or Marseilles. After much discussion we decided on the former; the task ahead seemed formidable enough, but we had the whole summer to do it in.

CHAPTER SIX

DISQUIETING EVENTS ON THE HOME FRONT

Whilst Chris and Dennis were on their 'cycling tour' of France, parents in England were becoming increasingly anxious as to their whereabouts. It took many days for soldiers returned from Dunkirk to find their way back to their units. In the immediate aftermath and ensuing confusion opportunistic conmen tried to take advantage of the situation.

It is highly unlikely family members in England would have known that the 1st Field Squadron was now attached to the 51st Highland Division, still fighting in France and falling back on Le Havre. When there has been no recent news from a 21-year-old son fighting in a desperate battle overseas any lead will be followed up.

This memorandum was prepared by John Lennon regarding events that occurred on 6 June, just two days after the last Allied boat left Dunkirk.

> On June 6th at 2pm a soldier in uniform called at my office and asked to see me. He asked me by name, if my son was in the BEF in France, and in a Tank or Armoured Division and if I had heard from him and when?
>
> I replied in the affirmative and that we had heard from him about 11 days ago.
>
> He said that his name was Philip Burger, Private in the Royal Welch Fusiliers.

Address: 27 Acton Garden Road, Wrexham, N.W.

His father owned a farm at Maescoed, Wrexham, and was known locally as Farmer Burger. He was about 5'4" in height of dark Jewish complexion.

He came to see me because he had been in hospital in the north of England, Preston, receiving spinal injections; that he had been discharged from hospital two days ago; that in the hospital in the bed adjoining his, a terribly mutilated soldier had been brought back from France with many other BEF; that the soldier had been unconscious since he arrived on a stretcher just seven days ago and could not be identified because his clothes, papers, etc had all been lost; that he had severe face and shoulder wounds; that he had been operated on last Saturday: that he had been all the time and was still unconscious except for a few occasional moments he was conscious when all that he could say was:

"Lennon, Shell-mex House."

He claimed that the invalid was being fed by the mouth, was receiving mercury treatment, and that by careful plastic treatment he would and could recover.

He gave the names of Drs Benson, Prebble and Woodrow as handling the case. Burger was entirely satisfied that this boy was my son. He asked me to show him some of my son's writing to compare with some notes which had been found on him and this he did and confirmed his entire belief as to his identity.

On leaving hospital Burger went to his father's home in Wrexham and on telling them about the "invalid" alongside him in hospital – in the 3rd ward, 3rd floor, 4th bed, left-hand side, they compelled him to come to London immediately to advise me about it. In doing so he was committing a serious breach of duty for which he could be court-martialled, because such accidents must be communicated through the proper military authorities direct to the parents.

He told me that I would not be allowed to see my son at present, nor for several weeks, because of his condition, but that I could be quite assured of his recovery. He had to go back to Wrexham and Preston for military duties, would be able to visit my son and would report to me by telegraph.

I insisted that I would go immediately to Preston to see him, but he said that this would be useless, that I would not be allowed in a military hospital in a Military Zone close to large armament works. The hospital in which my son was, was the hospital of the Armament Works.

I insisted on telephoning the barracks or hospital where my son was and this he pretended to do through my telephone exchange. He got on to someone, enquired for Major Woodrow, but could not get him. He then asked them if they could trace J D Lennon, an unidentified stretcher case and they replied that there was no record of such a case.

I still insisted on going to Preston. He then said he would meet me there 5 hours from London and take me to the Authorities and try and get permission to see my son.

We made a date to meet the following day June 7 at the Northern Hotel, Preston Road, Preston Station, just after arrival of the first train's arrival from Wrexham.

I accordingly reached Preston at 9pm and went to the Military Barracks, where they claimed to know Burger quite well. They kindly telephoned various hospitals but no trace could be found of my son. I then found Dr Major Woodrow. He knew Burger but knew nothing of my son. As it was then 10pm he could not pursue his investigations further. I then went to the Police Station at Fulwood and was there until 1am. They telephoned every local hospital, about eight of them and could trace nothing. They then phoned Wrexham and had the Police go to Burger's and his father's address, only to find after two hours' search that there were no addresses in Wrexham such as Burger had given me. Also there was no hotel in Preston of the name at which Burger asked me to meet him.

As I write this on a platform at Preston Station at 2.30am I find there is a train to London at 3am which will get me to the office at 8.30am as usual.

This whole story must have been an attempt by this unknown man Burger to extract money from me. I gave him £3.10.0 to cover his fares and expense. It has cost me nearly £6 for my own fares and expenses.

I told my wife that I was going to Liverpool on business. She knows nothing of the incident and I am glad to have spared her the anxiety.

P.S. Major Woodrow told me he had telephoned enquiries from the Southern Command to try and locate my son who was missing.

Burger had concocted a detailed and cruel story and it is very easy to see how an anxious parent could be taken in at a time when there were such limited forms of communication. There were few private telephones, automated telephone exchanges were not introduced for another twenty years, and the public were encouraged to keep lines clear for official war work. Making further calls to check up on the story would have been extremely difficult.

Lennon added a postscript:

'The man was eventually caught in London and got six months' hard labour.'

*

Having fought in the Great War, twenty-five years on it must have been difficult for Major Waters to know his son was fighting over the same territory that he had fought over so recently and at such great loss of life. Due to the time taken with getting the scattered BEF back to their respective units, it was not until 24 June that Major Waters received a telegram.

REGRET TO INFORM YOU THAT CAPT C D WATERS RE HAS BEEN REPORTED BY HIS UNIT AS BELIEVED MISSING FURTHER PARTICULARS WILL BE FORWARDED AS SOON AS RECEIVED = UNDER SECRETARY OF STATE FOR WAR

Receipt of this would have coincided with the arrival of a letter from the Squadron's Commanding Officer Colonel H Williams, who was himself recently returned from France.

> Longbridge Deverell Camp
> Nr Warminster
> 21st June 40

Dear Major Waters,
    What remains of the Field Squadron has been collected here during the past two days, having been evacuated in different boats from St-Valéry on June 12th. Chris has not arrived and from the scanty information available it seems practically certain that he did not get away.

The Squadron was acting in support of 51st Division which was retreating on Fécamp. During the 10th it was under continual fire all day and at 6pm was pushed back from St Geneviève via the direction of St-Valéry. A large proportion of the unit collected in the wood to the NE of the town. About noon next day the 11th, they were heavily shelled and the officers and men scattered in different directions. At 9pm that evening David Cleeve, Chris and some of the H.Q. Troop were seen at the edge of the wood. At dawn the next morning 12th David saw George Fenney who has returned and told him that Chris was "wounded but not seriously" and had gone on to see the M.O. at the R.A.P. David then went off towards the town and has not been seen since.

Those who got away embarked from the beach about 4 or 5 miles away from St-Valéry. According to Fenney no boats left the harbour. It is small and was under enemy m.g. and artillery fire.

A large proportion of the 51 Div including the General and his staff were captured in this area. The following are missing in the Squadron

> David Cleeve
> Chris
> 2/Lt Lennon
> 200 of the men out of 290

I am very sorry indeed to have to send you this news. Chris was with the Squadron when I took over command a year ago, and I have seen a great deal of him since. He was very young and junior to be a second in command but he made a very great success of the appointment and showed himself well worthy of it. I know that Col Broomhall the G.I. of the Division who was also captured and David Cleeve both thought very highly of him. He was very popular with the officers and men and will be greatly missed.

The Field Squadron was a very fine unit and did very well in France under very difficult circumstances. It is heart breaking now to see the handful of officers and men who remain. I sincerely hope that you will soon have definite news of Chris and that, if he has not escaped, he will in the not too distant future come back safe again.

If you do hear anything from him will you please let me know. I will let you know at once if I have any further news.

Yours sincerely

H. Williams

Colonel Harold Williams, later Lieutenant-General Sir Harold Williams KBE CB, was Commander Royal Engineers 1st Armoured Division during the Battle of France. After the withdrawal to the south of the river Seine he was amongst those evacuated from Le Havre whilst the Germans were concentrating their efforts on St-Valéry.

Colonel Williams wrote a similar letter to John Lennon on 27 June. This prompted both fathers to place a notice in The Times and their local paper.

> WATERS, CAPTAIN CHRISTOPHER DALMAHOY, R.E., 1st Field Squadron, R.E., officially posted missing. Believed wounded near St. Valerie June 12.—Any INFORMATION regarding above most gratefully received by Major R. S. Waters, O.B.E., "Lannock," Cunningham Hill Road, St. Albans, Herts.

Times 28 June 40.

The Casualty Branch of the War Office wrote officially on 29 July to confirm their sons were missing with no further news available at present.

CHAPTER SEVEN
WADING THE CHER
1-4 JULY

So on the morning of July 1st we set forth on the main road to Fontainebleau, although we left Paris by the side streets in case of police supervision. We were lucky to have got through Paris as early as this, as supervision later on became much stricter and we might easily have been questioned. Once questioned, and having no papers, we realized, of course, that we would be "sunk".

As we sailed down the main road towards Fontainebleau still with a following wind [every cyclist will realise what an immense difference this makes], we were alarmed by the vast columns of German vehicles proceeding southwards. Was this a preparation for the occupation of the rest of France, or was it, as was rumoured, the beginning of an advance through Spain to attack Gibraltar? As we approached Fontainebleau the concentration of troops became more and more dense, and we were becoming definitely alarmed, hardened though we were. At the entrance to the town we encountered a barrier where we at once saw that all civilian traffic was being stopped. After some quick thinking we turned off down another road, stopped, and had a good look at the sentries from behind the trees. Unfortunately one of them saw us performing this decidedly suspicious movement, and started walking towards us. Alarmed, we immediately turned tail and fled, turning off down a side track into the woods after a few hundred yards. The track fortunately led round into the town, and we soon found ourselves opposite a famous château. However, we were in no mood to appreciate the architecture expecting a hue and cry, and possibly a few bullets, at any moment. But all was quiet. As we came out of the town we saw another barrier. This time there was no turning off, so there was nothing for it but to ride straight on looking as innocent as possible. The sentry scarcely gave us a glance and we rode out of the town feeling very relieved.

In point of fact we were always over-suspicious of German guards. The Hun was far too busy organizing his troops to worry about "refugees" like us, and as long as they didn't get in his way or go into places where he didn't want them, we didn't think he cared much what happened. Fontainebleau certainly appeared to contain an unusual number of troops, partly because of the trees, partly because the Hun always chose the most beautiful parts of France to concentrate his troops, just to make sure we wouldn't bomb them. Doubtless H.Q. was in the château – it was all very cleverly worked out.

Fortunately we both looked young and innocent [?] *[N.B. their questionmark]* and nobody would have suspected us of being escaped officers, although perhaps we didn't look very like Belgians. Later on we found our youthful appearance cut both ways, as the French simply wouldn't believe that I was a Captain. The latter proved such a continual stumbling block that I had to reduce myself to Lieutenant. No French Captain seemed to be less than thirty-five, and they thought I was trying to be funny. [It subsequently appeared that the kind British Government had already done this for me.]*

We had great difficulty in finding a farm that evening, principally because this was not a farming district. Eventually we had to stay in an hotel, much against our will as our money was by no means inexhaustible. Here we met a young French boy who looked trustworthy, and as we were approaching the frontier into Free France, we thought we might get some information out of him. Unfortunately he couldn't provide any useful advice, and so we set forth next morning feeling rather lost as we had no idea which was the best direction to head for.

The main road was still thick with German traffic, and as we did not want another repetition of Fontainebleau, we decided to strike off due south. Passing though many villages – and incidentally buying a particularly good supply of butter, eggs and milk – we arrived that evening at Lorris which was thick with boche. I went into the "boulangerie" to get some bread, and was promptly asked by the woman if I was an escaped prisoner. Naturally this shook me a bit, but replied in my most innocent and offended tone that of course I was not. We subsequently discovered that the Germans had a lot of

---

*   It was the norm for officers on a temporary/acting rank to revert to their substantive rank after twenty-one days in the event of illness or injury. Presumably this also applied to capture.

French prisoners here who were working in the forests and fields under their supervision, and we presume a good many of them had escaped.

That night we spent in the loft of a very pleasant farm. The woman made us the usual omelette and told us that her husband was a prisoner, but she had no idea where he was. She and her two kids were running the whole farm themselves.

The following day we cycled through miles of forests where we saw many of these gangs of French prisoners working. For some reason Dennis received a very suspicious look from one of the German guards. I did not see this, but he said afterwards that he expected every moment to be stopped and asked a few awkward questions. The guard had probably lost one of his prisoners and was scrutinising everyone who came by, but it is amazing how one's imagination will work when one is afraid of being arrested.

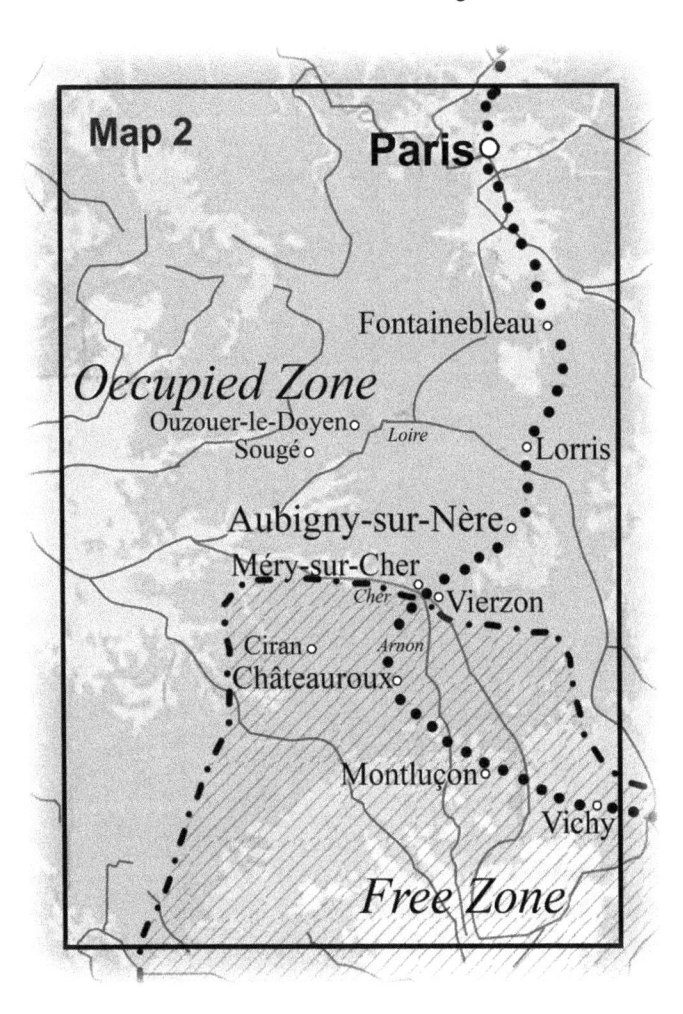

After an uneventful day, we reached Aubigny and stopped at a farm a few miles beyond it. We were now only twelve miles from the river Cher, which was the German boundary, and we decided to make a break for it on the following day. First of all we decided to make quite certain that we couldn't go straight across the bridge at Vierzon, as the Hun was sometimes amazingly casual. Next morning while Dennis was having his hair cut in Vierzon, I walked down to the bridge, but was disappointed to find two sentries who were stopping all traffic and asking for papers.

There was nothing for it but to explore the river into the country, and if necessary, swim it. We bicycled westwards towards Méry-sur-Cher, where we found a track leading down to the river. Turning down this we soon reached the meadows, which spread out on either side of the river, but unfortunately had to pass a collection of Huns in doing this. They looked a bit suspicious but we put on our best innocent air and rode straight past.

As we were pushing our bicycles across the meadows towards the river we heard what sounded like an alarm back in the village, and a few minutes later saw a German Cavalry Officer cantering up the river bank. Our time was up; a promising escape was to be baulked at the last moment. Hiding behind a hedge in a state of complete jitters we waited for him to get out of sight and discussed what to do.

However, we couldn't turn back now, and at the first favourable opportunity we pushed on to the farm we had in sight. Here we stopped and went into the farm, ostensibly to ask for butter, but actually to get some advice about crossing the river. The old man was evidently used to this sort of thing and took it almost as a matter of course, much to our relief. He told us that it was more dangerous to cross at night as the Hun increased his patrol out of all proportion. The only difficulty during daylight was this Cavalry Officer who patrolled up and down the bank, and might return at any moment. Just as he had said this we heard a horse round the corner, and as we were standing right on the track, we thought for the second time in ten minutes that our time was up. He was <u>bound</u> to question us. But he didn't. He simply rode straight on with a most benign expression.

Immediately he had passed, we had a look at the river, and seeing that it was only waist deep, decided it was now or never. Dennis was in great form and plunged straight in without even bothering to remove his boots, his bicycle under his arm. After removing my boots I followed suit, expecting a bullet in my back at any moment. The stream was very swift and at one stage we thought we would be swept off our feet; probably not many people have tried this particular trick with a bicycle, but it did not take long to discover that it was a handicap! The opposite bank seemed miles away, and the stream breaking against one seemed to make enough noise to attract the whole German army. At last we reached the island, and scrambling across it were relieved to see that the other half of the river wasn't so bad. Feverishly looking round to see if we could see anyone, we plunged in again and reached the other bank successfully. We were over, but we still had to cross the open meadows as we weren't going to rest until we were right out of danger.

Before crossing we had been told by superstitious people that the whole river was more or less "lined with machine-guns"! Although we never believed a word of this, we had an uncomfortable feeling that at any moment we might hear them, and it certainly drove us on. As we were crossing the meadows we heard shouting back at the farm and thought that the alarm had been given, so we increased our pace still more. After a few minutes, just as we thought we had reached the safety of the woods on the opposite bank, we were appalled to see that there was yet another river to cross. It was only about thirty feet wide but looked very deep. *[N.B. This was the Arnon, a tributary of the Cher. Both rivers have been flowing parallel to each other from the south but the Cher turns west as it approaches Vierzon. The Arnon on the inside is forced to follow suit just one kilometre to the east of where the escapees crossed. It then joins the Cher a kilometre further downstream.]* After a short and futile discussion Dennis said he was going to swim it, <u>with</u> his bicycle. Slithering down the bank he collapsed into the water. The mud gave under his feet and looking round I beheld the pathetic spectacle of Dennis, right up to his neck in muddy water, trying to support his bicycle, with rather a sorry expression on his face. Deciding immediately that this was no place for me, I went to look for a better place further up the stream; fortunately finding a shallow crossing point fifty yards up. I returned to find Dennis in exactly the same position and could not refrain from unseemly laughter at this absurd sight. Dennis didn't seem to mind much, and with a supreme effort got out and crawled up the bank. Together we ran to the shallower crossing, still in full view of the German side, and waded across the last obstacle. Having surmounted an almost impassable bank and crawled through miles of bramble we eventually found ourselves in a ride leading out of the wood. We looked first at ourselves, then at the bicycles and then our kit but, apart from being soaked, remarkably little damage had been done. Even the eggs were intact. Dennis's trousers were torn, but that was a thing we eventually took for granted.

CHAPTER EIGHT
A CHANGE IN FORTUNE
4-7 JULY

At last we were in free France, and our troubles were over or so we thought. We immediately celebrated by shouting English at the top of our voices to everyone we could see. Naturally they thought we were mad, but we didn't care – we were free! We met four Frenchmen on bicycles who asked us if they could get back to their homes in occupied France. "Oh yes, rather" we replied "just go down into that wood, swim the river and you're there". But they were not amused.

We soon got back on the main road and were amazed to see a line of cars stretching for miles. We were told they had been waiting for days trying to get back to occupied France, but the Germans would not let them go. Eventually they had to go back, but in the meantime the occupants were camping by the roadside, just waiting.

Arriving at the first town we stopped and celebrated our success at a café. Of course we told everyone who we were and we soon became the centre of attention; in fact for a few minutes we really earned the fruits of our hard work! We suddenly realized it was July 4th – Independence Day, and thinking it particularly suitable, we ordered more drinks all round. One had the feeling of having really accomplished something, and one could not help revelling in it.

Eventually we set forth again and soon found a little empty house where, with the permission of the owner, we lit a huge fire and dried our clothes. Next morning, having thoroughly cleaned ourselves up, we set forth for Châteauroux, where we had been told we could catch a train for the south.

From now on our luck began to change, and after a few days realised that our travels and difficulties had only just begun. First of all the weather decided we had been spoilt long enough. All the way down from Béthune it had been perfect; a north wind had blown us down all the time, and it hadn't rained once. But on our first day in free France it changed, and remained unpleasant for days. As we had no mackintoshes we could make no progress in the rain, and on this particular day we spent hours sitting miserably under trees and in barns. However, after some very hard work against a strong southerly gale, we eventually reached Châteauroux – actually it turned out to be our last serious day's bicycling in France so we shouldn't complain.

Châteauroux was full of refugees and no hotel accommodation at all. We were told by the police to apply at the local barracks; the Commandant gave us a ticket for two beds in a local hospital which they were reserving for stray officers and soldiers. We were the only English there, and I think they were a bit mystified by us, but allowed us in. So we got our free beds, and very comfortable they were.

We were too tired to find out about trains that night, and on the following day found we had missed the only available train at 7am. So we resigned ourselves to a day in Châteauroux – not an interesting town. That day, July 6th, the news about the bombing of the *Dunkerque* and other French ships, came out in the papers. We were as mystified by it as were the French, but it did not take us long to realize the full significance of it as it would affect us. It was particularly tactless of Churchill to have chosen this moment to do it – we said. But when we heard that diplomatic relations were broken off, the laugh was definitely on us, and the outlook became distinctly gloomy.

CHAPTER NINE

STUCK IN VICHY
7-19 JULY

Shortly after the Germans attacked France on 10 May, most of the vessels in French ports sailed to other harbours. A powerful French naval force was anchored at Mers-el-Kébir, just to the west of the French Algerian port of Oran. This force included the battleships Bretagne *and* Provence, *six destroyers, one seaplane carrier and two modern battle cruisers,* Dunkerque *and* Strasbourg. *These two* Dunkerque-*class battle cruisers were a major concern for the British Admiralty in case they should fall into the hands of the Axis.* Dunkerque, *which had been launched in 1937, was one of the most modern ships afloat. She was armed with eight 13-inch guns and capable of cruising at twenty-nine knots.* Strasbourg *had been commissioned in 1938 and possessed similar armament. Both vessels were more powerful than the German* Scharnhorst *and* Gneisenau *and faster than anything the British possessed except the battle cruiser* Hood. Bretagne *and* Provence *were each capable of twenty knots and carried ten 34 cm guns. [N.B. French warship guns were in centimetres not inches.]*

After several attempts at negotiation, during which the British tried to persuade the French authorities in North Africa either to continue the war or hand the French ships over to British control, a British fleet opened fire on 3 July, killing 1,297 French sailors. Bretagne *was blown up.* Dunkerque *was put out of action and finished off by torpedo bombers the following day. Heavily damaged,* Provence *was forced to run aground.* Strasbourg *was also heavily damaged although she managed to escape. In the space of a few hours, the world's fourth largest fleet had lost 84% of its operational battleship strength and had been reduced to a token force of light craft and submarines. Having severed all diplomatic ties with London on 8 July, the Vichy government officially came into effect two days later on the 10th.*

Next morning we left by the 7 o'clock train for Montluçon, and from there we caught a bus to Vichy, arriving late in the evening. One of the occupants of the bus had asked us to come and have dinner with him in Vichy, so we accepted and followed him to his flat. Having dined well he offered to accompany us to the station, where there was a train leaving for Nîmes at 4am. [French trains always seemed to run at unearthly hours.] During the meal, a French captain who was there advised us to see if we could get any help from the French government now that we were in Vichy, but in view of the *Dunkerque* and recent international developments we thought it wiser to steer clear of them and push on southwards. The next ten days proved how right we were.

On leaving the flat our host unfortunately lost the way, and after wandering about for about half an hour we encountered some gendarmes. "Vos papiers, s'il vous plaît." Of course we hadn't got any papers and were immediately taken off to the police station. We told them we wanted to catch the 4am train, and they replied sweetly that "of course that would be quite alright". But we had the unpleasant suspicion that it wouldn't be anything of the sort, and it wasn't.

We arrived at the police station at midnight and were greeted by an official who took our names and said it would be alright in the morning but of course we couldn't possibly go until we had seen the Chef de Police, and he didn't arrive 'til 8am. All hope of catching the train vanished. Meanwhile they took us along to a cell and locked the door on us. As we entered I noticed them having a pretty intensive look at our bicycles, which gave me a fairly uncomfortable night. That wasn't the only thing to cause discomfort; we slept on a stone floor in company with a dead drunk and two Russian refugees; the latter spoke English and were very interesting. They had fought with the French Army and were now trying to find work on a farm, but had committed the appalling crime of being without papers, and so we suppose they were suspected of being spies. Every ten minutes there was a fearful swish and roar as the latrine in the cell automatically flushed itself. Neither of us slept at all that night.

No light reached the cell and only by my watch could I tell that it was morning. Much to our surprise the door opened promptly at 8 o'clock and we were ushered forth, looking very dishevelled, into the main room of the police station. After a wait of almost an hour, during which there was a seemingly endless roll call of all the police in Vichy, most of them absent, the great man appeared. He was a kindly looking old man and we hoped that he at least would give us reasonable treatment. After some explanation and discussion he beckoned us forward and we were directed into the street, where we found a comfortable car awaiting us.

But they made quite sure we weren't going to escape by putting two gendarmes in as well, and the great man got in beside us. As we drove through the town we tried to make conversation but he wasn't very interested and we eventually gave it up; he was much more interested in the traffic control of the town.

We were taken to "La Place" or the military H.Q. of the town, which was temporarily situated in the Hotel International. Here we were put in the guard room, where the guards lay sprawling over their beds, and left to our own devices. After a hurried explanation to the Authorities, the Chef de Police departed. We had expected help from him and he proved nothing but a disappointment.

As we expected, the Authorities now completely forgot about us, or rather none of them wanted the trouble of dealing with us. The guard room was simply a room off the central hall of the hotel and we could see everything that was going on. Officers and all kinds of officials passed to and fro all day, but none of them took the slightest interest in us except to stare and sometimes point us out to their friends. We were gradually becoming furious; the guard commander was surly and would not let us leave the room except under guard; we were given no food though fortunately still had a supply of our own; we lay down to sleep on one of the beds, but the captain of the guard appeared and told us to get up – "no one was allowed to lie down during the day" he said, but this was palpably untrue as several of the guard were sound asleep. We discussed in great detail what we would do to him after the War, but it didn't help the present situation very much. He became offensive and asked us what we had done with all the sailors on the *Dunkerque*, but of course he was quite incapable of understanding that we could hardly be held responsible for them. We could scarcely believe that French opinion and behaviour could have turned so quickly.

The outlook seemed very black that evening, and we fully expected to be sent off to an internment camp. It seemed bad luck that after all our trouble to escape from the Hun we were to be treated like this by the French.

We awoke next morning, amid the snores of the guard, feeling depressed, but actually managed to get permission to go and wash. There were still no signs of food and even less of any action being taken about us, so later on while the guard wasn't looking Dennis boldly sallied forth to the Commandant's office. The latter evidently behaved like a normal gentleman, but like all the rest had no idea what was going to happen to us. "Tomorrow may find a solution." Needless to say neither tomorrow nor the next ten days found any solution whatever.

As we had not been fed for thirty-six hours, even the guard commander realised that we might possibly be hungry. So after a tremendous upheaval, during which probably almost every officer was consulted, it was decided that we could have an hour to go and eat in the town – at our own expense of course.

We duly repaired to a restaurant, and in five minutes realized that we were sitting next to a German. Knowing that there were several German agents in the town, this was distinctly alarming, and we began talking French again in our own style. Life wasn't to be quite so easy in unoccupied France after all.

It was already well-known in the town that there were two British officers being detained there by the Authorities, and it had even found its way into the papers. Naturally we feared that if the Hun spotted this, Free France or no Free France, he might order the French to hand us back.

On returning to "La Place" we found that we were now becoming an information bureau for English news. A young and very pretty girl *[Marcelle Dumas]* was awaiting our return, and having introduced herself, asked us if we knew anything of her English fiancé who was last heard of at Dunkirk. Unfortunately we could shed no light on this, but volunteered to do everything we could to trace him when we got back. A few days later we renewed our acquaintance with her and during our subsequent stay in Vichy she proved a most charming and kind companion. Although we continually refused offers of money, on the last night before we departed she gave Dennis a letter for her fiancé, and in it concealed a 1,000 Franc note which of course we didn't discover until she had left. As her family were refugees from Lille and were none too well off themselves, such generosity was wonderful.

> "I suppose it is the only way I can make you accept … but I should have been too much anxious to think that you could be short of money before you are in England.
>
> Good luck my dear boys! I hope very much we shall meet again some sunny day both of you and Jimmy [*N.B. her fiancé*] and me.
>
> God bless you
>
> Marcelle
>
> PS This is now grandmother speaking: Please, if it goes on raining, buy some kind of makintochs ? and a blanket. I think it most necessary for you to keep in good form whatever happens"

We now decided that if anything was going to happen we must take the necessary action ourselves, otherwise we should sit here for the rest of our lives. Dennis thereupon demanded to see the American Ambassador; strangely enough they allowed him to go without a murmur. He returned later to say that he found three Englishwomen who had promised to do what they could through an influential American they knew. The latter appeared at the guard room within half-an-hour and introduced himself in broad American. He was a Mr. Raldiris, had spent twenty-five years of his life in France, and "reckoned he'd wasted his time". We were naturally delighted to find someone who would help us, and we took an instant liking to him. He had a tremendous sense of humour. For the next few days he never ceased to give us help and advice, and although nothing eventually came of it, it was certainly not his fault. He would wait for us every day at an appointed time outside the very smart "Hotel Ambassadeurs", where most of the French Government were staying, and would never be in the least bit embarrassed by the two ragamuffins [our clothes were very tired by now] who appeared on very ancient bicycles. Then we would chat, and every now and then he would whisper "Come round the corner – Gestapo, Gestapo". He had a disconcerting habit of shaking your hand about 15 times before you really took your leave, and between each handshake would tell an American story. Most of these were about the 600 mph aeroplanes that America was shipping over to England; but we always suspected that of being a fishing story.

> Edward Raldiris was a New York State Assemblyman and architect who followed a career as a soldier with the 1st New York Cavalry Regiment. Having enlisted in 1906 he spent some time in Texas serving on the Mexican border. Promoted to Captain he was deployed to France in June 1918 where he saw heavy combat and was awarded the Silver Star for his actions. He resigned from the service in 1924.
>
> He designed a number of buildings in New York including The Lewis Morris in Tremont, Bronx.
>
> www.findagrave.com/memorial/58046782/edward-james_lyons-raldiris Accessed 5 May 2020

That evening as we sat in the guard room, feeling decidedly more hopeful, we were amazed to see two officers of our own division being escorted in. They looked even more ragged than we, and had been caught by the police just outside Vichy. They were intending to catch a train for Marseilles, but like us had been guilty of having no papers. The French [like all continental countries it seems] have an absolute mania for papers. Anything will do as long as it has a nice red seal on it and a little Gothic writing to help. They were quite incapable of understanding that if you were an escaped prisoner of war you had naturally thrown away any identity papers, which you may have had, long ago. We had to explain this in great detail to every official we met, and still he would ask "But haven't you got any papers at all?" in a shocked voice. [Incidentally the British soldier is not issued with identity paper at all, and an identity disc does not impress an official.]

Major P *[Potts]* and Captain B *[Besley]* were about as British as anyone could imagine. They could scarcely muster a word of French between them, and what they could had such an appalling accent that they might as well have admitted their nationality without further ado. They had an amazing story to tell of how they had been arrested a second time by the Germans but allowed to go free again. They had rashly admitted their identity to a refugee who immediately went and gave them away to the local Huns – this was in occupied France. Quickly changing their story they told the Hun they were Belgian refugees. Asked if they could speak English, B replied "A leetle" this he always narrated with great glee. Despite the fact that they searched his kit and found in it a complete suit of battle dress and an English book called the "Escape Club" they believed their story, and after making them scrub the floor and peel some potatoes they allowed them to go!

The following day we were all moved to a temporary camp for French soldiers awaiting demobilisation, just outside Vichy. It consisted of the local Stadium adapted for that purpose. Here they gave us quite good accommodation and food, and strangely enough complete freedom. The official attitude was certainly improving and it began to look as if they might give us some help after all.

The next few days were spent trying to pull all the strings we could think of. Dennis worked diplomatic wonders and managed somehow to see one of the most important people in the Foreign Office.

At the same time we worked away at other sources of potential help – firstly the American Embassy; they were polite and courteous and even wired to the War Office for us, but I doubt if the wire ever got there. Every day we arrived at the Embassy at 4pm sharp, but there was never any news or real assistance; it was always "Come again tomorrow and there may be some news". Secondly there was the Portuguese Ambassador, to whom Raldiris had given us an introduction. A really charming man, educated in England, and very interested in us. He wired to the British Embassy in Portugal, and got the reply "Why don't they go to Gibraltar?" but no hint or suggestion of assistance. They might as well have asked why we didn't charter the nearest aeroplane and fly to England. But as each wire took two or three days we were not prepared to argue this out.

Various other people whom we met promised to "see what they could do for us" – that hard-worn old phrase – but we gradually began to see that we were being steadily let down by everybody. By now the French Government had started to "pass the baby" – a most convenient way of getting rid of a difficult problem. You went to one department and were told the "matter was now out of their hands, and you must go and see so-and-so". We don't know how many times this happened – we lost count – but we do know that during our twelve days stay in Vichy we passed from Police to Military to Foreign Office to Minister of the Interior. And it was always the same story "Come back tomorrow and we may be able to help you", "Tomorrow may find a solution", etc. etc. In fact it became increasingly obvious that the French Government really had no idea what to do with us. To clap us in gaol perhaps seemed to them rather ungrateful after we had fought for them, but on the other hand they could scarcely countenance our proposed escape out of France "officially". But we felt that if we kept on pestering them too long they might get fed up, take the easy road and put us in an internment camp. Now that we are in Spain we often wonder if anyone gave the matter any thought whatever, as they were at that time busy forming the "New Constitution" for the "New France", and talking as earnestly as they could go about "the honour of the country", "the new spirit of France", etc, etc.

The remainder of our time in Vichy was spent sightseeing, drinking in cafés, and in one or two excursions into the country with our charming young chaperone [Marcelle]! In fact almost a real summer holiday. My birthday is remembered as being an extremely pleasant such excursion, with a bottle of champagne to celebrate and plenty of luscious fruit to eat, as we sat by the river – on a perfect summer's day.

Vichy was, of course, crowded out now that it had become temporarily the capital of France, and the shops and hotels were doing a roaring trade. It was all very interesting to see how hard "La Nouvelle France" could work to get itself in order again, and yet seemed to spend its entire day sitting in cafés. Interesting from our point of view at any rate.

One day while we were attending one of our meals at the Stadium we were astonished to see our friend the "German", who had sat next to us several days previously in the café, being brought in. He turned out to be a naturalized South African and a British subject, but German-born. He told us, in good English, of the terrible experiences he had had since leaving Alsace some weeks previously, where he had been living with his family. Having lost his family – he presumed that they must have reached Portugal or even be on the way to South Africa by now – he had been arrested several times by the French on suspicion of being a German spy but released on each occasion as his papers were in perfect order. But wherever he went he was looked on with suspicion and one day he encountered some particularly offensive Frenchmen – actually in Vichy we think. They decided to "test" him by making him repeat the words "Hitler ist ein …". He wasn't going to do this just for some unpleasant French, even though he was no friend of Hitler's. After repeated refusals they became violent and kicked him; worse treatment followed when he was hit on the head, had his hair pulled, his face punched, and finally nearly all his money amounting to some 20,000 Fr. removed from him. He was knocked temporarily unconscious and must have then suffered a lapse of memory as he talked vaguely about wandering about the country for days, covered in blood, and sleeping in nothing better than ditches until someone found him and took care of him. He was in a terribly nervous condition and almost cried with delight at meeting anyone who could speak English. It seemed an almost unbelievable story but it must be true as he told it with such sincerity and one could not help being very sorry for him. When he had regained some of his strength he told us all about himself – he had evidently been a very prominent man in the early days of the revolution in Germany, but had no respect for Hitler's methods and after some disagreement left Germany for good. Since when he had been to most European countries; brought up a son now a Rhodes scholar; become a naturalized South African and settled in that country. He told us with great pride that Bernard Shaw once stayed with him there.* *[N.B. Shaw visited South Africa in 1932.]*

After two or three days, during which time he complained to the French Police about his money and succeeded in persuading them for the umpteenth time that he was not a spy, he was allowed to go. But we were to see him again.

We had now decided that if we received no help in the next two days we would depart under our own steam, without any papers, to Marseilles. This was a change in our original plan, but we had been told that there was a British representative in Marseilles and so we thought it worthwhile going out of our way to see him. Besides which there was just a possibility that we might get a neutral boat to take us on. We also heard of a disquieting rumour that all the inmates of this camp were to be moved to a regular military camp within a few days, and it looked very much as if we might go with them if we didn't clear out. The following day this rumour proved to be true, and we busied ourselves making preparations to disappear without attracting more attention than we could help. We asked the Camp Commandant what was to become of us next day, and got the inevitable reply "Come back first thing tomorrow and I'll let you know". We were so used to this by now that we just roared with laughter, but it sounded a little too ominous to be worth risking and we decided to go before it was too late.

---

*   Notes in my father's file suggests his name was Johannes Uhlmann of Capetown.

CHAPTER TEN
FIVE DAYS IN MARSEILLES
19-24 JULY

After the usual arguments and discussions which always took place before any major decision was reached, we decided after a careful reconnaissance of the station and train timetables, to catch the 4.30 from Vichy next morning. So we crept out in our stockinged feet, with our bicycles, just as dawn was beginning to show, and a few minutes later *[together with Potts and Besley]* nervously entered the station. But there were no suspicious gendarmes or detectives about and the whole thing was just too easy, as we had already suspected. We had been told by almost everyone in Vichy that you couldn't possibly get onto a train without papers, but the fact remained that not one of them had actually tried. We were beginning to learn at last that what 99% of the people we met had to say about police supervision was not true. A few minutes later the train puffed out of Vichy and we were on our next stage. As was always the case when we were on the move, our spirits rose and we really felt we were getting nearer home, even though we <u>were</u> going in precisely the opposite direction! The journey took fifteen hours, but when we reflected it would have meant a fortnight's bicycling, we endured the heat and stuffiness of the carriage cheerfully. Not that we would have disliked the road journey. The Rhône valley, which neither of us had seen before, was magnificent, and in any other circumstances it would have made an ideal cycling tour.

As we sat watching the scenery we wondered what the Camp Commandant – a diminutive and rather petty lieutenant – had to say when he found his four British inmates had disappeared. He probably dashed off to report it to the Authorities whoever they were by this time, who equally probably replied "Thank Heaven for that. We needn't worry about them any more." But we still considered they might possibly have warned the police at Marseilles, where we would be most likely to go. However, they had not, and we walked straight out of the station, with no bigger worries than the fact that our bicycles were not on the train, but were expected to be on the following one. Feeling very bold we walked straight into the first hotel we saw and managed to get a luxurious room for 30 Fr. For the purpose of the hotel register we called ourselves Americans, and derived some amusement from trying to talk French with an American accent. We were tired that evening and after a light supper decided to postpone all further operations till the next day, and retired to bed.

Sketch of Notre Dame de la Garde by
Dennis Lennon[Lennon family]

We took a great liking to Marseilles and thoroughly enjoyed the five days we spent there. The weather was perfect and after some reconnaissance on our bicycles we found a perfect spot for bathing, where we spent whole afternoons, sitting on the rocks, discussing life in general, eating peaches and wishing we were back in England. The town itself has a certain fascination, or perhaps it is the number of different races and kinds of people that flock the streets; the market, indescribably dirty, and its tiny narrow streets; the old harbour with the hundreds of yachts and small boats anchored there; behind it the fort and Notre Dame de la Garde perched on top of the hill; and behind that the mountain ranges stretching for miles, all against a perfect cloudless sky. It was marvellous. Perhaps the fact that we were there at such a time, less than a month after our escape, seemed incongruous and made it all the better. Probably very few people would call Marseilles romantic, and I can imagine that after a long journey by boat or train, and arriving perhaps in dirty weather, it would appear far from beautiful. But to us it was glorious, and we spent hours sitting in cafés on the Vieux Port watching the people and the view, and wondering how long it would take to climb up to Notre Dame de la Garde; until one day we did it, and our efforts were repaid with a magnificent view.

Dennis's Certificate of Identity [Lennon family]

Needless to say we were not entirely on pleasure bent and the first morning after our arrival, our bicycles having arrived safely, we set forth for the British Consulate. This, of course, was no longer functioning officially. Due to a tendency to unpleasantness with the French, and even demonstrations outside, the Americans had taken the building under their protection. As a Consulate it was powerless – even the telephone line had been cut. All the British representatives could do was to give us a certificate of identity under the American Consulate. This turned out subsequently, however, to be a very useful bit of paper, principally because it had a large American seal on it. Nobody troubled to read the contents which stated that we were British subjects in small print, not even a capital B, so that no attention would be drawn to it – the Americans were very good about this.

Meanwhile we were told that there was a Sailors Mission at which we could stay and we went straight off there. It turned out to be a veritable colony of stranded British subjects,[*] run by a padre Rev Donald Caskie who welcomed us to his flock. Here we were given excellent food and a comfortable bed, and in fact "everything to make your stay in Marseilles happy and comfortable".

> Rev Donald Caskie was a Scottish clergyman who had fled Paris in May 1940 having denounced Nazism from the pulpit. He ended up in Marseille where he set up a refuge for stranded Britons at the British Seamen's Mission, having turned down a berth home on the last ship to leave Bayonne. He was dubbed 'The Tartan Pimpernel' having assisted over 500 Britons to cross the border into Spain as well as finding recruits for the French resistance. Arrested twice and saved from the firing squad by a German padre, he spent the last two years of the war in a Prisoner of War camp. When hostilities ceased he resumed his ministry in Paris, returning to Scotland some years later.
>
> 'The Tartan Pimpernel', *The Glasgow Herald* 28 December 1983

That afternoon we met our South African friend again, quite by chance, and he was as usual delighted to see us. He had been arrested again on the way down, but released and was now trying to get help from the British

---

[*] F/O Hawkins *[who was to join up with Chris and Dennis]* thought there were about thirty men, with twenty from the British army four of whom were officers.

representative and had cabled for money. He was in a desperate condition and wanted us to sign his Will as he talked of committing suicide – in fact he completely broke down and we felt more sorry than ever for the poor man. Naturally we didn't sign the Will, but took him off to the Consul [*Major Dodds*], who gave him permission to live with us at the Sailors' Home. From then on he was much more cheerful. Knowing Marseilles, he took us to a café he had evidently frequented before, and here we discovered the famous "Formidables" – large mugs of beer which more nearly approached real beer than anything we had found in France before. The "Formidable" became a standing institution every evening and a very pleasant one. Here we met some Polish officers who were trying to get to England; they gave us valuable advice and help and proved to be most charming people. We subsequently met them on the train to Spain and have every reason to believe they will reach England long before us as their papers are apparently in order.

During this time we were trying to get Spanish and Portuguese visas, but as it involved depositing 1,000 Fr. with Cook's [*N.B. Presumably Cook's Travel Agency*] we were naturally trying to get the Consul to do this for us, as we could scarcely afford it on the funds we had. There was apparently some hope of an arrangement with Cook's about this, but needless to say there was endless delay and we were as usual impatient. Meanwhile there had been unpleasant rumours that all the officers and soldiers were to be taken from the Seamen's Mission and "looked after" by the French Government in the "comfortable quarters" of Fort St-Jean on the outskirts of Marseilles. The rumour rapidly became a fact and we received a rude shock when on the morning of July 24th a police inspector appeared at breakfast and explained the procedure. He was quite amiable and told us that we should still have the freedom of the town, etc. etc., but nevertheless Fort St-Jean* sounded much too like prison for us. He showed no signs of having any guard about him, nor was there anyone outside the building, so we hurriedly swallowed our breakfast, threw our belongings into our bags and within five minutes we were safe in the crowd of Marseilles. We

---

* Fort St-Jean was built in the Seventeenth Century in response to an uprising against the local governor. Consequently the guns all point inwards to the town rather than outwards in defence of the city. During the French Revolution it was used as a prison. The army then took possession and over the next two centuries used it as a barracks and clearing station for the Army of Africa. The fort became the final stepping off point for recruits into the French Foreign Legion before heading for basic training in Africa.

decided to get as much money as we could from the Consul and then leave, papers or no papers, for Spain.

*

During our stay in the Sailors' Home we had met two other men with whom we often discussed plans, and we had gradually formed a syndicate of four in case we should have to move in a hurry, as indeed we did. In normal circumstances it was found unsafe to proceed in any number greater than pairs, as it tended to arouse suspicion; but on this occasion it looked as if our future plans might necessitate a small boat, and for anything but the shortest distance this would require a crew of four. Hawkins was a pilot-officer in the R.A.F. and could be counted on as a very useful man where any navigation was concerned, while Mayhew spoke French fluently and had a working knowledge of Spanish. So we counted ourselves lucky to be in with two such people.

These two had discovered a Greek boat in the docks and had managed to get on board and ask the Captain if he could take them. He was apparently very friendly and said he would have done so willingly, but he did not think he was leaving for at least a month. Dennis and I also explored the docks one afternoon, dressed up as near stevedores as we could. We had some difficulty in getting through the strictly guarded entrances, but our certificate of identity worked wonders. It was a nasty moment when we had to produce it, but we held our thumbs over the word 'British', and seeing that it had American Embassy printed in large letters on the top the guard immediately let us through without troubling to read it. In any case, of course, it was no more a permit to enter the docks than a cigarette card would have been; and yet they had the reputation of being <u>very</u> strict about permits. The docks had proved disappointing and the only likely looking ship was the [also Greek] *Alexandria*, but unfortunately she was at anchor in mid-harbour and we saw no means of reaching her. So we returned after a fruitless afternoon. That had been two or three days previously, and we were now confronted with the much more difficult problem of crossing the frontier, without papers, into Spain.

We managed to borrow £2 [350 Fr.] each from the British Government via the Consul, but needless to say the proposed arrangement with Cook's for the 1,000 Fr. seemed to have been delayed ad infinitum. It was now too late to negotiate for visas on our own as it would have taken two days, and we feared that the police would be on our trail by then. In any case we had been repeatedly told that Spanish and Portuguese visas were useless without an exit visa from the French authorities, and this we knew we could not get. So having prepared ourselves for the journey, taken a last look at Marseilles, and taken leave of the padre and friends at the Sailor's Home [we had to risk returning there later on in the day to do this] we caught the 7pm train for Perpignan. We had lost Hawkins and Mayhew that afternoon but were relieved to find them on the train. They had been making a final effort at the Greek ship but the Captain still did not know for certain when he would sail and they did not think it worth the risk of waiting.

CHAPTER ELEVEN
A NIGHT IN THE PYRENEES
24-27 JULY

After an uneventful journey through the night and an unpleasant wait at Narbonne we arrived at Perpignan early the following morning. Here for the first time we found we had to show our papers. Looking hastily round to see if there was any other way out, we held a hurried consultation and decided to risk the American identity certificate. I went first, with some trepidation, but as usual it worked like a charm and the others followed with equal success. It was a wonderful piece of paper, and had been well worth going to Marseilles for!

From Perpignan we took the road for the frontier and after a few hours steady bicycling, with a stop for lunch at Port-Vendres, reached Cerbère, the frontier town in the early afternoon. The weather was superb and the little towns dotted along the coastline here looked perfect against the deep blue of the Mediterranean. To the right rose the Pyrenees – mountain after mountain stretching for miles, and we began to realise the height of the obstacle we might have to cross.

For some reason the events of the next few days left rather a confused and dream-like impression, very much like the days leading up to the disaster at St-Valéry. We supposed it was for the same reason – lack of sleep, but on a much lesser scale. The preceding night in the train had been pretty well sleepless and the two following did not give us more than two or three hours altogether.

On arriving at Cerbère we held a hurried consultation and decided that our first efforts must be to try and get hold of a small boat and row round the frontier by sea. Mayhew went off to sound some fishermen about the possibility of hiring a boat or bribing one of them to take us round by night. Although he got every sympathy there was no-one willing to undertake this risk and the outlook in this direction was not at all promising. We were advised, however, to try the tunnel, to which we had already given some consideration, but a preliminary reconnaissance showed that there were two gendarmes sitting at the entrance, and nothing short of jumping on a train as it was about to enter the tunnel would have been possible. Besides which we had no idea what sort of guard we should encounter at the Spanish end.

The entrance to the train tunnel at Cerbère [vintage postcard]

It was now getting late and we were beginning to arouse suspicions by our rather obvious intentions, so after a hurried meal, we decided to go back in the Port-Vendres direction and see if we could get hold of a boat we had noticed in one of the bays. This would mean further to row, of course, but we calculated we could do it under cover of darkness. However to our disappointment it turned out, after a search of the beach in the gathering darkness, that the boat was no longer there. It was now almost dark so it was decided that we should have to postpone operations till the next day. Hiding our bicycles as best we could we lay down in the open to sleep. Never had any of us spent such an unpleasant night. The mosquitoes were appalling and every inch of one's body had to be covered, including one's head, with the result of course that one was then overcome by the heat. We were all relieved when the dawn came.

There now seemed only one alternative – to abandon our bicycles and a good deal of our kit and cross the mountains on foot, and having decided on this we proceeded to make the necessary preparations. It was with regret that we parted with our bicycles but there seemed nothing for it – they had carried us half way across France and stood up to it with scarcely any attention, except of course the inevitable punctures.

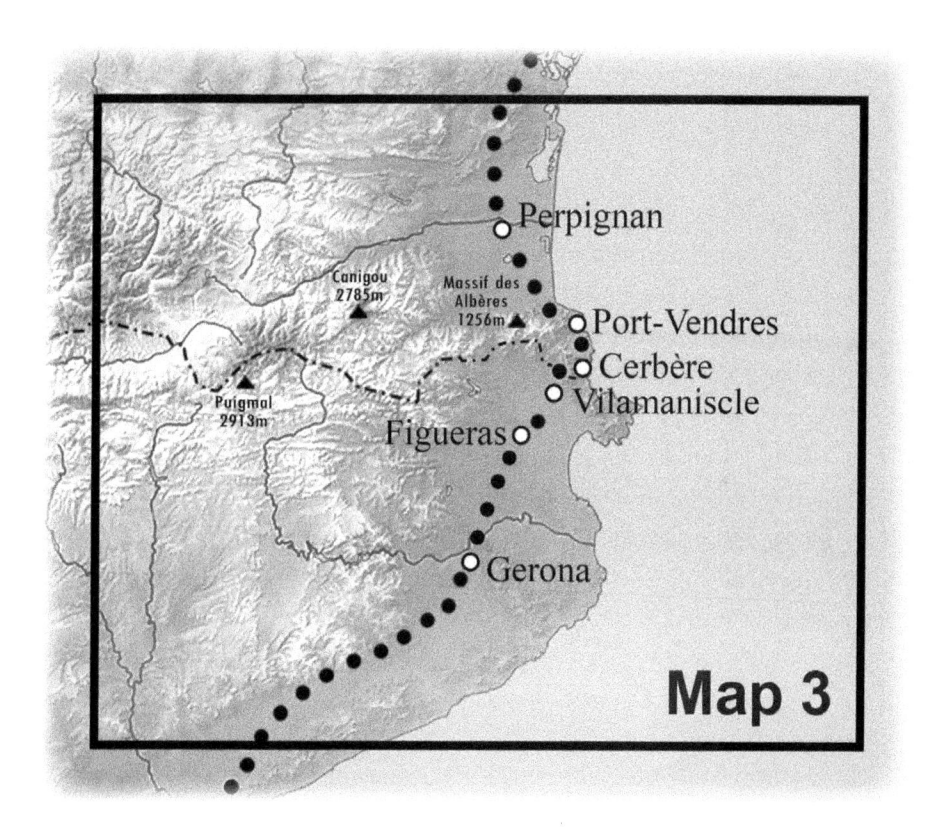

Map 3

The day turned out <u>very</u> different from what we had expected. After tackling the first ridge, we found ourselves descending into Cerbère again [we had started some way back]. We soon met an old man working in the vineyards and after questioning him he affirmed that there was no need to go trudging about the mountains when it was perfectly easy to get out of the country without any papers at all! This seemed so fantastic that we naturally didn't believe it, but the walk over that first ridge had been so difficult that we decided to try the experiment. The Customs House stood up on the mountain on the opposite side of Cerbère, so it meant going down into the town again, which we duly did. On the way down we met a gendarme and spent an unpleasant few minutes wondering if he was going to arrest us.

But no, it all seemed too good to be true. He was most obliging and helpful and said he would take us down and show us the best way up to the Customs House; scarcely believing him, and expecting at any moment to be led back to the police station, we followed him down. But he was as good as his word and after pointing out the quickest way he took his leave. Here was a man who was supposed to be guarding the frontier calmly showing four dishevelled looking tramps the best way over. It was incredible. But more was to come.

Arriving at the Customs House we asked if we could go through. "Well, you'll have to wait till 2 o'clock when the customs officer comes up, but he's sure to let you through" was the answer. This was too good to be true, and we sat down to lunch in the company of a voluble Frenchman whose permanent job seemed to be advising people how to get into Spain without being caught. It was amazing. He promised us a guide and told us we must be ready to start at 7 that evening. And we hadn't even shown the only paper we did possess, our American identity certificates, although we did say that we were English. Doubtless they would not have allowed Frenchmen to leave the country like this, but we had given no proof of our nationality and in any case, nobody was "supposed to leave the country without papers".

The customs officer duly appeared, a rather tired old man in civilian clothes who immediately sat down in the shade and began to read a novel. He took not the slightest interest in us, and when asked if we could go through, just nodded his head rather irritably, as if annoyed at being asked such a trivial question. It was quite typical of the French that while the Government in Vichy was spending days making all sorts of laws about who could leave the country and who could not, here at the frontier was a doddering old man who didn't even ask for any papers and had probably never heard of Vichy. We had been repeatedly told that there was no hope of getting out without a 'Visa de Sortie', but we don't think the old boy here had even heard of such a thing.

Having recovered from our astonishment and still scarcely believing our ears, we settled down to an afternoon's siesta, and by 7, after a hurried supper, were ready to move. Our guide proved an amicable and confident man, and we set forth at a brisk pace up the mountains. Just as the night was beginning to fall we reached the first crest and for the first time looked over into Spain. It was a great moment. There were still three more ridges to cross, and after a long and detailed explanation of the route, our guide left us. We gave him 100 Fr. and set forth with a feeling of loneliness which one experiences without a guide, even though there were four of us.

Darkness had soon completely fallen and any further progress, until the moon came up, was dangerous, so we settled down to a sleep. It was extraordinarily warm considering the height about 3,000 ft. but nevertheless we woke up two hours later shivering, but soon got warm again as we set off. The moon was now up and we continued our rather slow progress over the rocky ground. The visibility in the moonlight was wonderful, and we could see the silhouette of the mountains for miles, while behind us the Mediterranean lay spread out like an enormous pond. Lights twinkled from the villages and towns which lay spread out on the plain ahead of us, and we tried to make out which these were from the map. This was not a very successful operation as by now we had little idea of our own position. The guide had advised us to keep to the top of the ridges as far as we could, and this proved very sound advice as we could always see where we were heading for.

As soon as one leaves the ridges in these mountains it is remarkably easy to lose one's sense of direction; however, the stars were out and the elementary knowledge of the Pole Star proved invaluable. But keeping to the ridges had its disadvantages – sometimes these were literally 'knife edges' with a sheer drop of two or three hundred feet on one side which did not tend to make the going exactly fast! In fact our first resting place turned out to be unpleasantly near one of these; we woke up in the moonlight to find we had been sleeping right on the edge of an almost sheer and seemingly bottomless drop! Towards 2am the going rapidly became worse and we began to feel decidedly depressed; it was no use trying to disguise the fact that we were lost. It was annoying having to waste the valuable moonlight, but there was nothing for it but to await the dawn so that we could get some ideas of the best way to proceed. So choosing a somewhat safer spot than before we lay down to sleep.

We awoke an hour later frozen stiff. It was much cooler now and a wind had got up so we walked up and down trying to get warm, anxiously awaiting the dawn. The guide had told us that we must get out of the mountains by 6am, when the 'Carabinieres' started their patrol and we hadn't got much time left. Dawn came much later than we had expected and it wasn't till 5 that we could see enough to decide on our route. We had only one hour to get down to the plain beyond, and it seemed impossible. Scrambling down the mountainside we soon reached the intermediate valley, and after filling our water bottles at a much needed stream we started up what we hoped was the last ridge. Fortunately there was a path up here, and after some steady climbing we were surprised to find that we had reached the crest by 5.30. Looking over the top we were thankful to see that it was indeed the last ridge, and Spain lay spread out before us. Flinging caution to the winds we set off down the mountain path. At the bottom of the slope lay what looked like a farm – perhaps we should be able to get some provisions here. There were people already up and about – in fact almost too many people. It began to look a bit suspicious. Too late to turn back. At 6am, as we reached the lower slopes of the mountain, the notes of a bugle floated up, and our worst fears were confirmed. We had run into a frontier post. There was nothing to be done as they would certainly have seen us by now; all we could do was to hope they would be as casual as the French and let us through. A vain hope.

An outpost guard was awaiting us at the bottom of the path. He had evidently watched our entire progress down the mountain and immediately took us in charge and brought us along to the fort, as it proved to be. We had paid for our carelessness, and with dejected expressions we followed the guard to our interview with the officer-in-charge.

Figueras August 1940

CHAPTER TWELVE
SPAIN - AT THE BORDER
27-28 JULY

We had made the fatal mistake of assuming that the Spanish police would be as disorganised and inefficient as the French, but we had been in Spain not more than an hour before we found out how wrong we were. We soon discovered that the frontier guard had indeed seen us the moment we started down the mountain, so that even if we had avoided the track we should have stood very little chance of getting away, and a very considerable chance of being shot at.

The guard took us in charge and directed us round to the back of the fort where we awaited the C.O. The latter appeared after a few minutes, was courteous and offered us breakfast which we gladly accepted. Naturally he began to question us, as we had not exactly come into Spain by the usual way. Unfortunately, as we then thought, we had not prepared any kind of story for such an emergency; this lapse seems quite unaccountable as it was obviously one of the first precautions, and we subsequently decided that it was the fatigue and lack of sleep that had made us too careless to worry. We were, therefore, somewhat alarmed when Mayhew, who was the only one who could speak the language, proceeded to tell him that we were British officers escaped from France. We produced the only paper we had, our American identity certificate, but needless to say this did not work the wonders of which we now thought it capable. In fact he was not in the least impressed, and we quickly began to realise that we were in captivity for the third time.

As we ate our breakfast the soldiers gathered round us and stared, unable to believe that four such ragged apparitions could possibly be British officers. We were having our first glimpse of the Spanish army and were not precisely impressed either. Their uniform consisted of khaki shirt and "jodhpurs", with rope sandals or shoes – usually very untidy and dirty, like the soldiers themselves. As we came to learn the officers usually appeared rather better, wearing much the same as we do but nearly always badly fitting or too small. It is of course more difficult to appear smart in this hot and dusty country, but the characteristic untidiness of the whole country does not seem to stop at the army. They still rely mainly on horse transport and have many mules to carry their machine guns and mortars, etc. All their animals are remarkable for being kept very badly, and every horse and mule appeared half starved. Their only mechanical transport seems to consist of extremely old and decrepit lorries.

It was in one of these that we were now put, together with a number of soldiers. The Sergeant, in whose charge we now were, appeared with an evil-looking double-barrelled shot gun, made quite sure that it was fully loaded, and clambered in beside us. The lorry was well up to standard, the tyres were right down to the last layer of canvas, ready to burst at any moment [presumably they just drove it on and on until they did burst], the tail-board was tied on with string, the cab wobbled dangerously and looked as if it might fall apart from the chassis at any moment, and <u>everything</u> rattled. But nobody seemed in the least perturbed and we assumed it must be quite the normal procedure, as indeed it was.

After an appalling drive along what seemed to be nothing more than a dried-up river-bed we were dumped at the first village we came to, called Vilamaniscle. Having heard that Spain was the dirtiest country in the world we were prepared for anything, and the village of Vilamaniscle confirmed what we had heard. Outside the post office we awaited the decision of the "Guardia Civil" in whose charge we now were. This was our first view of these gentlemen and their remarkable hats, which appear to serve no purpose whatever, least of all that of keeping off the sun. The Guardia Civil are the traditional civil police, as opposed to the new party of Fascist police, and are quite a different type. They were on the whole very polite and courteous to us, and always willing to help us as far as they could although, like all Spaniards, they would say anything that suited them at the time.

While our guard was telephoning to find out what to do with us, we sat disconsolately on the pavement trying to find small patches of shade from the blazing sun, for at this time of the year the heat is appalling. It was our first view of this parched and arid country, so different from the France we had

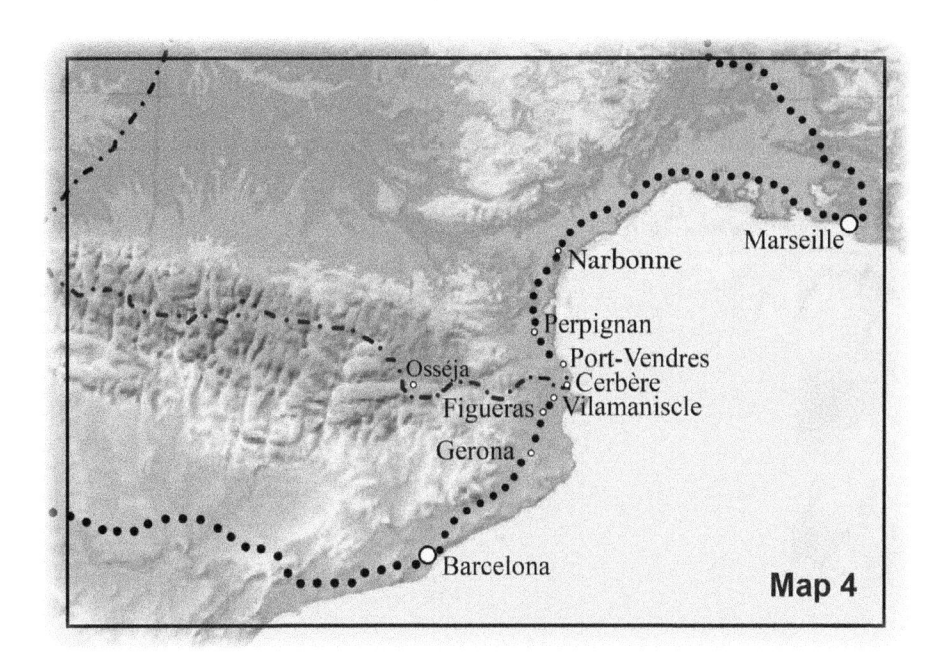

Map 4 — Marseille, Narbonne, Perpignan, Port-Vendres, Cerbère, Osséja, Figueras, Vilamaniscle, Gerona, Barcelona

left only the day before; the Pyrenees form a very definite dividing line both geographically and climatically, and nowhere in France had we met this dry heat which shrivels everything up.

But the heat was nothing compared with the flies. The Spaniards appear to make no effort to deal with these and in this particular village they thrived by the million; this was natural enough as the streets, if one could call them such, were filthy and no effort appeared to be made to clean them up. Even in the bigger towns there seemed to be little effort to combat the fly, and fly-papers are evidently unheard of. On market-day in Figueras it was a common sight to see foodstuffs completely obscured by flies – but nobody seemed to mind.

It was now becoming increasingly obvious that we were not going on to Figueras as we had been promised, and our guard eventually appeared and confirmed our fears. We were to stay in Vilamaniscle until further orders and despite much argument on Mayhew's part we were marched off to what appeared to be the only possible place of confinement, the "village hall". Here we were locked in and left to be devoured by the swarms of flies whose habitation we had disturbed.

The situation was not promising, and it looked very much as if internment was going to be our lot. Unless they took us to Figueras, where we knew there was a British Vice Consul, there seemed little prospect of getting in touch with the British authorities. The Spaniards, so we thought at the time, were quite within their rights to intern us for the rest of the war, and the prospect of a Spanish prison was far worse than a German prison-camp. We sat about disconsolately on the bare forms, the only furniture provided, until the guard reappeared with his wife who brought us food and wine. Water is almost unknown as a drink in Spain largely replaced by an unlimited quantity of the inferior type of red wine – very raw compared to French wines, and as most of us subsequently found, very disturbing to the stomach. However, food and drink were very welcome; the guard then informed us that we were to see the "Jefe" of the village at 3pm so we settled down to wait patiently. Needless to say it was not until 5 that the guard returned and we all followed him up to the village, with an extra guard behind just to make quite sure that we weren't going to bolt for it.

The Jefe was a surly looking devil and shouted his instructions at us at a range of not less than six inches. It appeared that we were all to fill up identity papers stating our names, ages, professions etc. Quite unprepared for this we held hurried consultations as to how much truth we could safely tell, but in view of the fact that we had already given ourselves away there was little to hide. One thing we were careful to make clear however was that we were not regular officers [quite untrue] and made up various civilian professions to suit the occasion. We thought this might possibly help in future diplomatic wrangles. As it turned out it didn't make the slightest difference, but it seemed to impress this gentleman. After a lot of backchat and tremendous volubility on his part he promised that we should be taken to Figueras on the following morning. As to our future prospects, he waved his hand airily and said "oh, then you'll be sent off to Portugal and so back to England", but we set no great store by that remark, for how could he possibly know what the higher authorities would do with us? However, the promise of being sent to Figueras was encouraging, and we departed back to the village hall under escort, with the invitation to dine with the old boy later on. Meanwhile the guard's wife became very generous and gave us mattresses to sleep on, for which we were grateful enough. The summons to dinner did not arrive until very late. We ate with the whole family who were very good-humoured. We laughed and smiled pleasantly, pretending to understand what they said, and after a simple meal retired to some much needed sleep.

The following morning saw us washing and shaving at the village pump, under guard, much to the amusement of the villagers. Of other sanitary arrangements there were none, and we had to use a ruined building for the purpose. I mentioned this sordid fact only to show that the Spaniard has no idea whatever of sanitation and cleanliness.

After endless delays, and with the usual delightful unpunctuality, we were escorted down to where we were to meet the transport. After another long wait we heard the distant sound of singing, and shortly afterwards an army lorry, similar to the one we arrived in the day before, hurtled round the corner and came to rest with a scream of brakes and tyres. It was absolutely crammed full of soldiers, all standing up and hanging on to each other like grim death. We wondered how on earth we were going to fit in, but we did somehow, together with our guard. The lorry started off with a fearful jerk and careered on its reckless and perilous journey. Immediately the soldiers all started to sing again, in perfect unison, and quite spontaneously; they appear to have a fund of literally endless songs, rather like chanting, which can go on for ever without becoming in the least tedious, and they certainly sing them well. This continued all the way to Figueras, and we were very impressed indeed, as it was magnificent, although our attentions were almost entirely centred on not falling out of the lorry. The latter seemed to present no difficulty to the soldiers, to them it was a matter of practice, rather like ski-ing.

CHAPTER THIRTEEN
FIGUERAS
28 JULY-22 AUGUST

Eventually we arrived at Figueras, and passing the Gran Hotel, where we had heard the Vice Consul was staying, drew up outside the police station – or rather the "Jefetura de la Frontera", where we were told to get out, and hustled into the guard room of the police station. Here we found many others in the same plight, I think they were mostly Spanish refugees from the civil war who were returning from France. After an hour or so we were taken up to see the Jefe and Mayhew explained who we were; the Jefe looked gloomy and muttered a few words amongst which we picked out the dreaded "campa di concentration" and our hearts sank. Mayhew then asked to see the Vice Consul; the Jefe said there wasn't one in Figueras, but he knew very well there was and after a lot of persuasion he rang up the Gran Hotel. Yes, a British representative had just returned from Barcelona, what luck, and would come round that afternoon. We were ushered back into the guard room in better spirits; but even yet we feared the concentration camp and held lengthy discussions as to whether we would escape before we got there, or await a more favourable opportunity.

We had no Spanish money, so we were taken to eat at the local soup-kitchen, where we were given an immense bowl of beans and broth. On our return to the guard room we tried to snatch a little sleep in one of the cells, but very soon discovered the inevitable lice; the prospect of a night there was appalling, and we sat gloomily looking into the street, where a small child was pulling the wings off a half-dead bird. The guard was watching this edifying sight with an amused smile. Our first views of Spain were not inspiring.

Eventually we were summoned to the office again and met the British representative – a Mr. Rapley, who was evidently only temporary pending the appointment of a new Vice Consul. He looked at us suspiciously, and particularly at Mayhew who was fairly obviously not of British birth, while his accent also betrayed him. However his attitude was perfectly correct. We might easily have been communists trying to get into Spain under false pretences, and this, of course, is what the Spaniards were so frightened of. The effects of the Civil War were still very obvious, and they did not attempt to conceal their fear of elements subversive to the new regime. In fact, there were said to be 2,000,000 political prisoners at that time.[*]

However, Rapley was soon convinced that we were genuine and began to plead with the Jefe. The latter was quite reasonable and said he would wire to Madrid for instructions; meanwhile we would be allowed to stay at a small hotel opposite the police station and report ourselves every morning. Our luck was in, and we expressed our gratitude to Rapley most effusively.

The "Fonda Mallol", our hotel, was unpretentious but comparatively luxurious to us, and we were given a large room, with four beds in a row, which looked out on the dingy little street with the police station opposite. Every evening we saw new batches of wayfarers being brought in – we never discovered who these were, but they evidently had no papers and were therefore suspicious characters.

The occupants of the hotel regarded us with great interest and we became quite friendly with an officer who eventually turned out to be the governor of the local prison, he gave us a Fascist salute whenever he saw us and we wondered if it would pay us to return it, but we feared he might think we were laughing at him.

We were allowed the freedom of the town but were forbidden to go outside it; however, one of the first things we did was to reconnoitre a way of escape in case we should need it, and we soon discovered how thoroughly policed the town was. Every road had a guard on it and there was little hope of getting past these without being asked for one's papers. We also explored the station and its approaches, for we had given some thought to jumping a train. Meanwhile we saw many signs of the civil war; many buildings in Figueras had been bombed and the work of rebuilding had scarcely begun. There

---

[*] This is probably an exaggeration: it is estimated that before the civil war, in 1933, the prisons of Spain contained some 12,000 prisoners. By 1940, one year after the end of the civil war, there were 280,000 prisoners contained in more than 500 prisons throughout the country.

was an enormous dump of worn-out and shattered cars. There were bullet marks on many of the buildings, including the Gran Hotel; and the general tone of the town proclaimed that "things were not what they were". For this was Cataluña, which had put up a stubborn resistance to the new cause, and had always prided itself of being independent from the rest of Spain. So now they were treated with extra special care, and were not allowed to forget for one moment that they were defeated. The Catalan tongue was forbidden in public; as also were the traditional dancing and festivities on the Rambla. The place was dead. Prices were appalling. The peseta was equivalent to about five-pence and many prices were prohibitive to the ordinary inhabitant. Food was scarce, butter was unheard of, the bread was coarse and brown and tasted musty. There was no beer, and all drinks were subject to the "Subsidia al Combatente" tax. Everywhere were pictures and posters of "El Caudillo" *[Franco]* smiling down at you, with the usual slogans of "Arriba España" and "Viva España", and all the rest of it. "Plato Unico" was instituted, on Mondays, but in the big hotels this was a mockery.* In fact, all was modelled on the Nazi line. But in spite all these wonderful new ideas and taxes there was nothing to show; the people were discontented, the cafés almost empty, the local prisons full, and the standard of living lower than before.

Propaganda was strongly anti-British; the principal outlet was of course Gibraltar and there were offensive notices, pinned up on the trees by the local Falangist youth, to the effect that Gibraltar must be returned to Spain where she rightly belonged. The newspapers were the same, in varying degrees, and any blame for poor conditions of living was laid on the British. One day there was no bread, so the papers announced that we had sunk their supply ship. Another morning we opened the paper to find that our Cabinet Ministers were now reduced to eating grass for lack of better food. London, of course, was a mass of ruins after the first few raids, while the Italian conquest of Somaliland was greeted with tremendous enthusiasm.** The local paper shop displayed German and Italian papers, but of any English literature there was

---

* Plato Unico, introduced by Franco as a symbol of austerity, was a day of the week when only single-course meals could be served.

** In 1887 Britain signed a treaty to establish a protectorate in an area opposite the outpost of Aden which became known as British Somaliland. With garrisons on both sides of the entrance to the Red Sea she was now able to protect communications with India and the Far East. In August 1940 Italian, Eritrean and Somali forces of Fascist Italy attacked British positions forcing an evacuation. In March the following year Somaliland was back in British control having been recaptured by two Sikh battalions of the British Army and a Somali commando detachment.

no sign. We derived much amusement from all this, but were rather horrified to see one day a picture of a German officer giving orders to an English "Bobby". This of course, was displayed very prominently, and it was not until we read the lines below, in very small print, that we discovered it had been taken in the Channel Islands some months previously.

But it was all very impersonal and the Spaniards themselves, at any rate in that district, bore no grudge against us and we ourselves became quite well-known in the town and were treated very well. No-one showed any sign of being rude to us, and in fact I think they were all for us, although, of course, they dared not say so. No-one could trust his neighbour, and it seemed that Gestapo methods were much the same as in Germany. We, of course, were careful what we said, but were often tempted to pull the notices about Gibraltar off the trees; but it wouldn't have helped our position. However, we used to amuse ourselves when at cafés by toasting loudly to "Hell with Hitler".

We soon got tired of the Fonda Mallol. The food was bad, and we were all ill for the first few days being unused to the oil in which everything was cooked, and the raw wine; and the heat was terrific. We quickly gave up reporting to the police station, and as nobody worried we decided to go to another hotel, partly for better conditions and partly to find out just how close a watch the

Sketch of market day at Figueras by Dennis Lennon [Lennon family]

police were keeping on us. Mr. Rapley suggested that we should join him at the Gran Hotel, as the manager offered to have us at special cheap terms; to this we quickly agreed and soon found ourselves in luxury, though still in our old rags. However, the consulate provided us with 250 pesetas each and we were soon looking like "perfect gentlemen"; they, of course, were also paying all our expenses, and in fact doing us very well as far as comfort was concerned.

We were always impatient, however, and were beginning to wonder if anything was being done about us at all. The Vice Consul from Barcelona had been up and wasn't too hopeful; he told us that we ought never to have said we were soldiers, and we cursed ourselves anew. Dorchy,* whose job as Press Attaché to the Embassy had been forbidden [the Germans had 90 press attachés in Spain, which accounted for the noticeable bias!] came up and promised to get us out, by fair means or foul if necessary.

The new Vice Consul, Mr. Whitfield, arrived and we got to know him very well – a charming man with a great sense of humour. He was always complaining how abominably the authorities treated him and put every obstacle in his way, as indeed they did, but he took it very well, and pursued his work with limitless energy. He did not trouble to disguise his feelings about the new regime, without needlessly prejudicing his position. One morning the paper so infuriated him that he tore it up and threw it out of the window. It was he that instituted the evening toast consigning Hitler to the nether regions. He always kept us amused and interested; the Duke of Windsor's passage through Spain was always a thorn in his flesh. He and Mrs. Simpson had left a trail of trouble behind them, and Whitfield spent days trying to rescue one of her maids from France. Two enormous lorries had to be hired to take all the

> The Duke and Duchess had fled from the north of France south to Biarritz to avoid capture by the Nazi Germans. They continued to Spain in June 1940 and on to Portugal the following month. They left Lisbon on 1 August bound for the Bahamas.

---

* To counter the anti-British news there had been much pressure and lobbying for approval from the Ministry of Information and Foreign Office for a network of press and information offices in Spain, North Africa and France under direction of the Embassy in Madrid. Paul Dorchy was deployed to Barcelona to help communicate British propaganda but had to fight hard for funds from the British Government.

luggage from the Riviera to Lisbon, and endless formalities gone through to ensure the drivers were not in the pay of Soviet Russia. Incidentally we seriously considered smuggling ourselves to Lisbon on one of these.

One day we had the surprise of our lives when we heard that Raikes and Hogg, who had escaped a week before us, had arrived and were locked up in the local prison. A few days later I was also amazed to hear that my cousin *[Jimmy Johnson]* was in a French concentration camp at St-Cyprien, just over the border. *[N.B. Sapper Joseph Richards, whose escape account can be read in Chapter Twenty Five, had brought the news.]* It was evident that many British soldiers had come over the border and been either locked up or taken to concentration camps without being able to get in touch with Whitfield, and of course the Spanish authorities could not be bothered to do that. Some arrangement should have been made to prevent this and warn them that Spain was almost impossible to cross without being caught. At one stage there was a spate of them coming over, and Whitfield was in despair trying to get them out of jug. We had been in luck being almost the first arrivals, and were in fact the only ones who had not seen the inside of a Spanish prison or concentration camp.

At the instigation of Whitfield, we spent some of our time buying food and necessaries for Hogg and Raikes and one afternoon I went up with Rapley to see them. This was a most illuminating experience; visitors were allowed ¼ hour to talk to the prisoners. This performance was carried on through iron grilles, and a bar ran along the front to prevent one getting close enough to pass anything across. All food, etc. was sent in baskets and inspected before being sent in and a guard was posted at the end as an additional preventative; it did not, however, prevent Rapley giving them some money which he somehow managed to do while the guard wasn't looking. As there were about fifty people all trying to talk at once one had to shout at the top of one's voice to make oneself heard. I had never yet seen a closer human resemblance to a monkey-house. Fifteen minutes was not long to talk, but they seemed to be bearing up under the disgusting prison conditions; most of the prisoners were evidently political and had been there since the end of the civil war. This meant that Raikes and Hogg were popular guests, for, of course, they all wanted England to win the war and put an end to the Fascist regime when they would be quickly liberated. The prison conditions were evidently foul and abominably overcrowded, the place abounded with flies and lice and there was nowhere to sit down; they had to sleep on the bare stone floor, and as for sanitary arrangements, they were so inadequate as to be almost useless. We were very sorry for them, but there was nothing we could do, and after a fruitless interview with the Governor, who waved his hands and said "I must obey my orders", Rapley and I left.

We were becoming profoundly bored with Figueras and were as usual considering escape. Actually our situation was much improved and we had at least got into communication with our families and been sent money; English papers and books from the Consulate also relieved the tedium. But that didn't really get us any nearer home, and we were becoming very dissatisfied with the Consulate and Embassy for not letting us know what the situation was. We had received no answer to our letter to the British Ambassador, written 3 weeks previously, and even Whitfield was left completely in the dark; needless to say, he was as angry about it as we were, but unable to do anything.

However, something evidently had been happening, for on August 22nd a policeman appeared and informed us that we were going to Gerona with Raikes and Hogg. This sounded bad, as we thought it would mean the prison or concentration camp, but were reassured to hear that we were all going to stay there in an hotel. Why we couldn't stay in Figueras no-one could understand, except that Gerona was the capital of the province and the orders evidently came from the Governor of Gerona.

Raikes and Hogg duly appeared looking somewhat dishevelled and after affectionate farewells to the hotel staff who had been very kind to us, almost their only residents, we were escorted off to the station in the local taxi. Petrol incidentally was 12/6d *[62.5p]* a gallon, so motor traffic was not precisely abundant. *[N.B. In England, petrol was about 2/- or 10p a gallon in 1940.]*

CHAPTER FOURTEEN
NEWS FOR THE HOME FRONT

A month had passed since the surrender at St-Valéry. With no further news from official sources families in England were getting more and more anxious. It had been a hot summer's afternoon when the telegram arrived from the War Office to say that Chris was missing. Chris's brother Lee recalled his mother had frozen in anguish, whilst his father adopted the manner of a man who had sacrificed his son for his country as a means to hide his own turmoil. They had almost given up hope when, the day after Chris's birthday, a telegram arrived from Vichy saying:

ALL SAFE = CHRIS

Those three words were received with such enormous joy and relief. Then possibly frustration due to the lack of any further information. However they were soon followed by a very welcome surprise when, in early August, John Lennon received a telephone call from Major Tom Rennie of the Black Watch who had just returned to England and had come across Chris and Dennis on two separate occasions in the south of France. Rennie was able to answer many questions which would have reassured the families of both men.

Tom Rennie had also been taken prisoner at St-Valéry escaping nine days later – possibly the same day as Chris and Dennis. He managed to make his way back via Spain and Portugal, returning to England just six weeks after his escape. Although he had some papers and documents he too had found difficulty in crossing the French/Spanish border, but eventually did so at night over the mountains. He finally reached London on 4 August. Rennie had come across Dennis when the latter was examining the possibility of escaping via the train tunnel at Cerbère which they both turned down as impractical. Having been successful himself, Rennie felt able to reassure John that Dennis and his comrades would eventually find a way out of Cerbère to the British Consul in Barcelona.

Whilst Chris and Dennis were kicking their heels in Figueras he wrote to Mr Lennon as follows:

Solizarie,
Blairgowrie, Perthshire.
13 August '40

Dear Mr. Lennon,

Thank you for your letters of 9 & 10 August. The confirmation of my telephone message is correct with the following amplifications:-

1 At Marseilles he was in the process of getting a passport from the U.S. Consul General and visas for Spain and Portugal. Before procuring these a certain number of Soldier escaped prisoners at that time accommodated at the Sailors Club were taken over by the French authorities and accommodated in a French barracks. Your Son and his friends who were also at the Sailors Club decided things were becoming too official and to avoid internment in France decided to make away without waiting for papers.

2 We came across them again at Cerbère when they were investigating means of entering Spain. With no papers their problem was to cross the frontier and make for Barcelona and the British Consulate there. In order to do this they naturally had to get their bicycles across. When we left them – we had decided to cross the mountains on foot avoiding the frontier post by some three miles – they were considering taking a boat from Cerbère into Spain. They had plenty of French francs but might have considerable difficulty changing these into Spanish money in Spain as regulations there are pretty strict. On reaching the Consulate at Barcelona they would have little difficulty in obtaining papers and money from the C.G.

By National Law an escaped prisoner is not liable to internment. *(See Chapter Final Thoughts.)*

They were a fully capable quartette and I was pretty confident of their getting through. At worst they might have been arrested in France or Spain.

CONFIDENTIAL

The Embassy at Madrid are interested in getting escaped prisoners out of France and they know the conditions as we gave them full particulars when we were there. They were, I think, sending a representative to Marseilles to clear up the situation. We told the Embassy about your Son and his party.

I suggest you communicate with the Military Attaché at the Embassy, Madrid, asking if they have information. This should be done through the W.O. in cypher – War Office MI9 would help you if you went to see them I'm sure. I would deprecate any communication with Spanish officials at this stage as there are 3 or 4 others now in detention in Spain and the Embassy are dealing with the situation and hoped to get them out in due course.

The other men with your son were an R.A.F. Officer, a Soldier in the R.A.S.C. fluent French speakers an Officer in the R.E. also in the guard with your Son probably Capt. Waters but I thought the name was Arthurs. I'm sorry not to be more definite about this but we only saw them for a few minutes.

Yours sincerely

Signed T. G. RENNIE

P.S. I would be grateful if you could let me know when your Son gets home. He should have an interesting story as I believe they came through Paris when the Germans were in occupation.

My father annotated his copy of the letter with a handwritten note saying 'Rennie was killed on 24 March 1945 when commanding 51st Division in Rhine crossing'.

On 17 August Major Waters received the next telegram, confirming the safe crossing into Spain:

PLEASE TAKE MY PASSPORT FOREIGN OFFICE INSTRUCT FORWARD BRITISH CONSUL BARCELONA URGENT LOVE = CHRISTOPHER

Finally at the end of August an official letter from the Casualty Branch bore the news that Second Lieutenant J.D. Lennon was at present detained by the Spanish authorities and efforts were being made to secure his release.

> Having returned to England Thomas Gordon Rennie was made Commanding Officer of the 5th Battalion, Black Watch in 1942. He led the battalion at El-Alamein in October 1942, and then led the 154th Infantry Brigade during the Allied invasion of Sicily in July 1943. In December 1943 he was given command of the 3rd Infantry Division and took part in the Normandy Landings in June 1944. Now a Major-General he was given command of the 51st Highland Division. Rennie was killed in action by mortar fire during Operation *Plunder*, the crossing of the Rhine.

CHAPTER FIFTEEN

FOUR WEEKS IN GERONA
22 AUGUST-19 SEPTEMBER

A plain clothes detective accompanied us in the train to Gerona, where we duly arrived and were escorted to the "Hotel Peninsular", evidently the hotel of the town, a pseudo-modern but shabby building. Here we were handed over to a new "stooge", a most unpleasant and sinister looking man whom we soon christened the "black stooge", on account of his black hair, glasses, eyes and clothes. "Sleek" just wasn't the word to describe him. Rapley had come with us and after various negotiations he returned to Figueras. We had been given to understand that we should be allowed to go out into the town, but as soon as he had gone the black stooge reappeared and told us we were to be confined to the hotel and were not allowed to telephone or communicate in any way with the outside world. We were naturally disgusted at this treachery, and Mayhew was unfortunately rather rude to him, and asked him if the Spanish ever kept their word! This naturally infuriated him, but it was worth watching.

We immediately wrote off to Whitfield and informed him that dirty work was afoot, posting the letter via a passer-by out of the window. The stooge and his assistant sat at the entrance to make sure we didn't go out, and we had the greatest pleasure in keeping them up till 3am that night, just out of spite. They subsequently tried to get their own back by accusing us of having "drunken orgies".

We spent exactly four weeks in this hotel. The only fresh air we could get was by sitting up on the roof, which commanded an excellent view of the city. Here we used to sunbathe for hours on end, except when the wind was in the wrong direction and the smoke of the town drove us downstairs again. The black stooge and his assistant eventually disappeared with orders to the hotel manager to report us if he saw us going out. Despite this we used to slink out when he wasn't looking and wander round the town. However, someone must have seen us as the black stooge reappeared one day and threatened with dire oaths to cast us into prison if we did not obey orders. He also forbade us to talk to anyone in the hotel, but this was too absurd, particularly when many people came and talked to us. The telephone rule was relaxed and we frequently rang up Whitfield or the Consulate at Barcelona to find out if anything was being done to obtain our release.

Life was uneventful and our impressions of Spain were naturally limited to the confines of the hotel. We made several friends, most notable of which was Juan, a young Spanish officer of the Ski Corps [they have them in the Pyrenees] whose mother was English. He had been educated in England at Stonyhurst, and became a naturalised Spaniard at the outbreak of the Civil War, when he fought for the Fascists. His father was murdered by the Communists, and his collection of books, one of the largest in the country, burned around him. He told us how he took infinite pains to avenge this, by obtaining an entrance to the prison, as a visitor, where he knew the gentleman responsible for this was locked up. With a chair, the only article of furniture in the cell, he belaboured the said Communist and apparently killed him.

He entertained us well and used to bring some of his girl-friends, and we danced to an ancient and decrepit gramophone. The Manager, however, a surly fellow, objected to this, and before long the black stooge was in again accusing us of further "orgies"! So he forbade us to talk to them, and even ordered them not to see us any more. So that was that, except Juan continued to talk to us, as of course the army was in a strong position not to worry about trifles like that. Every Saturday the local garrison marched past and we had a good view of their equipment – very primitive and poorly turned out. But we gathered that the soldier is really tough and capable of marching for miles in blazing sun or freezing cold, both common enough, with very little food or sleep. The Military Attaché, whom we subsequently met, said he was very impressed by what he had seen of this.

The hotel had an unfriendly atmosphere, but as there were now six of us we formed the larger proportion of the permanent residents so it didn't matter to us. There was a popular bar attached where we spent much of our time and money; occasionally we made surreptitious efforts to turn the wireless on to the English news, and it was then one discovered how thick with stooges the place was. They all leapt up from various corners and shouted across at us, forbidding us to do it. The only way was to get Juan to come and do it for us. The only people we were really friendly with were the waiters, who complained to us in low voices of the new regime and bad pay, and how glad they would be when England won the war. One of them even wanted to come back with us and join the army.

We had to find some outlet for our energies and were eventually reduced to throwing water at each other's windows across the courtyard. This was not popular either, and I well remember Dennis being chased at full speed down the passage, clad only in a pair of pants, by a furious hotel night-porter. Hawkins was always in trouble, one of his best efforts being to fall through the skylight above the lift shaft; he made a habit of sunbathing on this, until one day it broke, and only by the greatest good luck did he manage to hang on to the edge while we rushed to his rescue. Glass fell all the way down the shaft and created a panic, so that the Manager immediately rang up Whitfield at Figueras who came rushing down to Gerona, only to find that Hawkins was suffering from a few cuts.

After a fortnight of this we again began to get desperate and started thinking, for the umpteenth time, of escaping on our own. Someone suggested

Gerona rooftop 1– l to r: 'Berlitz' Mayhew, Mrs Dorchy, Montie Hogg, Peter Raikes, Dennis Lennon, Ron Hawkins, Chris Waters [Author's collection]

Gerona rooftop 2 – l to r standing: 'Berlitz'Mayhew, Dennis Lennon, Ron Hawkins, kneeling: Peter Raikes, Chris Waters, Montie Hogg [Author's collection]

writing to the Military Attaché *[Brigadier Torre-Torr]* at Madrid, so we penned a desperate letter saying that we should escape if nothing happened in the next few weeks. A few days later he rang up and told us for God's sake not to do anything so silly but to wait patiently; he would soon have us out. This was the first intimation we had had that the Embassy knew anything about us, and so, of course, we were enormously pleased and duly celebrated. Up to then we felt that we were being entirely neglected, and possibly that the Embassy had not even heard of us. This was the only thing we had to blame them for, if only they had let us know weeks ago that something was being done, however slowly, we should have been saved weeks of anxiety and useless talk of escape. Not that our worries were of much importance to the Embassy, but we might in fact quite easily have gone off under our own steam, ignorant of the fact that we were a "test case" – as we subsequently discovered. And that would, of course, have scarcely improved the negotiations of the Embassy.

So we waited patiently and the promised freedom duly arrived – exactly four weeks after our arrival in Gerona; the black stooge appeared with the good news that we were going to Madrid and must be ready to catch the 7 o'clock train on the following morning September 19th. It seemed strange hearing of any good news from that dreadful man, but it was true. After exuberant farewells to our friends – we weren't worrying about not talking to anyone now – and having completely flooded the passage between our bedrooms with a final water fight, we retired to bed in high spirits.

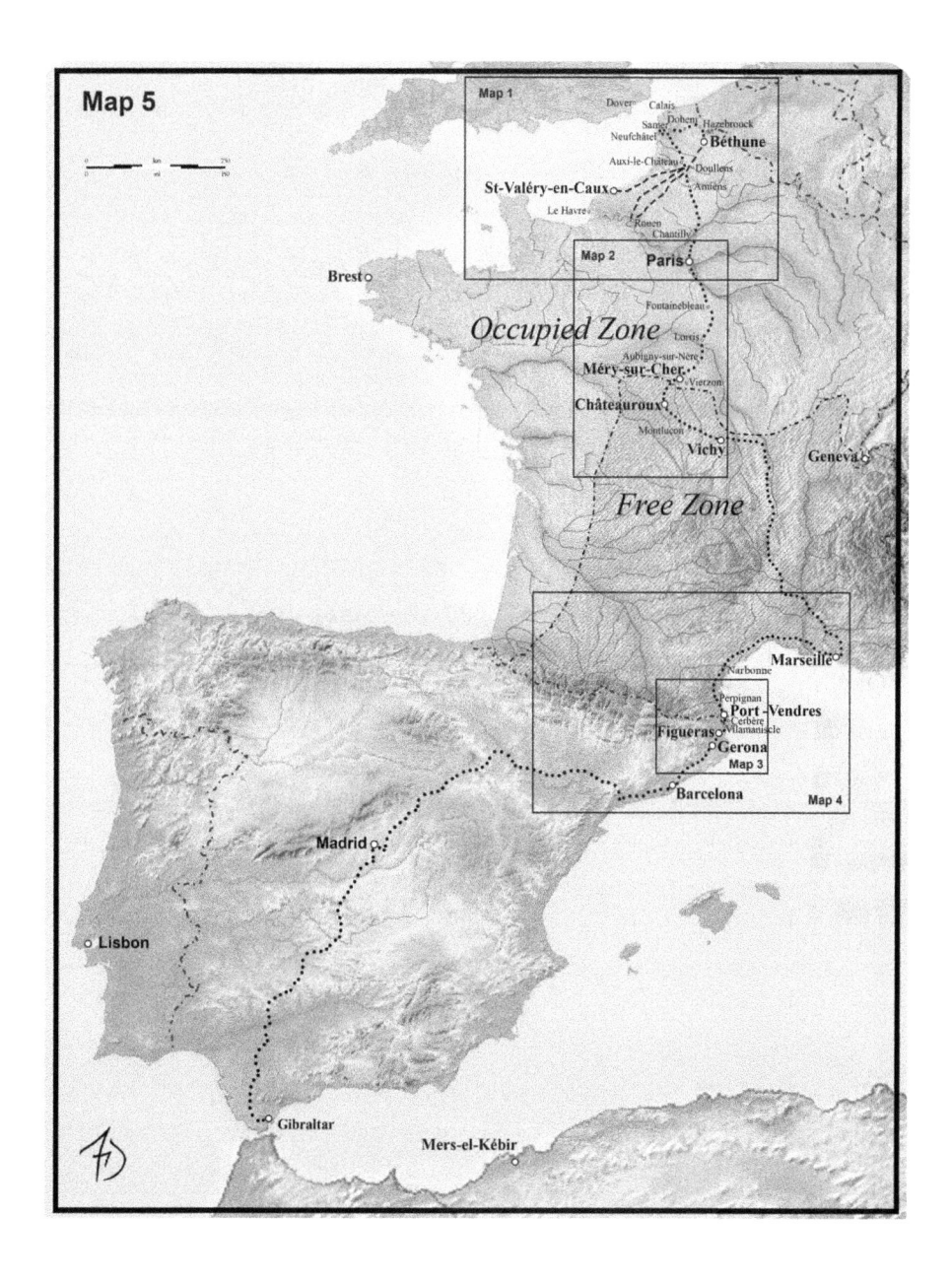

CHAPTER SIXTEEN

OILING THE NEGOTIATIONS

There was a strong suspicion that, as part of the overall negotiations for a supply of oil to Spain, Sir Samuel Hoare included the release of British internees from Spanish prison.

When the Spanish Civil War broke out in 1936, Nazi Germany sent units to assist the Nationalists under General Franco with the aim to gain combat experience for his men and test some of the latest military technology including the Luftwaffe's *Dorner* bombers and *Stuka* dive-bombers. The United Kingdom recognised Franco's regime in February 1939 with the last Republican stronghold surrendering on 1 April.

Sir Samuel Hoare, later Lord Templewood, was the British Ambassador in Madrid from 1940 to 1944. Hoare had been a senior Conservative MP, with positions including Foreign and Home Secretary and First Lord of the Admiralty. However a condition of Labour's agreement to serve in the coalition government was that he be removed from office as he was seen as an appeaser – someone prepared to make concessions to an aggressive power in order to avoid conflict. Churchill, who knew Hoare well and had opposed him during the passage of the India bill,[4] recognised Hoare's negotiating skills built from years of experience, appointing him as Ambassador to Spain from May 1940. In this challenging role he was to somehow dissuade Franco from drifting towards the Axis powers and to remain neutral. Requested by Hoare and sanctioned by Churchill, MI6 spent large sums on bribes to prevent Franco joining forces with Nazi Germany.[5]

Exasperating both MI6 and MI9 in London, Sir Samuel would not encourage British internees to make any plans to escape from Spanish custody, preferring to negotiate with the Spanish authorities for their release. This concurs with the account given by Captain Besley *(see Chapter Twenty Five)*.[6]

With the fall of France the United States complied with the request to halt its considerable oil exports to Spain as the Allies feared the Spanish would re-export petroleum products, especially aviation fuel, to the Germans. With no other access to oil Franco acceded to the demands for neutrality in return for an allotment of oil.[7]

CAPTAIN
JIMMY JOHNSON

AND

CAPTAIN
TOMMY TRYTHALL

CHAPTER SEVENTEEN

AN AFTERNOON ESCAPE

17-27 JUNE 1940

The rumour that had been circulating amongst the patients at the Royal Picardy of the Germans' plans to separate the different nationalities now became fact. On 17 June Jimmy and Colin were told of a transfer to an English hospital and that afternoon were taken away in ambulances to Camiers on the other side of the river where a base hospital had been established.

As in the Great War, Camiers, with its many hundreds of beds [possibly as many as 2,000] had become a British Base Hospital receiving wounded from many of the Clearing Stations at the front line. It was glorious to return to an English atmosphere again and English doctors. Everything seemed so clean and there did not seem to be any shortage of equipment. However once again there was a shortage of food due to the Germans having taken all the emergency supplies and extra cigarettes and chocolate belonging to the hospital. One morning porridge was made of mashed biscuits and oats, and the bread was rationed to two or three rounds a day.

Camiers lay at the foot of the downs beneath the shadows of the tall chimneys of a cement factory. Before the war it had been a TB sanatorium composed of two modern concrete blocks. There was a road running at the back of the hospital building and behind that the preliminary construction of a large permanent camp. Round the whole area was an eight foot high wire mesh fence. Based on the two main blocks a tented base hospital camp had been pitched. One of the main blocks was reserved for German wounded, the other acted as the administration centre for the hospital. This latter building had the advantage of a large flat roof on which patients were allowed to sunbathe. From here they could see not only the surrounding country, but everything that was going on in the camp. There were two entrances, both

Sketch of Camiers [Daphne Newton]

heavily guarded. By day patrols went round the camp outside the fence at irregular intervals, but by night all ranks were confined to their tents. It was given out that anybody outside their tent at night, when both dogs and sentries patrolled, was liable to be shot without warning. Certainly shots were heard at night, but there was never any report of casualties! The road was patrolled occasionally by day and there were guards at all the exits in the fence.

21 June

Diana Darling,

I am getting on very well now. Another fortnight should see the thing completely healed up with luck. I am at last able to use my arm more. We are being well looked after.

It is very tantalizing here as we do not get much news so do not really know what is going on. What a marvellous day your first letter will be but I suspect it is still some time off – I think your only hope is to try writing through the Red Cross. Keep well and get some fun out of life if you can. Write to my family won't you as I can't.

Love from Jimmy

This postcard arrived 9 September.

Although Jimmy and Colin had been considering escaping, Colin's wounds were such that it would have made things very difficult and he would not have been able to carry anything. Jimmy too was still very weak, plus they only had about 400 Francs between them. The hospital at Camiers had some 800 patients and once again Jimmy met many men from the RWF, including Corporal Codd, Fusilier Thynne, Lance Corporal Williams, Hughes 87, Evans 57 and Evans 74.[*] He also befriended men from the Royal Artillery including Captain Harold 'Tommy' Trythall.

26 June

Diana Darling

A short letter, we are only allowed to write on one side. I am still in hospital and progressing well. The wound is nearly healed up but I am still having a little trouble with the nerves. At one of the other hospitals at which I was I saw Clough who I think will be all right – he was shot through the leg. Jim Lewis is also in the offing but I have not seen him, he is a little ahead of me. I don't think he was wounded but his broken thigh gave out.

I am looking forward to hearing from you, but I am afraid it will be some time yet. It is funny you know but it is quite hard to know what to say. There is so much one would like to say but can't. Do you know I got the final copy of Esquire but had to abandon it with some of my kit the same night.

All my love.

News came on the hospital grapevine they were to be moved to a convalescent camp about twenty miles away. Conditions were rumoured to be better there but the guard more strict. They immediately set about scrounging clothes, washing gear and collecting together odds and ends they thought they should want for a journey.

Standing on the flat 'sunbathing' roof studying the form, Jimmy was approached by Trythall who asked whether he had thought of escaping. 'Yes' was the reply, but the idea had been temporarily abandoned as Colin was still not fit enough to undertake the task.

---

[*] Soldiers had numbers during the Great War, officers did not; until after WW2 numbers were in regimental blocks. In a regiment like the RWF you could have sixty or seventy Joneses and as many Williamses. The last two digits of their number differentiated them; sometimes there would be two men with the same last two numbers, in which case the last three would be used.

Tommy said he had made up his mind to go the next day, if he could get somebody to go with him. He had heard the clerks were making out the lists to move the nearly able bodies to Germany. 'Would Jimmy be interested?' Tommy had some money, about 1,600 Francs, or £5 *[about £270 at today's values]*, and also a plan. Briefly, this was to leave the camp just after lunch, a period of great inactivity when the guards would not be on the look-out, unlike the night time. There was also a good chance of being mistaken for members of a French working party who appeared to be moving outside the camp without let or hindrance. This fitted in very well with an observation of Jimmy's. He had noticed that the guards would head for their lunch at the cookhouse on the south side of the camp around 12.30pm. Patrol of the whole perimeter, which took about an hour, would not resume until after 2pm. Importantly on the north side there was a part of the fence that could not be seen from within the camp, except from the flat roof, because of a dip in the land and the long grass. This meant they would have about two hours in which to get away.

Jimmy mulled this over before approaching Colin. He was very nice about everything, admitting that he did not think he could 'compete' at the moment and if Jimmy thought he had a chance he should take it at once instead of waiting for him. Deciding to go, the rest of the day was spent making plans.

On the morning of 27 June, a week after Chris and Dennis had jumped through the hedge, Jimmy and Tommy carried out their preparations. The first thing was to get their kit ready. In order not to be too conspicuous in khaki they decided not to carry a haversack, although this meant limiting what they took. They wore, and carried, bearing in mind that this was June and therefore hot days and cold nights, thick woollen vests and pants, flannel shirt, cardigan and battle dress. In their pockets were handkerchiefs, Jimmy counted five, then shaving kit, pocket books, knives, scissors, socks, compass, map, dressings for the wounds and seventeen cigarettes. Jimmy also had photographs of his wife and two-year-old son and a dud cheque which he had written in Le Touquet but failed to cash, carried in a case given to him by his father-in-law Lord Keyes. They raided the 'deceased persons clothing store' for some form of hat to keep their heads warm at night. Tommy found an ex-Tank corps beret and Jimmy a French forage cap. Something they wanted badly and were unable to procure for some time was a 'housewife', that is, a small sewing kit. Finally although they wanted to take ground sheets they decided against them feeling they would look too obvious.

At this point in his notes Jimmy gave a description of his companion. 'Tommy Trythall was fairly tall, about 5'10" or 11", aged 45 with hair going grey, which he brushed straight back without parting. He was very thin and light. In civil life he was a banker in a south coast town. He served in the western desert *[i.e. in Egypt]* in the last war as a trooper in the cavalry. He had the heart of a lion, nothing appeared to frighten him and nothing would deter him from doing what he wanted. He only had one idea in his head and that was to get back to England and fight the boche again. This time he had got a commission in the Gunners Searchlight. He was a silent person to travel with, quite incapable of talking nonsense and only made statements after careful thought. We got on very well and never had a "row" the whole time, in spite of our being always rather on edge.' Tommy was equally impressed with his fellow traveller, describing him as 'an awfully good fellow and I could not have had a braver companion. He is a great chap.'

Before lunch they again reconnoitred the fence and decided they would have to cut a hole in it. This required a pair of wire clippers, which were eventually found in the tool box of one of the ambulances, a number of which were lying idle in the grounds. Having found the cutters and tossed for the job, Jimmy went up to the roof of the hospital to keep a look out for patrols whilst Tommy, watching out for signals, went to the selected spot and cut the wire. This was done successfully without any scares. Colin was told that they were going. He said he would try and keep their departure dark. Jimmy later found out that there was a rumour round the camp that night, but the Germans did not know until the next day.

In order to conceal their absence, Colin apparently ate their tea for them. The orderly therefore failed to notice their departure and presumably the night orderly thought they had been moved elsewhere. In any case he could not report any absences as he too was not allowed to leave the tent once he went on duty. The remaining British officers were confined to their tents for two or three days as a punishment which would not have been too popular.

Too keyed up to eat much lunch, at 1.15pm there was a last look round from the roof and the decision taken to start. With Colin and one other remaining as lookout on the roof the two men walked slowly out of the hospital, crossed the road and subsided into the protecting long grass and bushes on the other side. Tommy had done a beautiful job with no sign of the cut wire unless looked at very carefully. Jimmy wondered later as to whether or not it was ever found. One after the other they lifted the flap in the fence, which had been cut so they could roll through lengthwise, then fixed it again afterwards to leave no sign of their departure. It was a thrilling moment. Being a keen horse rider Jimmy likened it to the start of a Point to Point race. Then, in full view of the hospital, they crossed the patrol track and walked very slowly up the slope of the field, restraining themselves from looking round. There was only one open field, the rest being terraces of wheat. Reaching the first wheat field they sank to their knees and crawled through until they had reached the far side which took nearly half an hour. It was hard work with their thick woollen vests and weak arms.

About 3pm they took a breather under the lee of a hedge, removing their cardigans and jackets which were then carried over their shoulders. Donning their hats and lighting cigarettes they continued to climb up the downs away from the camp. Turning a corner they saw, about thirty yards away, a man in blue uniform trousers just taking off his coat, preparatory to lying down for a sun bathe. On seeing the escapees he jumped to his feet and started pulling his coat back on.

They thought their last moment had come and they would be arrested. 'Act natural' said Tommy. There was nothing to do but put a bold front on it and stroll past. Saying 'bonjour' with a friendly wave, Jimmy, the only one of the two to speak French, continued to converse with Tommy as if they had a right to be there. The German said nothing and directly they were out of sight the two escapees went off as fast as they could. In hindsight they came to the conclusion that he must have thought they were part of a party who had been working about a mile away in the morning. Of course it might have been that he was not supposed to have been there himself.

Soon after they reached the top of the hill from where the view seemed like the promised land. Having previously decided to head due south through German-occupied territory they arrived at the outskirts of the village of Widehem where they found villagers harvesting in the fields nearby. They had walked about ten kilometres and were absolutely beat. Jimmy asked if there were any Germans in the village. It seemed that one or two came in the evening to graze their horses and in the morning there would be foraging parties. Jimmy asked for something to eat and drink whereupon an old man, wearing the blue peaked cap that appears to be the privilege of French 'oldest inhabitants', led them to his back fields. He produced raw eggs, bread and butter and two bottles of home-made cider. His wife, who was rather frightened, threw lettuces, tomatoes and some fruit over the hedge, but would not enter the field.

The farmers were reluctant to offer them a bed for the night, directing them to the next village. Being very unfit the escapees rested a while then, at 7pm, headed to the other end of the village where they saw a barn with a car inside. Nobody was about so they got into the car thinking that even if they could get nothing to eat they had at least got cover for the night.

A little later Jimmy went round to meet the farmer's wife. La Patronne was very pro-British and said she would be delighted to give them dinner and yes, they could sleep in her car. That meal was the best they had had for several weeks. Soup Bonne Femme, chicken and vegetables, an omelette, cheese, bread and butter, cider, coffee and eau de vie de cidre. The cold night passed uneventfully in the car and they set off at 4am, helping themselves to two empty sacks as they left.

CHAPTER EIGHTEEN
TURNING SOUTH
28 JUNE-29 JULY

The plan was to proceed to the area of Dieppe or St-Valéry to see if they could get a boat, in the belief that all the boats between Boulogne and the south of the Somme were guarded or made unserviceable. Anywhere near Le Touquet was definitely out of the question as the beaches were closely guarded and there might be a hue and cry after them. For three days they moved mostly by night using the cover of darkness to cross main roads unobserved. With the child's compass to guide them they travelled across country on field paths or small country roads, but were making very little progress.

There were a number of discussions as to whether to try and get civilian clothes. They did not wish to be taken as spies, on the other hand they wanted to avoid attracting attention. In the end three days were spent in khaki, travelling at these awkward hours, before changing into rough farmer's clothes. However they kept their khaki trousers as they had noted that everyone seemed to be wearing some bits of uniform – whether it was French railway staff or Belgian refugees in their blue army uniform trouser – so khaki did not look out of place. Their overcoats and jackets were transferred to the sacks. They also began to notice that French farmers would set off for their fields around 6 in the morning and return to their homes about 5 in the evening. So Jimmy and Tommy joined in with the visible movement of the country by walking two or three hours every morning from around 6am and another two hours in the evening, thus were able to cover greater distances – up to sixteen miles each day.

The route was generally in a south/south-westerly direction except for skirting Montreuil. Taking just under two weeks, some of the villages they

Map 6

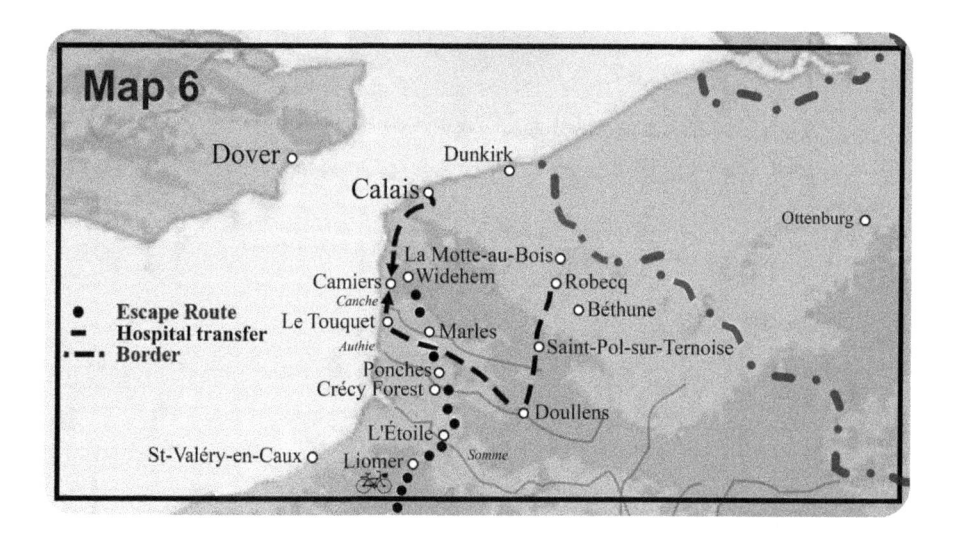

- Escape Route
- Hospital transfer
- ·—·· Border

Dover, Dunkirk, Calais, Ottenburg, La Motte-au-Bois, Camiers, Widehem, Robecq, Béthune, Canche, Le Touquet, Marles, Saint-Pol-sur-Ternoise, Authie, Ponches, Crécy Forest, Doullens, L'Étoile, St-Valéry-en-Caux, Liomer, Somme

walked by were Frencq, Cormont and Marles where they got their civilian clothes. They crossed the river Canche near Brimeux and on to Buire, Saulchoy, Douriez and Tortefontaine. Crossing the Authie near Ponches, they passed Gueschart, Yvrench, Coulonvillers, Bussus-Bussuel, Francières and Bouchon. The Somme was crossed near l'Etoile by an unguarded bridge and on to Riencourt, Camps-en-Amiénois and Liomer.

The chief difficulty was crossing rivers and railways. They had been told that all bridges were guarded and it was necessary to have either a pass issued by the local *Kommandantur* or to have papers to prove identity. The first river they encountered, the Canche, was guarded but eventually they found a small bridge that was not.

It was the same with the Authie and the Somme and it appeared that the Germans were only really taking trouble with the larger crossings. Also they had begun to learn that the guards did not tend to question people in the early morning or evening when large numbers of workers were crossing to and fro. Once again by blending in with the visible movement of the countryside they could move much more freely.

The country through which they were walking was open and undulating, the only cover being around the villages or farms and in the river valleys. The majority of crops seemed to be grain. The difficulties were enormous as neither of them were as fit as they had thought and they tired very easily. They slept in barns, under haystacks or hedges, and sometimes were lucky enough to get a bed. Although barns provided shelter they were also full of rats which would crawl over them while they were asleep. On waking the men would find their clothes covered in urine trails or droppings which had to be washed off. They quickly learnt to cover their arms and heads with their overcoats. The first week was hot, the second, by which time they were feeling stronger was rainy and they managed one day's break from walking to rest up and get some washing done. The Germans were everywhere.

About the tenth day, after they had crossed the Somme, they passed through an area where a French Division had been decimated and laid down its arms. This gave them the opportunity to pick up a number of items such as pairs of shorts, and in particular a pack so that they could carry their belongings, which included their uniforms, more easily.

They were also lucky enough to pick up two old bicycles which speeded their progress, despite being difficult to ride as they were not the right size for either man. The wheels were missing many of their spokes which did not help either. But they were now able to travel much more quickly covering up to twenty-five miles a day with little difficulty.

Food was a problem. They found the local inhabitants were generally very helpful as long as they 'did not strike anybody too rich'. The farmers would help out with bread, cheese or butter and with their few francs they could supplement their meals in small village shops. However it seemed the bigger the landowner the less prepared they were to help. They avoided people on the roads not knowing who they were.

It was near Liomer, where they obtained their bicycles, that they became aware of more and more troops on the coast. Even though they had not heard of the fighting in the area, St-Valéry-en-Caux was ruled out in favour of the Channel Islands.

Travelling on through Beaucamp, Ronchois, Conteville, Sommery, Montérolier, Bosc-Edeline to Saint-Aubin-lès-Elbeuf just south of Rouen, they crossed the Seine by passenger ferry – a rowing boat. Feeling bolder, they proceeded to Lisieux via Giverville, Fumichon and Hermival-les-Vaux. They had hoped to borrow some money from an acquaintance of Tommy's but this proved to be unsuccessful as they failed to make contact. Lisieux was full of German troops and the garages seemed to be used for billeting accommodation. They continued to Benerville near Deauville on the coast via Beaumont and Tourgéville, to look up another French friend. Cycling up to the house they had the alarming sight of two German sentries standing on the steps. Dismounting from their bicycles they said 'Sorry, wrong place,' and walked out, without looking round. Back on the road they quickly moved on, thankful for their rag tag appearance. It appeared that the majority of the civilian population had been evacuated as most of the houses were occupied by German troops. Immediately behind Benerville on the hills there were 'a great many direction-finding lorries and apparatus'; a big château gave the appearance of an obvious HQ with the insignia of the Black Eagle.

They had been heading for St Malo but learnt at Tourgéville that the Germans now occupied the Channel Islands and the coasts were so well guarded that it was impossible to get a boat. After a hurried consultation the decision was made to make for the French non-occupied zone about 300 miles away and then Spain as Jimmy could speak a bit of Spanish too.

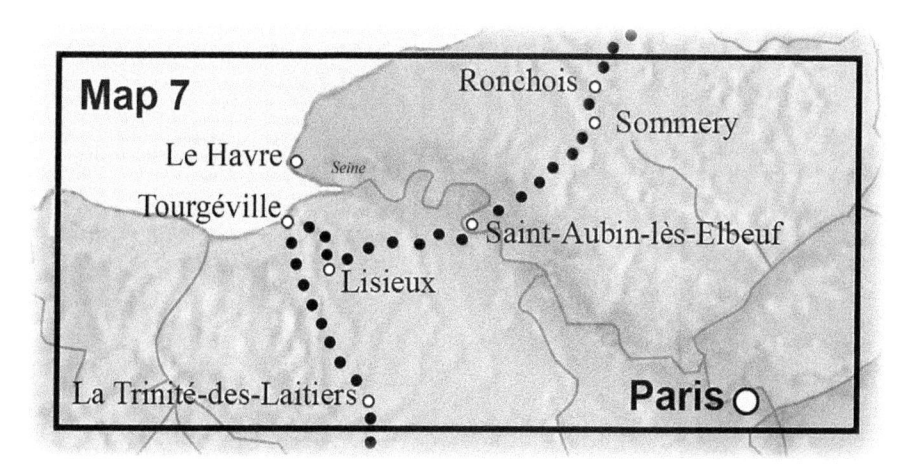

Map 7

Le Havre
Seine
Tourgéville
Ronchois
Sommery
Saint-Aubin-lès-Elbeuf
Lisieux
La Trinité-des-Laitiers
Paris

Turning south they followed the course of the river Touques. Feeling tired as evening approached they headed for the river. On the bank above the road they passed an 'enormous' old Frenchman digging in his fields with a long handled spade, wearing his First World War medals dangling from a long piece of string. They stopped and asked if they could sleep in his barn that night. His house too was above the level of the road. 'Who are you?' the farmer asked. 'British officers' and they showed him their English uniforms in their pack. 'I will ask Madame' came the reply. [They had learnt by now that Madame always made the final decision on all household matters, including guests.] Madame was produced and after a bit of a talk said they could sleep in the barn but must be away early in the morning because of the German patrols in the area. Jimmy and Tommy had not realised they had left the coastal area where the main concentration of German forces were assembling for Operation *Sealion*, the invasion of Britain, but were now in an area where the German support groups were based. Occupied with building up airfields and recreation facilities for their own troops, they were not particularly alert.

The old man 'who must have been aged around 70' and his wife led Jimmy and Tommy up to their house. Despite being very short of food themselves, the farmers gave them something to eat and showed them the barn. After eating, the old man said 'I have something to show you' and went outside the front door of his cottage, pulled up a brick and exposed a key hidden underneath. He put the brick back into place and led them to the barn. Inside were two enormous Normandy barrels, oval things. The smaller one had a lock on it which the key fitted. Opening the lock he produced three glasses of cider. Closing it he said 'that's my special cider'. Then he locked it all up and returned to the house, putting the key back in its place under the brick and dusting it over so that his wife would not know where it was. This procedure was followed whenever Madame requested any cider too. The farmer repeated 'You can sleep in the barn but we'd be grateful if you were gone as soon as daylight comes.' After a good night's sleep on the hay in the barn they moved off south. The farmer's name was M. Marguerite; Jimmy returned to visit him after the war.*

The journey now took them through Manerbe, La Boissière, La Trinité-des-Laitiers, St Gauburge, Moulins-la-Marche, Mortagne-au-Perche, Préaux-du-Perche, Le Theil, Théligny, Saint-Agil, Rocé and Villerbon. The bicycles were running truer and easier than before as they had managed to mend one or two of the spokes in the wheels. It was easier to travel down the roads too, having decided which direction to take. However they found themselves travelling at different speeds. Tommy always wanted to go like hell, whereas Jimmy would say 'we're going to try and do forty or fifty miles today, so we will go

---

* After the war Austria was divided into four zones – each controlled by different powers, the Soviet Union, United States, United Kingdom and France. The British and French sectors were adjoined allowing military personnel to organise sporting competitions against each other. Jimmy was based in Austria from August 1945 and often competed in polo tournaments against the French. When an international tournament was held in Deauville to celebrate the resumption of polo in Normandy Jimmy was invited to enter an official *British Troops in Austria* team.

Once the tournament was finished Jimmy, along with his wife and now ten-year-old Robin, took the opportunity to visit some of those who had helped with his escape. A half hour drive took them back to the farm where M. Marguerite was still working the land. He showed them a Guest Book with the names of Allied men he had fed and sheltered during the war. Jimmy and Tommy were the first two entries in a list of nineteen names.

quietly and take frequent rests.' As a regular soldier it had been instilled in him to march at a steady pace and rest for ten minutes every hour. A greater distance could be covered this way therefore it was a pattern he continued on his bicycle. Accordingly they would generally travel alone. Tommy would set off ahead and if there was a decision on whether to turn left or right he would stop and wait for Jimmy to catch up.

They carried on this way until they reached the Vendôme, a prairie like area growing wheat and other cereals on enormous farms. Stopping in a village they found a priest and enquired about lodgings for the night explaining they were escaped British officers. By this time they were aware that French priests would not let them down on anything like this as they had had a lot of help from priests at various times. This particular priest advised them to avoid a family who lived just down the road who were extremely rich and not a very good lot. Instead they should travel another five miles.

On arriving at the next farm, and after the usual due inspection by the farmer's wife, they were able to stay for two or three nights. This gave them the opportunity to wash their clothes and have a bath. The farmer was a tenant farmer on a very big estate, and when the owner heard about the escapees, as the farmer had obviously told her, she demanded to see them. Jimmy and Tommy tidied themselves up as best they could and went off to see her. The owner was a charming old lady, wearing a collar ruff round her neck and living in a beautiful old house which she took delight in showing them. Taking them for gentlemen from England she gave them a drink and 2-300 francs each saying 'I hope you get home and really it has been absolutely delightful.' They returned to the farm in the back of the farmer's van. The word RAVITAILLEMENT *[i.e. food supplies]* was written on the side, as did all the vans that carried bread and other foodstuffs around the countryside. This meant it could travel around France without anybody inspecting it. The two even spent a pleasant day travelling round the area with the farmer.

The Loire was crossed on 29 July by another small ferry at Cour-sur-Loire. This area was very full of Germans with scarcely a village without at least a platoon in it. The troops did not appear to be from first line divisions as they were not dressed as smartly as those at Benerville.

By now they knew the boundary between Zone Occupée in the north of France and the Zone Non-Occupée in this area was the river Cher – a tributary of the Loire, a sizeable river about the size of the Thames. Although only fifty yards wide at this point, approximately thirty-five kilometres

Map 8

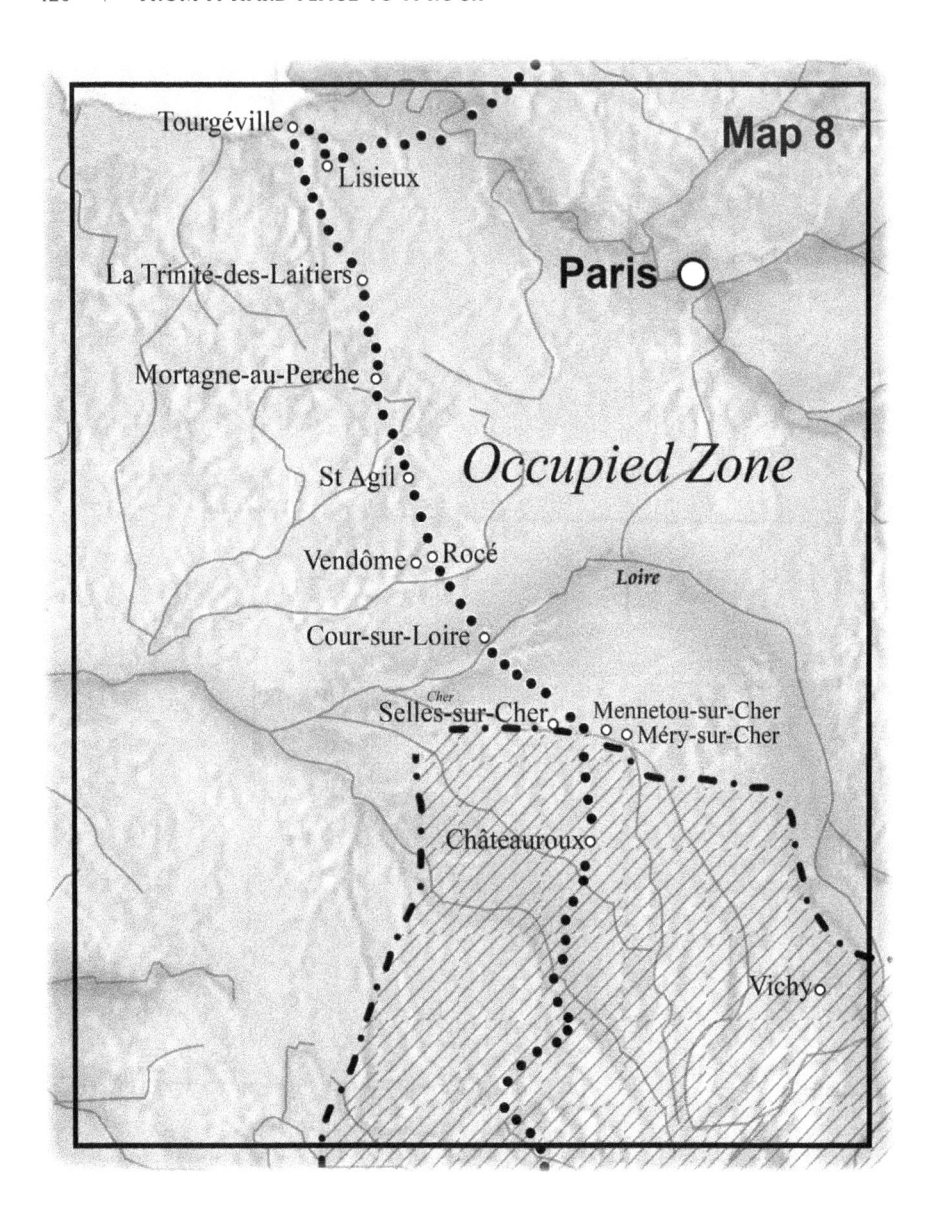

Occupied Zone

downstream of where Chris and Dennis had crossed, it was now fast flowing. Both the Cher and the Loire are in an area known as the Château District with enormous houses and properties. Many of the farmers had land on both sides of the boundary and would regularly cross over to check their herds. The Germans would patrol both sides of the river on foot, bicycle or horseback, at unspecified hours but which began to follow a sort of pattern. With the help of a nearby friendly farmer and his boat, they waited until they heard a patrol passing on the far side before loading themselves and their bikes into the boat, shoving off and were across the river and in hiding before the patrol came along on the northern side.

They had travelled over 700 miles on foot and bicycle and were now feeling very fit. From the moment of their escape they had found the French people had shown great kindness, offering assistance wherever they could, some even pressing a few Francs on them. They had managed to avoid guards and patrols at all the main river crossings, and now on the southern side of the Cher were feeling relaxed and a little excited, wondering what lay ahead for them.

CHAPTER NINETEEN
INTERNMENT
30 JULY–23 SEPTEMBER

It was 30 July when Jimmy and Tommy crossed to the Zone Non-Occupée. They were running out of funds and Châteauroux was about sixty miles away. Thinking the French would continue to look after them reasonably well they cycled down the road in that direction.

About ten miles short they were stopped by a gendarme who asked to see their papers. 'Like mugs' Jimmy later wrote, they hoped to 'wangle some Laissez passer' out of the Gendarmes. They admitted to being English, trying to get back home. Unable to help, the gendarme escorted them on his bicycle to the nearest post where they were put in a van and taken to the military headquarters.

They were interviewed by General Martin who was the Commander of this particular military area. He was quite friendly but had a typical French outlook and would do nothing outside the letter of the law to help. He suggested they stay 'en parole'* for a month whilst they tried to get some

---

* En parole *[to have given one's word]* is an agreement between captor and PoW. In exchange for not attempting to escape or take up arms against their captors for an agreed length of time, a prisoner would be given special privileges including freedom of movement. Prisoners would report to the guard regularly, at times specified by the captor. Once the agreed time period had expired the PoW was at liberty to move on. The prisoner could withdraw their parole at any time by informing their captor verbally or in writing; the captor could then give a period of grace for the PoW to continue on their way before taking any action. Parole could be a convenient arrangement for the captor as he would not be responsible for feeding the PoW; it was also very convenient for the escapee as it gave opportunity to rest and accrue funds for the next stage of escape. Jimmy was never sure if they had given their parole as he thought it was forbidden at that time but he, Tommy and the General had made a verbal agreement. Plus they had bought some time in which to plan.

money, of which they were in urgent need. At the end of that period he would then release them. Desperately needing funds the men agreed.

In spite of their being pretty grubby and scruffy the Adjutant, who did not quite know what to do with them at this stage, allowed them to eat in his Mess. However they were asked to find somewhere else to sleep.

So they headed into town to make enquiries, unsuccessfully. After a while they began to realise that although the French were not going to do them any harm, neither did they want to get involved in case the Germans turned up. Again they met a priest and explained their situation. He suggested they may be successful in the dormitory accommodation in the old girls' school down the road and took them there himself. This worked. Finally they were able to wash and clean up before returning to the French headquarters for their meals, becoming honorary members of their popote or officers' mess. Someone suggested they write to the War Office in London to apply for exchange with French Officers in England.

After a couple of days the Adjutant visited them saying arrangements had been made. They were to report the following evening 2 August with all their kit when they would be put on a train with a guard of two soldiers and were to travel to Port-Vendres near Perpignan. He added 'Of course you will have every advantage along the way' and started winking and nodding. Jimmy and Tommy stood 'like stupid people' not understanding what on earth he was getting at. In due course they were put on the train and went all the way down to Port-Vendres via Toulouse and Narbonne.

What they had not appreciated was that the French officer had arranged that the soldiers should pay no attention to them at all so they could escape off the train at any suitable place where the train went slow enough. It never occurred to either man or they would have withdrawn their parole before leaving. Instead they duly arrived in Port-Vendres where there was nobody to meet them. They disembarked from the train and marched towards the barracks, where they were not expected. The officer of the day greeted them saying 'I don't know who the hell you are but I think we'd better put you in here for the moment, and maybe we had better incarcerate you because we've got an inspection from the Germans coming soon and we have to say what people, travelling through the area, we have in custody.'

By now both men were anxious to write home to reassure families of their whereabouts. Although it was difficult to say a great deal in letters sent through the Red Cross, 'an opportunity arose' for Jimmy 'to send a letter by another route,' and it was this letter which listed the towns and villages they had passed through together with a rider saying 'To follow our route you will have to get a good road map Michelin – as most of them are very small.'

3rd August
Port Vendres
Par Perpignan
France

Diana my darling,

I hope you have not been too worried during the last six weeks about me. I wrote to you from hospital via the Red Cross to let you know I was all right. Since then I wrote a short note to Liz *[N.B. Diana's sister]* because it was not advisable to write direct to you. In any case I doubt very much if that letter will arrive.

This letter I shall send via the Red Cross so you should get it. But one is not allowed to say much.

I cannot tell you where we have been but suffice it to say that I came with a man called H B Trythall, a Captain of 45 in the Gunners, who in ordinary life is the manager of the branch of Barclays Bank at Bognor Regis, and could not find any direct means of returning home. At the moment we are stuck having been interned by the French military authorities in non-occupied France.

For various reasons we are not in a position to do much at the moment. Finance is one.

I believe, at least we have been told, that there is a possibility of exchange with French officers in England and we were told to write officially, which we did. Perhaps this avenue might be explored. In the course of the next few days I shall write again and let you know how we are getting on and where we are. Don't write to this address as we are leaving here tomorrow. I am well and the wound has healed up well leaving only a small scar in my back.* We bathed this morning. It was lovely. We shall bathe again tonight.

---

*   Six months after his return, his son Robin, who by then would have been three years old, vividly remembers sharing a bath with his father and being able to fit his fist into the hole in his father's back. The fist sized hole remained for the rest of Jimmy's life.

All my love darling to you and Robin. Don't get downhearted.
From Jimmy

This letter did not arrive until 20 November.

Tommy also wrote to his wife. It too must have been sent through this 'other route' due to the amount of detail it contains. Although the letter had been penned in Port-Vendres, it was headed with St-Cyprien as the return address.

> From Captain Trythall RA
> Etat-Major
> Camp Anglais
> St-Cyprien
> Sur Perpignan France
> 3 August 1940

My Dear Lucy,

What anxiety you must have had . . . I too have had a hard and dangerous time . . . First of all I will give you a short history of what I have done since I last wrote to you.

22nd May: We were near Calais. I had not been able to write to you for some days. I had to go into Calais and I took a bag of mail to a ship and asked the Captain to post it in England . . .

23rd May: German attack intensified. We had to abandon our searchlights and go into Calais to defend city.

24th May: Worse still. We were acting as infantry in redoubts.

25th May: In the morning, Deighton and two more officers wounded, D badly. I sent them to Hospital and was left alone in charge of battery. All officers having gone! In the afternoon I was wounded in left shoulder, but because the men would have been without a leader I refused to go to Hospital but stayed with the Battery. German attack intensified.

26th May: I was weak and almost delirious, was captured by Germans and sent to a French Hospital at Le Touquet, under German control. The French Medical Staff treated me well and although my arm was painful, it did not prevent my getting dressed and walking about the hospital. The Germans too were very good. The food was adequate but not what we were accustomed to. I was quite happy at Le Touquet but anxious about you . . . . Planned to escape.

23rd June: Was moved to British Hospital at Camiers near Etaples. Food not too good. Planned to escape from there, because I knew I should soon be fit and sent to Germany.

27th June: Made an escape in company of Captain Johnson of Welch Fusiliers. We got away in daylight, under the very nose of the sentry. We had decided to work Eastwards and then South through the German lines. The difficulties were enormous. We also found we were neither of us to be as fit as we thought we were, and tired very easily. We have about £5 in money. Johnson is an awfully good fellow and I could not have had a braver companion. He is a great chap.

The details of our journey must be left. We slept in barns, under haystacks, sometimes we were lucky enough to get a bed. The Germans were everywhere. Our chief difficulty was crossing rivers. There are six big rivers. The Clanche [sic], the Authie, Somme, Seine, Loire and the Cher, all guarded at every bridge and patrolled by Germans . . . I feel that without God's help we should never have got through. We found unguarded bridges in two cases, in the others we found small boats to carry us across. We crossed the Seine and the Loire in this way.

On the 3rd day we changed into civilian clothes – rough farmer's togs. We carried our uniforms in a sack. About the 10th day, we were lucky enough to buy two old bicycles very cheap. Thereafter our progress was quicker. We intended to make for the coast and try to get a boat to Jersey. On the way we went through Lisieux to try to find Mr Martin but could not contact him. The town was full of Germans. We then went to Benerville near Deauville on the coast to find another French friend – their house was occupied by Germans and they had gone. We found that the Germans occupied the Channel Islands and the coasts so well guarded that it was impossible to get a boat.

We then decided to make for French non-occupied zone, about 300 miles more journey. We crossed the Loire on 29th July and the Cher on 30th July. We were safe from the Germans at last.

We were running out of funds and decided to go to a big town Châteauroux to try to cash a cheque. All the way down the French people had been most kind. In most cases they gave us food and drink and would not accept our money. Only once did we pay for a bed! I shall never forget their kindness. Three times we had money thrust into our hands! They were unbelievably good.

On 31st July we decided whether wisely or not I cannot say to report to French authorities for advice. We were immediately put under restraint, but not in the sense of imprisonment. They are treating us with the greatest courtesy and our condition is infinitely better than being under the Germans.

2nd Aug. We were sent to a place called Port-Vendres on the extreme end of Mediterranean Coast near Perpignan.

There is so much to tell, but space will not allow, also time. The boys will be most interested to hear of my adventures. I have had some exciting times and have carried my life in my hands . . . It is so beautiful here. Like a picture from an ancient gallery. You would love

Port Vendres, 1928 by Roger Fry [Philip Mould and Company]

it. We move on to St-Cyprien tomorrow. I don't know what awaits us but I hope it will bring me nearer home.

I must not raise your hopes too much, but I feel there is a possibility of our being repatriated in some way or other . . .

We travelled upwards of 700 miles on foot and bicycle. It took over a month to get through. We have also travelled some 800 miles by train to get here. I am now hard and fit and bronzed by the weather. I should not like to go through the experience again, although I am prepared to take any risks in order to get back to England. For the present I am safe and well looked after! Today I have been to swim in the Mediterranean. It is lovely here. The mountains tower above the sea.

I forgot to tell you that when I got to Camiers, I found Deighton there in the hospital. He was not able to get back to England. He was getting better . . .

We are in almost complete ignorance about conditions in England here, as all the wireless is taken away and we only have German news.

Yours

St-Cyprien was one of a number of camps originally set up to accommodate some of the hundreds of thousands of Republican refugees fleeing from the Civil War in Spain. Suffering its own economic and social crisis, France was totally unprepared for this huge wave of migration. The government passed decrees by which "undesirable foreigners" could be confined to permanent surveillance centres thus providing the legal cover to imprison the refugees in concentration camps. Fleeing Jews, as well as Belgians, Germans and "potentially hostile foreigners" found themselves joining the Spanish contingent at St-Cyprien, although the Germans with Nazi tendencies were released after the Armistice with Germany.

The first refugees to the area had been imprisoned on the beach without any shelter from the elements, but tents were provided when St-Cyprien opened. These were replaced by huts, housing fifty people per hut, offering rudimentary shelter from the elements, though little protection from the winds that would whip up the sand every three to four weeks. There were unbearable numbers of flies and mosquitoes and prisoners slept on straw mattresses infested with lice. Sanitary arrangements were inadequate, potable water was badly filtered and supplies of food were insufficient. Dysentery was commonplace and there was an outbreak of typhoid.[8] [9]

After staying at Port-Vendres for two days, they were moved to the camp at St-Cyprien. Their accommodation was outside the perimeter of the concentration area where the 'Jews, doubtful Belgians and Germans' were. Jimmy and Tommy were given a cook called Gewurtz. He spoke English very well and was given rations for them. Despite the sand, wind, flies and other insects it was a beautiful spot.

The camp was also used as a place for collecting African troops prior to their being sent to North Africa for demobilisation. There was one small riot due to discontent amongst these troops through seeing the slightly better feeding arrangements that had been made for the internees. As the troops' feeding arrangements were very bad indeed, their complaint was justified. There was a great deal of graft in the camp and anything could be got by money, including various forms of passes, extra food, spirits, etc. The chief culprits were the Garde Mobile who were responsible for guarding the camp.

The men were woken a few days later by the sounds of hammering outside and looked out to see barbed wire being erected around them. When they looked closely however they saw it was just one strand. On enquiring they were told that the Germans were coming to inspect the camp and the French had to show them 'any Jewish or peculiar people we don't know about who are in custody, and you are in custody.' As Jimmy said, you only had to step over the wire and you were out of custody! But that was enough for the French to be able to say they had people in custody. At this stage the French were not as scared of the Germans as they would be later. Nor were they overly impressed with the Vichy government so did not follow every rule.

With parole still running there was ample opportunity for a spot of R+R. They would go out all day exploring the countryside or swimming in the Mediterranean [bathing was permitted twice a day] as well as conducting a flurry of letter writing.

One day Jimmy got severe toothache. Having little money in his possession he visited the Vice Consul who was French and lived in Perpignan. He explained his problem of requiring dentistry and the lack of means by which to pay. Could a kindly dentist be recommended? One was and a filling was required. The dentist then said he had just heard on the news that day that the post and telephone was open between the Zone Non-Occupée and England. Jimmy and Tommy immediately telegraphed their wives.

The assistant Commandant was very pro-British. Jimmy approached him asking if, as prisoners of war, they were entitled to some pay. The Commandant checked the books and confirmed that under the 1929 Geneva Convention, having been prisoners of the Germans now detained in a neutral country, they were indeed entitled to some pay. Checking the rates they duly received, from the French army, a nominal sum. It was only a few francs but it was a great help. As prisoners of Vichy France their official position was much the same as a prisoner of war, with officers paid at half the rate of their equivalent rank in that country.

On 4 August Jimmy wrote a similar letter home as that sent from Port-Vendres. His further letters give an insight into their daily life:

c/o Camp Commandant
St-Cyprien
8 August 40

My Darling,

I do hope that by now you will have heard from me, and will have got some idea of what we are doing. For the moment we are going to stay on here. Firstly to try and get money – secondly in the hopes of hearing from you. We have discovered that the American Consul in Marseilles will 'occupé de nos affaires'. We have written to him asking for money and we hope that he may be able to change cheques for us. I don't suppose we shall hear from him for a few days yet. The question of whether there is any immediate prospect of our exchange with French officers in England has a great effect on our plans. You might perhaps find out how the land lies. We have no intention of being stuck here all the war.

When you write to me you won't forget to give me any regimental news. I would like to find out who is still alive and kicking. We meet all sorts of strange people and nationalities here so I am trying to polish up my Spanish a bit but I have to ask questions in French when I get in difficulties which complicates matters a bit. I bathe twice a day which is nice – generally in the nude. I hope to get nice and brown. I am very well but I think about due for a go at British tummy. It seems to be a universal complaint round here. I haven't found time to be very heavy on my hands as yet. There are too many small things to do like one's washing, letters to write, acting as interpreter, picking up the languages. We have managed to collect an Austrian cook who is excellent with the simple means provided. I have kept a species of diary since we left the Germans so one day I should be able to tell you the whole story. I have got well accustomed to French cigarettes and find the very few English ones that come our way rather mild affairs. The moustache is blossoming. It's a bit of a soup strainer at the moment but will soon grow out of it.

I don't imagine that you and Robin have left Tingewick although I expect you are doing some sort of War Work. I shall have to visit the dentist soon which is annoying. Give my love to everybody and let me have what news you can. I love you more and more darling.

From Jimmy

PS Got fed up with my moustache after lunch and cut the majority of it off.

Dear Robin, can you read this yet? Hope you are well and being good. Love from Daddy

Again 8 August

My Darling,

Again not a very long letter. But it is nice to write to you even if the letters take a long time to arrive. I have tried to get in touch with you by telegram today. I don't know whether I shall be able to or not. I have also written by Croix Rouge and by Tangiers. I hope that some of the various methods will be successful.

Our future plans are still in the melting pot. We are waiting here to try and get money and to hear from you. After that I don't know. We are able to get the news such as it is. The papers are of course not up to much as they are controlled.

This is in some ways an interesting place. Every nationality is here. It was originally one of the several Spanish refugee camps. There are still many Spaniards left. I am trying to polish up my languages a bit. My French is quite reasonable now and has progressed beyond the kindergarten stage.

I am very well and getting brown from bathing. I wonder whether you have got in touch with Mrs Trythall yet? We have managed to get hold of an Austrian cook and so are eating well. The American

Consul at Marseilles is looking after us. But we have not seen him or heard from him yet. So we do not know what our chances of getting back legally are.

Will write again soon. All my love to you and Robin and the family.

11 August

Diana Darling,

No news from you. But I don't really expect any for some days yet. We have not heard from any of the consuls we have written to. But the post is pretty peculiar here.

I am taking my sun bathing very gingerly as I do not want to be unfit for any emergency. I wrote to Joan McLennan yesterday. I suppose the letter will turn up in about 3 months' time. But it's funny how nice and comforting it is to write to people, even if the prospect of the letter's arrival is doubtful. I am longing to hear from you. Our own efforts to telegraph our address to you were of no avail. The post office would not accept them.

12th Last night we had rather an amusing evening. The cook, Austrian, said would we like some music? He himself was on the halls with his mouth organ at some time in his varied career. We said yes and eventually 3 more Austrians or Jews or something turned up. One with an accordion which he played very well, one a comedian and one a singer. We got hold of some red wine at about four pence halfpenny a bottle. We invited our Spanish friends in and during the evening more and more people kept drifting in. One or two French, some

---

Joan McLennan was Private Secretary to the Governor of Tasmania, Sir Ernest Clark and the first woman to hold the position of official private secretary to an Australian Governor having studied law and accountancy as well as being fully trained as a private secretary. She had become a personal friend to Jimmy and Diana when they lived in Hobart. Writing to Joan could have been an attempt to unofficially contact another consular office. *The Mercury* (Hobart, TAS) 6 July 1951

garde mobile all together about 20 people. A more cut throat looking crowd I have never seen. But it was great fun being our first party of any sort for ages. It is wonderful how easily one is pleased in this life.

No news but we live in hope. It is a bit cooler today which is something as our hut is terribly stuffy when it is very hot and there is no wind. Send me a photo of yourself and Robin some time if you get a chance. We have some plans now and have some idea what we are going to do.

Must stop. All my love darling. I am just longing to get a line from you.

16 August 1940

Diana Darling,

No news from you, but I expect it will still take a little time. We are starting to get a few things moving. But we have not actually got our money yet. We have heard from the Consular at Geneva and the American one from Marseilles. So with luck we should be in touch soon.

Today we went into Perpignan to see the American Consul's representative. He helped us a bit but could do nothing about the money as that has to be done in Marseilles. I hope to get there to settle things up quite soon. In spite of all this sunbathing I am not getting awfully brown. Good salmon colour seems to be about my mark. Perpignan is an interesting town. Old of course – very narrow streets. Very like Spanish towns. We listen eagerly for the news here but it is difficult to get.

There is so much I should like to tell you but can't.

Yesterday we spent making ourselves a veranda from bamboos and reeds. It is rather successful but has a tendency to increase the already plentiful supply of mosquitoes. I bought myself a pair of respectable cream trousers today and so when clothed can go about a bit cooler. Generally I go about in a state of comparative indecency, but I suppose it is healthy.

I can't tell you how I am longing to hear from you. But don't delay writing too long.

It is very hard to find news to write because from our point of view there is none to speak of.

All my love darling

17 August 1940

Diana Darling,

I cannot remember whether I wrote to you yesterday or not. We had a day in Perpignan having got permission to go there. We left at 7 in the morning catching an empty lorry in the camp to St-Cyprien about 2 miles away. Then we caught a bus to Perpignan about 10 miles away. We wanted to find out if there was any American Consul in Perpignan. There was not. But we found the representative of the Red Cross *[a Danish commissioner]*, working under the American Consul. He could not help much. He was very interesting. We have not got our money yet but things are looking promising. I bought a pair of trousers for Fr 100. The seam has already split, but it won't be very difficult to sew it up. I am getting much better at these odds and ends now and it only takes me about ten minutes to thread a needle.

We had lunch at some restaurant, quite nice but not very exciting. Rationing makes things very difficult for the restaurants. After lunch we took a tram out to Canet Plage which had a bank holiday crowd and then walked 5 or 6 miles home along the beach.

With luck by now you should know where we are. It gets very hot here in the afternoon. It is too hot indoors and too many flies. And too hot outside even with our bamboo veranda unless there is a breeze.

The more I see of life, particularly here, the more I realize how important it is to be able to speak other languages. It has made all the difference to us the little bit I know. And maybe even more useful in the near future.

Incidentally a small thing you might consider is as follows. You know that I have about £1500 not invested with our marriage settlement. You might consider, with the aid of Peter, using it to buy a cottage somewhere. It would be of no immediate value but might be very useful after the war. Property values must be very low near aerodromes now, but like after the last war jump up when all is over. It is worth thinking about if nothing else. I hope you have been able to manage all the Income Tax questions etc all right. Must stop my darling. Hope you and Robin are keeping well. Give my love to your family and mine, to whom, the latter I mean, I wrote the other day but don't know how long the letter will take.

One of the letters written to the numerous Consuls paid off as on 21 August the War Office was able to write to Diana:

I am directed to inform you that information has been received from Berne that Captain J R Johnson, The Royal Welch Fusiliers, has escaped from German captivity and is now interned at St-Cyprien, near Perpignan.

22 August 1940

Diana Darling,

Still no letters from you. The last week's news has been quite heartening for us. We went into Perpignan to get a little money the day before yesterday. Not much but something to get on with. Our other money looks as though it will arrive at the end of the month. It will be a great relief to us when it does come.

I now have more or less proper Spanish lessons every day. I teach a man English and he teaches me Spanish and when we get into difficulties we have to explain to each other in French. We learn with the use of a rather advanced French English grammar and exercise book, plus French Spanish and French English dictionaries, but we have only a phrase book directly between English and Spanish. This makes it a bit complicated. On the other hand this man before the Spanish War was a master in a school in Madrid. So we have a good deal of scholarly method.

Today we have been undergoing an almost continuous sandstorm. The wind is causing quite a bit of damage to the huts, which are not very strongly built. When you get a clear spell you can see the sand being carried right up to the Pyrenees.

I think my Spanish lesson is about to commence so I must stop. There is absolutely no news. We are getting a little impatient but are tied up until we get our money. I heard the report of Winston's speech. Very good sounding it made to us.

I wonder whether you got in touch with Trythall's wife.

Must stop my darling. I do miss you.

Diana finally heard from the War Office and was able to telegram Jimmy, copy of which is unfortunately missing. Jimmy replied:

26 August 1940

IN GOOD HEALTH WE HAVE RECEIVED THE MONEY
THANK YOU FOR THE TELEGRAM WRITE BY AIR = JIMMY

27 August 1940

My Darling,

I seem rather to have neglected writing to you for the last few days. It was lovely to get your wire. It just made all the difference to know you were safe and sound.

I was surprised to get it because we had been told that it was impossible. But I wired back the same evening. I have not had a letter from you yet but I expect that will take a few more days. Anyhow I am quite happy now. Somehow the last few days have gone very quickly, there has been a lot to do. We got a little money from Switzerland but for various reasons which I can't explain it is not enough. Hence my telegram to you today. I hope you will have been able to arrange it and that the money will get here before the 30th. After that I am afraid it will be no good.

My Spanish lessons go on from day to day. I think I am making some headway. But I spend so much time talking my ungrammatical French that it takes me a little while to change gear into Spanish. But one does get better.

On Monday I went into Perpignan as my clothes have given out and bought myself an indifferent pair of French flannel trousers and what they call a "blouson", a sort of pseudo golfing jacket with zip fasteners in all the wrong places.

We have been suffering from the tramontane *[i.e. a cold wind from the Alps]* but it has improved a bit lately and we can bathe again, although I have not as my tummy is not quite right again today. I found I had made an elementary error the other day in writing to you about the camp "houilles". Of course the word is "huit", but such is my French I did not realize it in ordinary conversation.* I would love to get a letter from you by the end of this week. I am longing to know which of my letters you got saying I was here or whether you heard from one of the consuls or from the War Office.

There doesn't seem to be any news as such.

All my love darling to you and Robin

The reference to a telegram is a little confusing but as the envelope has a postmark date of 30 August there was possibly a second request for funds, copy of which was also not retained.

As is hinted at in these letters the men were planning their next move. A number of others who had escaped at a similar time were turning up at the camp. Jimmy started to formulate a plan to try to get about ten people over the Pyrenees into Spain. However the newcomers were not quite ready to move on as quickly as Jimmy and Tommy would have liked.

Money had been acquired from various sources including the British Consul at Geneva, a contact of Tommy's in Switzerland and the pay from the French army. In the end Jimmy and Tommy decided on just one extra, R Clubbs, a Platoon Sergeant Major of the Gordon Highlanders, 'a splendid chap'.**

With relief, the day parole was up they made their move; St-Cyprien had become a very unpleasant place to stay. *[Conditions deteriorated so much that in December of that year it was closed 'for sanitary reasons'.]* Planning a route

---

* The letter referred to does not seem to have been retained and the reference is puzzling. It is possible the 'camp huit' could be huîtres or oysters. The pronunciation is similar and could also partly explain the tummy troubles.

** The rank of Platoon Sergeant Major, or Warrant Officer Class III, was introduced in the infantry in 1939 because there were too few young officers. PSMs usually commanded one of the three platoons in an infantry company, the other two being commanded by Lieutenants or Second Lieutenants. The rank was phased out after the war.

Map 9

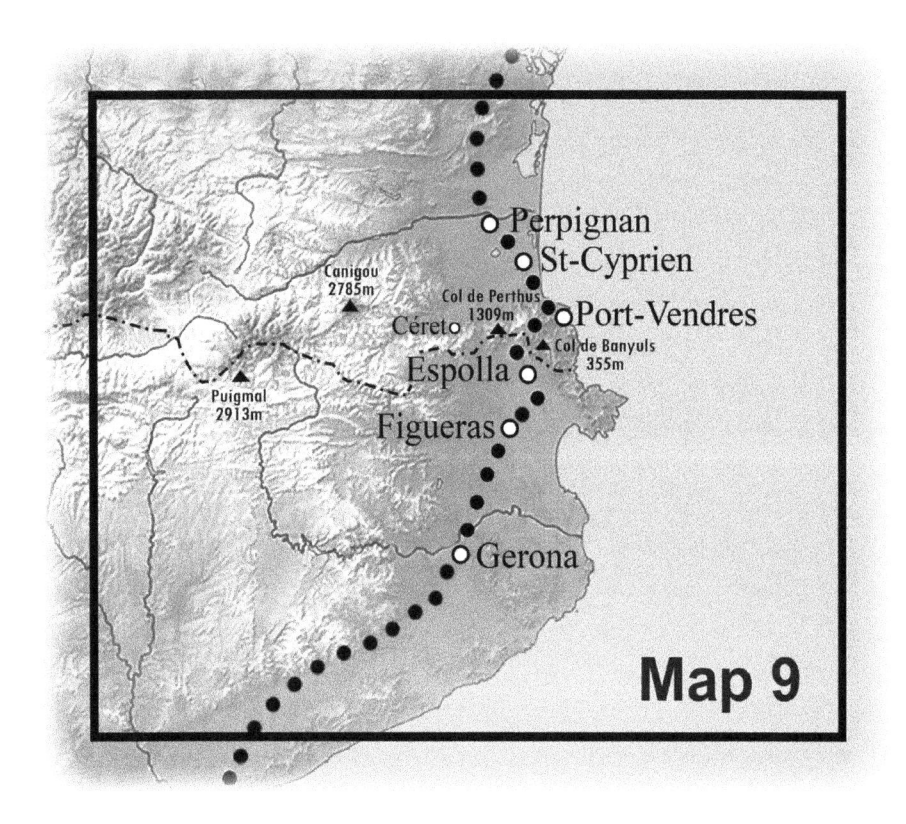

had been much harder work than they expected because although they had kept asking people where and how to get over the Pyrenees, the answer had always been 'to go the way the smugglers go' without saying which way that was except for asking at every farmhouse en route.

The three men set off on 29 August travelling from farmhouse to farmhouse. They crossed over into Spain about ten miles north of Portbou by means of a smugglers' pass midway between Col de Banyuls and Col de Perthus. The mountains were about 4,000 feet high which was a tough climb, and they spent a very cold night sleeping on the very top with just newspapers for cover.

It was a Sunday when they climbed down the far side – to be met by the Carabineros, enjoying their day off shooting partridges. Both parties were somewhat surprised. The shoot was reluctantly stopped and the trio taken to the nearest police station in the village of Espolla. After a wait of two to three hours they were interviewed by the Civil Guard and promptly imprisoned in a room that was the village mayor's stable and junk room combined. They claimed to be American citizens therefore were treated fairly, apart from having their money taken away.

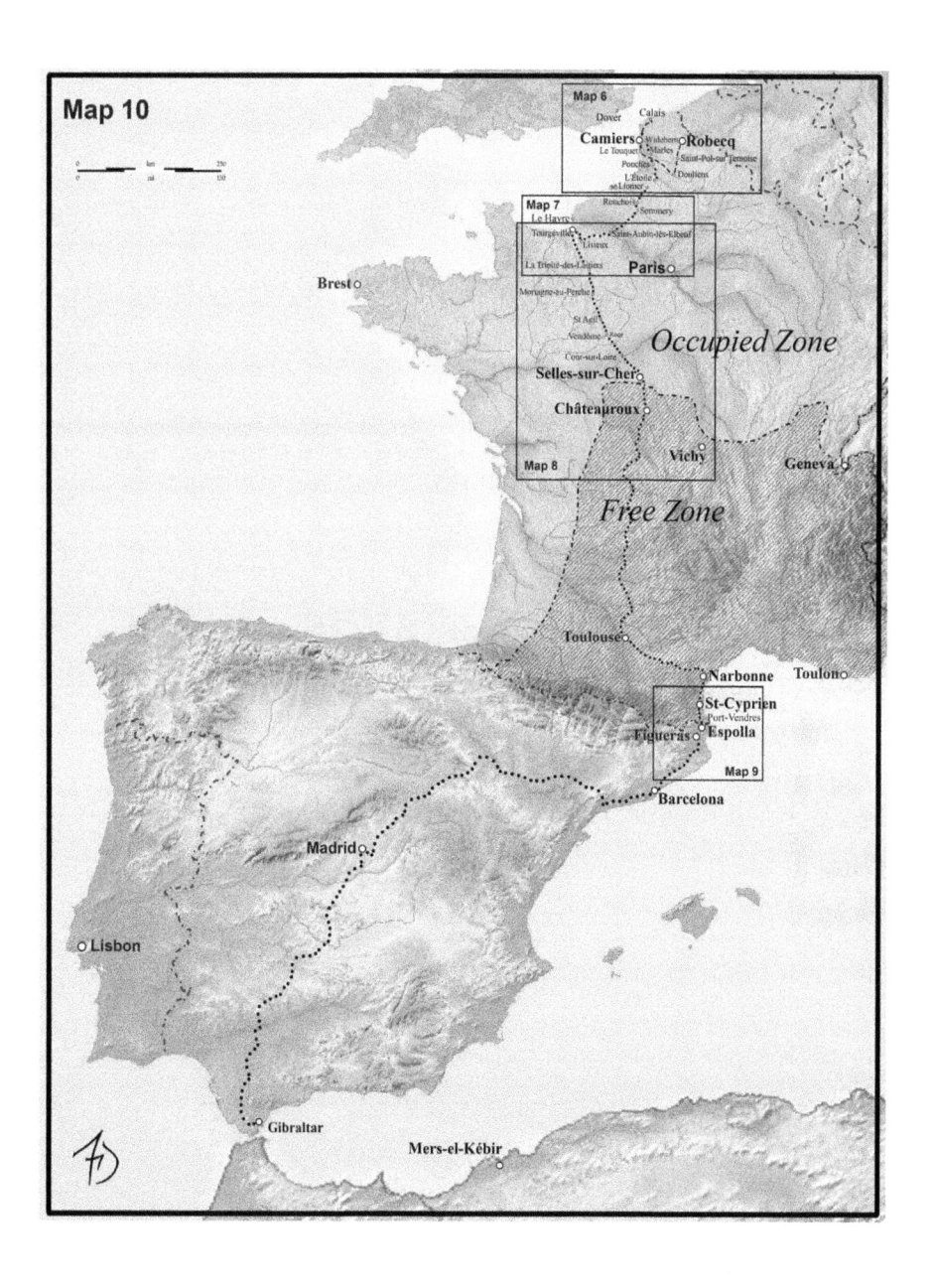

On Monday they were transferred to the civil prison in Figueras where they were sentenced to be detained for up to thirty days on the grounds that they had been smuggling currency and breaking frontier regulations, unless claimed out *[Jimmy's phrase]* by an Embassy or Consular official. Conditions here were not good. The prison housed about 100 prisoners with two lavatories at one end. The last people in were always bedded down next to the lavatory and as the stay became longer they would get promoted further away from the lavatory. It was rather an unpleasant time, sleeping on one blanket on a concrete floor next to the lavatory with people coming and going all day.

There were eight other escaped British soldiers imprisoned there. Being the most senior officer and the best Spanish speaker Jimmy was appointed to speak on behalf of all the British prisoners. Having already claimed to be an American citizen from New York, he asked and was given permission to write to the American Consul in Barcelona. In the letter he asked the Americans to contact the British Consul.

Within a few days Jimmy received his first visitor. To his astonishment it was his cousin Chris, loaded with bunches of grapes and melons! Having heard from Sapper Richards that Jimmy was just over the border in France, the Vice Consul Mr Whitfield had been waiting for news of his arrival. Whitfield arranged with the authorities to collect Chris as he passed through Gerona on his way to Figueras. This was the first time the cousins had seen each other since the start of hostilities. Jimmy was to dine off the 'bunch of grapes' story for years to come.

Wheels were now in motion for their release; Jimmy, Tommy and the other British prisoners had been claimed out. At the end of ten days Whitfield was able to arrange for their removal to the Military Prison at the Castillo in Figueras, 'a wonderful old building' though a bit of a disappointment as they were not allowed as much liberty. However they were occasionally able to bribe a guard to get a litre of wine, something they had not been able to do at the civil prison. Hearing about the bombing of London, Coventry and other English cities, Spanish prisoners they had befriended suggested they should stay in Spain. 'You would be safer' they said, 'away from the bombs.'

Mrs D Johnson   10th September 1940
Tingewick House   Consulate-General, Barcelona
Buckingham

Madam,
    Referring to our previous communication I now have the pleasure of informing you that Capt J R Johnson RWF has reached Spain,

where he has been temporarily detained by the Authorities. Every effort is being made to ensure his prompt return home.

Your obedient Servant,
Dorchy,
His Britannic Majesty's Vice Consul, Barcelona

Seven days later Jimmy, Tommy and Clubbs, along with the other British prisoners, were on the move, heading for the Hotel Bristol in Barcelona.

CHAPTER TWENTY
BACK ON BRITISH SOIL
19-23 SEPTEMBER

The two escape stories have converged. We return to the journal which Chris and Dennis finished writing in Gibraltar, with a few interjections from Jimmy and Montie Hogg.

The following morning saw us in Barcelona where we were met by one of the consular staff. After various negotiations with the police we were taken to see the Consul himself, and after a short talk went off to the Hotel Bristol where we were to stay the night. We were very disappointed that we were not allowed outside the hotel, and so had only a limited view of this famous city. The balcony, however, looked out on the main square, and some excitement was provided by a fire in the shop next door.

That evening we were amazed to hear that Jimmy Johnson and Trythall with nine other ranks, were also arriving. We had heard previously from Whitfield that they had also found their way into Figueras prison, and now they were being released and sent to join us. They all arrived that evening looking remarkably well despite the rigours of prison life.

We had now become a large herd of seventeen and were shepherded on the following evening by the Consular staff to catch the night train to Madrid arriving at about 10 the following morning. Here we were met by a member of the Embassy staff who informed us that we were catching the night train to Gibraltar, and were to stay in an hotel in the meantime. After further police negotiations we duly repaired thither and were regaled with an enormous and sumptuous lunch.

> Montie recalled everyone was very tired after the long overnight train journey. However arrangements at the station were very efficient and everything so well organised that the weary travellers quickly reversed any negative opinions of the Embassy that had formed during their imprisonment in Spain. They were taken to the Hotel Nationale where each man had an individual interview with a member of the Embassy staff. Montie was pleasantly surprised to see one of his senior tutors at Peterhouse College, Cambridge amongst the Embassy staff.

As usual we were confined to the hotel and so saw very little of Madrid, but in any case there would have been no time. That afternoon we were visited by Sir Samuel Hoare who asked various questions about our escape and Brigadier Torre-Torr, the Military Attaché who had evidently done all the diplomatic work to get us out.

> Montie had been particularly nervous about meeting the Brigadier who, with Sir Samuel, made a point of speaking to each man in turn. Montie had been appointed communications officer by Chris and Raikes with his many duties including a telegram* to London and a terse telephone conversation with Torre-Torr during which he threatened that he and the others were planning to escape from Gerona. However Torre-Torr could not have been nicer, and apart from a twinkle in the eye, no reference was made to the call.

Jimmy was delighted to also meet a few friends from the days when he was stationed at Gibraltar.

> The interviews were followed by a group briefing for the onward journey to Gibraltar. Chris, Dennis, Jimmy, Tommy, Montie, Raikes, Hawkins and Lord Cardigan, who had been held in Miranda de Ebro prison following his remarkable solo escape, were to travel in one carriage. Clubbs and the other men in another.

---

* STUCK HERE WITH FIVE OTHERS – EMBASSY VERY SLOW – CAN YOU HELP HOGG HOTEL PENINSULAR GERONA T.N.A FO371/24507

After a hurried dinner we were bundled into the Gibraltar train, which was crammed full of soldiers bound for Morocco, and had some difficulty in forcing our way into the reserved carriages. We were now under the escort of two stooges, but they were at the other end of the train and weren't in the least worried about us.

In the early hours of the following morning we peered out of the window, hearing some commotion. To our surprise a Guardia Civil was crouching underneath the stationary train with his revolver trained at something we couldn't see. After smothered curses and some yells from the other side of the train he leapt to his feet and hared off at full speed down the line in hot pursuit of what we supposed must be an escaped prisoner under escort. It was a remarkable sight and quite typical of the new Spain. Train journeys were great experiences; plain-clothed stooges appeared periodically and inspected everyone's papers with the utmost care. We happened to travel with some British subjects on one of the trains, and the stooge was completely baffled by the passports they presented, and spent hours trying to decipher all that wonderful stuff on the first page.

More stooges appeared at odd intervals and poked your baggage to make sure you hadn't got any chickens or potatoes on board as these were forbidden between Figueras and Barcelona for some peculiar reason. Sometimes they used to peer underneath the carriages and on the roof, to make sure there were no improper travellers. As this was exactly what we had been considering doing for the last month, we felt we were well out of it! Hawkins' face always fell when he saw this, as he had always maintained that it was just too easy to tie yourself to the axle and travel for miles like that. We saw some magnificent country between Barcelona and Madrid, particularly just at dawn when the colours were really wonderful. Between Madrid and Gibraltar the country was less spectacular, but the colours of the soil are remarkable.

We were due in at Rosas, the junction north of Gibraltar at 11am the following morning, but the train was exactly twelve hours late, due partly to a train smash a few hours previously, and partly to the rottenness of the line on the last stages of the journey, when the average rate of progress was approximately ten miles an hour. We noticed that the line was being repaired in a truly Spanish fashion, in a most casual way.

At Rosas we were met by a bus and taken to the frontier post where we saw the last of the stooges. After turning out the frontier guard and various negotiations between numbers of officials, most of whom we were too tired to notice, we arrived in Gibraltar after midnight on September 23rd. We were again on British soil, our escape was accomplished and were we pleased.

A detailed Historical Report covering the first ten months of the 1st Field Squadron RE can be read at the back of this book. This report was included with my father's manuscript and I believe it to have been written by him. Of the 290 officers and men who embarked for France in May 1940, 200 were taken prisoner. Chris and Dennis were the only two from this RE Squadron to escape from a Line of March and make their own way back to England.

FROM A ROCK TO HOME

CHAPTER TWENTY ONE
UNFRIENDLY FIRE
23-25 SEPTEMBER

Gibraltar, the gateway to the Mediterranean Sea, had been under Moorish control from 711AD until 1462 when it was captured by Castillian forces and declared Crown Property by the Castillian King Henry IV. In 1700 King Charles II of Spain died without leaving any descendants. This led to the War of Spanish Succession with claims to the throne from both France and Austria. England and The Netherlands sided with Austria which resulted in the Austrian Archduke Charles being proclaimed as King of Castile and Aragon, whilst the French Phillippe of Anjou was proclaimed King of Spain. An Anglo-Dutch fleet laid siege to Gibraltar in 1704 demanding unconditional surrender to the Austrian Archduke. Troops were landed and took control of the Rock and the peninsular linking it to the Spanish mainland. English rule dates from this time. The Treaty of Utrecht which ceded the territory to the Crown of Great Britain in Perpetuity was signed in 1713.

The strategic importance of Gibraltar has long been recognised; Oliver Cromwell had considered seizing it in 1654. Spanish monarchs wanted to regain control and first laid siege in 1727. The four year Great Siege occurred in 1779 when Spain joined forces with France, who were supporting the rebellious American Colonies in the American Revolutionary War, with Spain's primary aim being to seize Gibraltar. In 1782 a complex system of underground fortifications began to be tunnelled out by the established British Garrison to repel the besiegers, now reinforced by French forces who took over command. The siege was finally lifted in February 1783, a factor in the Peace of Paris negotiations which ended the American Civil War. The Battle of Trafalgar in 1805 was fought nearby. After HMS Victory was towed into Gibraltar with Nelson's body on board, some of the British sailors who had died during the battle were buried in the cemetery just outside the city walls. Britain and Spain were later to become allies against Napoleon during the Peninsular Wars.

Between 1808 and 1814 Gibraltar acted as a supply base for the British and allied field army in Catalonia as well as Wellington's main army further north.

In 1938 the racecourse on the isthmus, the only large piece of flat land, had been converted into an emergency short airstrip. [N.B. The longer concrete runway was not built until 1941-2.] During World War II Gibraltar once again became a fortress, then a military garrison when the citizens were evacuated.* The Allies had control over the entry to the Mediterranean and with its safe harbour the Rock was able to play a key role in the supply lines to Malta and North Africa, Italy, Greece and most important of all, on to the Suez Canal.

With the formalities at Rosas completed, it was almost midnight when the seventeen men finally arrived at the frontier post only to be refused admittance; the border to Gibraltar was closed. Having spent the previous two nights on the move, the men were very tired and now hugely unimpressed. Lord Cardigan insisted an officer with sufficient seniority was found resulting in the men finally being allowed through at 1am on 23 September. Several other escapees had arrived independently at the border. Under the cover of darkness they too managed to enter Gibraltar alongside the party from Madrid without being detected. It was a huge relief to finally be on British soil. Formalities were cleared and they were all allocated accommodation.

It may have been dark, but Jimmy was able to point out some changes that had been made since his last visit. The road into town now crossed a runway which ran almost the full width of the isthmus and the harbour to the right was filled with the outline of naval vessels, including the battlecruiser HMS *Renown*. He was able to identify many more vessels later in the day. After a night's rest they walked down to the Post Office in town. It became obvious to all that the large civilian population had been replaced by military personnel, with only civilians in essential jobs remaining.

Chris and Dennis, Jimmy and Tommy, Raikes and Hogg together with Lord Cardigan were allocated to the Royal Army Medical Corps (RAMC) mess, Lamorna. At the time of Jimmy's 1932 posting this had been the mess for the post and telegraph headquarters. Medical personnel stationed in Gibraltar were also accommodated there.

Lamorna was described as a comfortable house, situated on South Barrack

---

*   Between May and August 1940 approximately 22,000 civilians were evacuated to England, Madeira and Jamaica, some staying away for up to ten years.

Road, outside the old city walls just off the main Europa Road. Overlooking the bay right at the end of the great mole it afforded its occupants a clear view of the ships in the harbour. Europa Road extends from the town of Gibraltar, past the Trafalgar Cemetery, Botanic Gardens and Rock Hotel *[where Field Marshall Montgomery and General Eisenhower were to stay when planning the invasion of North Africa]* to the southernmost part of the Iberian Peninsula, Europa Point, from where Africa and the mountains of Morocco can be seen.

Flying Officer Hawkins was quartered in the RAF mess of No 202 (General Reconnaissance) Squadron. From there he sent a signal to the Air Ministry Intelligence Department giving the location of suitable targets and other military information which he had noted and written down, hiding the paper in a bar of soap. He also wrote a very brief paper on 'Hints for prisoners escaping from north of France'. This was sent by flying boat to Flight Lieutenant A J Evans, the expert in escapes at the Air Ministry who liaised with MI9, hoping it might be of use to anyone unfortunate enough to be shot down whilst bombing the northern ports of France.

Since their arrival the men had been sending telegrams home, acquainting themselves with Gibraltar and checking out the various military messes for any familiar faces.

24 September

ALL WELL WITH DENNIS AND JIMMY MAY BE SOME TIME BEFORE SAILING FOR HOME ADDRESS LAMORNA SOUTH BARRACK ROAD LOVE = CHRIS WATERS

The cables took twenty-four hours to reach their destinations in England. Lucy Trythall must have been overjoyed to learn it was just a matter of waiting for the next convoy. In late May she had received a telegram from the War Office stating her husband was missing, believed killed, but now he was nearly home. Tommy was even able to send his sons a jigsaw of a map of Europe that he had bought in Perpignan.

Lunch was being prepared on 24 September when the air raid warning sounded. Being some way from the centre of town the residents of Lamorna took to the balcony to look through the broken clouds to attempt to see from which direction the danger lay. There was much speculation as the French fleet at Mers had been bombed some months ago. An attack of some sort was obviously expected as *Renown* was already in full steam. Not wishing to be a sitting target she was making her way out of the Gibraltar breakwater with light guns blazing as a wave of Vichy bombers suddenly flew overhead. Onlookers held their breath as two bombs narrowly missed *Renown*. However they cannot have caused any damage as the battlecruiser did not falter as she continued to make way.

The cloud cover made it very difficult to defend the harbour. HMT *Stella Sirius* was at anchor waiting to refuel with HMT *Arctic Ranger* on the mole. [N.B. Hundreds of commercial trawlers had been requisitioned by the Navy to be used as minesweepers and in an anti-submarine role.] The destroyer HMS *Firedrake* was on the main wharf also preparing for sea. Amongst the onlookers on the balcony were medical staff who had been present during previous raids. They confirmed it was the biggest raid on Gibraltar to date but were relieved to see once again many bombs falling harmlessly into the sea. A number did land ashore with one causing a large fire when it landed on property in the old town. Two hours later the all clear sounded.

The skies were clearer on the morning of 25 September and Jimmy took the opportunity to send a telegram to Diana.

HOPE SEE YOU SOON STAYING LEMORNA [sic] SOUTH BARRACK ROAD THOROUGHLY ENJOYING LIFE CABLE ME LOVE = JIMMY JOHNSON

Montie Hogg was looking forward to lunch. An invitation had arrived that morning from an officer in the Royal Signals, a friend of his from the Royal Military Academy Woolwich. The officer's fiancée was also stationed in Gibraltar and would be joining them. Montie tried to persuade Raikes to come along as well but he declined.

It was a pleasant downhill walk into town. Having enjoyed a pre-lunch cocktail they were about to start their meal when an orderly came over and whispered news of the approach of aeroplanes. Asking Montie to look after his fiancée the officer left. At 2.30pm the air raid siren began its warning alarm followed closely by the sound of aircraft. Montie and the officer's fiancée ran as fast as they could to the nearest ARP Shelter – the caves in Prince Edward's Road – with debris starting to fall around them.

The occupants of Lamorna were settling into their new routine of relaxing after lunch. Cardigan had gone out for a walk leaving Waters, Lennon, Johnson, Trythall, Raikes and two medical officers [Lieutenant Ball and one other] in the house. As the air raid siren sounded they too heard approaching aircraft. The sky filled with even more French bombers than the previous day – they sounded like Bristol 42s though they were in fact Douglas DB7s, LeO 451s and Glen Martin M 176Fs. Initially the occupants stood on the balcony to watch. Once again they had the impression the pilots did not have their hearts on the job. Although the ships in the harbour were the prime target, bombs seemed to be 'dropping all over the shop from Algeciras to Ronda up in the hills' with many loads being dropped in the sea. Having watched the bombing raid of the previous day, after a short time the onlookers retired to their rooms, leaving Tommy alone on the balcony. Jimmy went to lie down on his bed on the top floor, recalling the words of the Spanish prisoners who had suggested that they stay in Spain away from the bombs.

Then a bomb landed on Lamorna. Jimmy would never forget the sound it made as it fell through the roof and on through the floors. 'You would be surprised to know you can hear a bomb coming, but you can.' Bang, bang, bang. First floor, second floor, third floor. Bang. Then dust and straw coming down, very frightening, and being unable to move, pinned down. Eventually a voice shouting 'Anybody about?' and Chris saying 'Yes, I'm here I think.' Jimmy, who with his bed had fallen all three floors, also replied 'I'm here I think.' Chris had been blown over backwards which somehow prevented him from being buried. Shakily rising to his feet he was able to make breathing space for the two who were calling out nearby. By chance a soldier passed the house, returning to barracks. With the soldier's help Chris was able to reach Jimmy who had ended up wedged in a corner. Moving very carefully the two were able to remove debris from Jimmy's head and a beam that was pinning him down thereby freeing him. A fire bucket had flown through the air and lodged upside down on his head saving him from more serious injury.

The three men, Jimmy, Chris and the soldier, now tried to cross the floor to help the two still pinned underneath, but Dennis and one of the medics cried out for them to stop. The rocking of the floor caused dust to shake down making it impossible for them to breath. Jimmy was unable to help with any lifting. Covered in blood, with a broken hand and punctured ear drum, he inched his way as quietly as possible out of the room and out onto the street upstairs to look for help. It seemed to take ages as he had to walk down to the local headquarters to find any troops.

Help finally arrived and the soldiers started to dig through the debris. Chris, shaken but all right, had made progress with rescuing Dennis and the medic, both unharmed. Then they found Tommy Trythall. He must have been killed instantly. He had remained on the balcony, standing exactly where the bomb landed. Peter Raikes had also been killed along with Lieutenant Ball RAMC.

At the sound of the All Clear at approximately 5pm Montie left the shelter of the cave and escorted his friend's fiancée home before walking slowly up the hill, past The Rock Hotel and back to Lamorna. He was completely unprepared for what he saw. He immediately set to helping the soldiers to clear debris from the remains in the search for survivors and bodies. Badly shaken by the death of his comrade and without any belongings other than the clothes he was wearing, he later found himself wandering about in a daze shopping for basic necessities. Like the other survivors he rarely spoke of the events of that day.

Lamorna September 1940 [Gibraltar National Museum]

At the time of the bombing the families of Captain Trythall and Captain Raikes were receiving telegrams sent the previous day announcing their safe arrival in Gibraltar, and the news that they would be returning home on the next convoy. Both men were buried in Gibraltar.

CHAPTER TWENTY TWO

A LETTER FROM SIR SAMUEL HOARE

Sir Samuel Hoare and Sir Roger Keyes knew each other personally. Both men served as Conservative Members of Parliament and in 1936 the latter had sent a letter of congratulation when Prime Minister Baldwin appointed Hoare as First Lord of the Admiralty. Although relationships may have become strained when the two men took opposing sides on the Agreement that had been reached by Neville Chamberlain in Munich [Keyes, along with Winston Churchill, withheld support from the government on this issue], having successfully arranged the release from Spanish internment of this group of Allied servicemen Hoare was able to find time in his busy diplomatic schedule to write a personal and illuminating letter to Keyes.

British Embassy,
Madrid
26 September, 1940

Dear Sir Roger,

    I am writing this line to say how delighted I was to succeed in getting your son-in-law released from internment in Spain. He will himself tell you the story of his adventures. I will only add from my side that it has taken us here many weeks of continuous effort, first of all to find out where the British prisoners of war were and secondly to get the innumerable and conflicting authorities to take action. Anyhow, by continuous protests and rows we have got the ex-prisoners of war out to the number of nearly fifty and I am very glad that your son-in-law was amongst them.

I wonder greatly what you are doing at this moment. So far as I am concerned it never entered my head that I should find myself as Ambassador in Madrid, and I am not sure that I should have done so if I had realised the troubles and difficulties that surround the post. All the same the fact remains that when I came here it looked as if I should only be here a few days, and I have now been here four months and Spain is still out of the war. It is worth putting up with a good deal of personal worry and irritation if the result is to keep the Atlantic ports and the Straits out of German hands.

Yours,
Samuel Hoare

Admiral of the Fleet, Sir Roger Keyes, Bt., G.C.B.,
Tingewick House,
Buckingham[10]

CHAPTER TWENTY THREE
HOMEWARD BOUND
26 SEPTEMBER-28 OCTOBER

A total of twenty-four military servicemen and six civilians were killed during the raids of 24 and 25 September. In addition to the damage on land, HMT *Stella Sirius* had been sunk with the loss of fifteen sailors. Funerals for the deceased were held a few days later. Tommy was buried at sea about one mile offshore with full naval honours.[*] His coffin was draped with a Union flag and a salute fired after the committal.

Captain Raikes and Lieutenant Ball were buried in the North Front Cemetery. Still badly shaken by the events of that afternoon, those that had survived the bombing of Lamorna attended both services.

The men were rehoused at the Grand Hotel lower down the hill, with Jimmy joining them on his release from hospital. Along with Montie, Chris and Jimmy had lost all their belongings. Dennis must have been in a room furthest from the balcony. He was the only survivor to return to England with all the papers and mementoes acquired since leaving Vichy. Incredibly he must also have had the manuscript he and Chris were still writing, otherwise their story would have been lost.

---

[*] It has not been possible to ascertain why Tommy had a naval burial. With so many having been killed on HMT *Stella Sirius* during the same raid, maybe the decision was taken to commit his remains with them.

30 September

THANKS TELEGRAM LAMORNA DEMOLISHED HAND SLIGHTLY DAMAGED SLIGHTLY DEAF OTHERWISE GRAND NOT WRITING LETTERS BUT WILL SEND WIRE EVERY 4 DAYS UNTIL DEPARTURE REPLY GRAND HOTEL INFORM MY FAMILY LOVE = JIMMY JOHNSON

Gibraltar - Catalan Bay
Montie Hogg   Lord Cardigan

Three members of The Garrison

Dennis Lennon
Chris Waters

The next two weeks passed quietly. Time was needed to recover from the loss of their companions as close friendships had been forged over the preceding weeks. The survivors rested, sunbathed, swam and played sports to help them assimilate the events which would remain with them for the rest of their lives.

There are photos of them sunbathing on Catalan Bay Beach, from where they swam every day. Montie seemed to have a knack of bumping into friends and acquaintances. The latest was Captain Prynne, the elder brother of a fellow cadet at Woolwich who offered them the opportunity to go horse riding. The racecourse may have gone, but horses were still available. Chris was a keen horse rider having competed in many prewar regimental point to points and Montie was prepared to learn. Appropriately mounted they found themselves riding around the airfield and along Catalan Bay. Once out of hospital, when not joining the others on the beach, Jimmy caught up with friends he had known from his earlier posting. With an arm in plaster and a damaged ear drum he had to be cautious with his activities.

Military Hospital
Gibraltar
1 October 40

Diana my darling,

I am glad you got my first telegram from here all right. I was delighted to get your answer. I wired you again yesterday saying I would wire every 4 days or so. Incidentally I suppose you have been notified that I have been wounded again. We were in Lamorna taking shelter when they scored a direct hit. There were 7 of us there and 3 including Tommy Trythall were killed. I will write to Mrs Trythall soon but it is rather hard work writing at the moment. Of those that got away with it none were badly hurt. Luckily one of us was scarcely buried at all and he was able to make breathing space for the other two and clean some of the stuff off my head. Then he got a soldier nearby to give him a hand. They half cleared the other two and after lifting a beam off me got me out. I went and got a rescue party who got the other two out. It was not a very pleasant experience. As far as I am concerned I got a cut in my right hand which had to be cleaned out and stitched up and 2 fractured bones in the hand. I also got a bit of a bump on the head and am now rather deaf in one ear. This may improve with luck.

I gather you have been making enquiries from your end as to when I am likely to get away from here. I don't suppose they will be able to tell you because ship sailings are kept very secret. I don't know myself. I said in the telegram I was not writing letters to stop you writing and to stop you worrying in case you wondered why you had not got one from me. I must stop now. It is very hard writing with one's hand in bandages and the alternative of writing left handed is very long work.

All my love darling and God keep you both well. I'm longing to see you.

News from the Under Secretary of State for War did not arrive until 5 October:

REGRET TO INFORM YOU OF CONFIRMATION OF REPORT RECEIVED FROM GIBRALTAR THAT CAPTAIN J R JOHNSON ROYAL WELCH FUSILIERS WAS INJURED IN AIR RAID ON 25 SEPTEMBER

The Grand Hotel
6 October 40

Diana darling,

Since last writing to you I have had my hand put in plaster of Paris so I can't hold a pen with it at all. Hence this left hand effusion. We don't know when we are likely to be sailing yet, and we are getting very bored. I don't think I told you before but Trythall was killed by the same bomb. But I will wait until I get my hand out of plaster and until I get back.

There was then a paragraph listing four or five friends he managed to see and news of others they had known from their days on the Rock.

I can't tell you how much I am longing to see you. I shall continue to wire every four days or so. So when my wires stop don't send any here. Must stop my darling. I hope all the family are well, give them my love. I do love you so. Life would be very hard without somebody like you to love. Which reminds me I have lost all the photographs they are still in Lamorna.

*

Germany was aware that as an island nation Britain was dependent on imports, much of which travelled across the Atlantic Ocean from the Americas. The German Kriegsmarine *intended to curtail these imports. The Battle of the Atlantic commenced on 3 September 1939 when the liner SS* Athenia *was mistaken for an armed merchant cruiser and sunk by a U-boat. In the first seven months of the war, submarines or U-boats would account for 222 of the 402 Allied, British and neutral ships that were sunk.*[11] *Churchill wrote in Volume II of his history of the war that, 'The only thing that really frightened me during the War was the U-boat peril.'*[12]

There was just one last danger to face – the journey home. Ron Hawkins was the first to start the final leg. On 7 October space was found for him on an overnight flight in a Sunderland flying boat which arrived in England the following morning. A keen pilot, he had not been idle during his two week stay in Gibraltar. Somehow he had managed to persuade the commanding officer of No 202 Squadron to allow him to fly on operations. He flew on two sorties as aircrew, both of which were uneventful anti-submarine patrols.

Two days later, on 9 October, the remaining escapees received orders to report to the harbour with all their kit. They were allocated berths on the MV *British Coast* a small 1,000 ton cargo ship carrying scrap iron sailing with convoy HG45. They were all given single berths except for Montie and Chris. They had both admitted to being poor sailors so it was decided that they should share, with Chris on the top bunk and Montie below, as they were bound to be seasick. And they were. As the convoy rounded Cape St Vincent off the south west coast of Portugal it was met by the full force of a north-westerly gale.[13] Its speed dropped from seven to four knots, which was the best many of the ships could do with their heavy cargo. The convoy even had to hove to for a period of time as the weather worsened further.

The most stable part of a boat is nearest the centre as it is less affected by the rolling action of the sea. A cargo ship therefore carries its load in this area with crew accommodation as far forward and back as possible. On *British Coast* the sleeping berths were in the bow, whilst the galley and mess were in the stern. To get from one end of the boat to the other entailed crossing the open deck. A strong line was attached fore and aft across the deck to be used as a handhold in bad weather. The soldiers admired the ease with which the

---

Scottish built MV *British Coast* had been requisitioned by the Admiralty in October 1939 to carry cans of petrol to the BEF until May 1940. Having run in a number of convoys from 1940-1944, she took part in the D-Day landings again trying to meet an insatiable demand for petrol which continued for many months until the PLUTO programme was finally made operational. She was sold to a Newfoundland company in 1964 and renamed *Newfoundland Coast*. Her last journey was in July 1981 when she ran aground off the Turks and Caicos Islands.

www.clydeships.co.uk>view>vessel=British+Coast, December 2020 merchant seamen traversed this line while the boat was pitching and rolling, whilst they viewed every crossing with a great deal of trepidation.

Travelling through these rough seas it was a week before Montie got his sea legs and was able to join the other three who had been passing the time playing cards. This would have pleased Jimmy as there were now four players for a rubber of bridge. Chris finally recovered ten days into the voyage. From then on, Montie recalled, he and Chris, occasionally joined by Dennis, spent many hours in intelligent conversation putting the world to rights. They became close friends during those days and it was always Montie's regret that due to the mode of operation of the regiment that he was never to meet either man again.

Convoy HG45 consisted of forty-nine ships of various sizes.[*] Forty-two of the boats were either carrying pit props for the Welsh mines or iron ore for the steelworks, although *Lapwing* was recorded as heading for Glasgow with a cargo of wine. The convoy's Commodore was in SS *Ardeola* a passenger/cargo ship which had been requisitioned by the Admiralty in 1935 as a naval supply ship.[14] The minesweeper HMS *Gleaner* acted as escort for the entire journey with HMS *Wishart* seeing them safely out of Gibraltar waters and HMS *Firedrake* and *Hotspur* from Force H accompanying them the first week. Twice there were alarms with German bombers coming over and *Firedrake*, with assistance from other vessels, sank an Italian submarine three days after leaving the convoy.[15]

Travelling in lines of three across, the convoy was seven to eight miles long. Montie reported an interesting way the boats kept their position in line to avoid breaking radio silence. Each boat would drop a long piece of rope off the stern with a big drum attached to the end. The boat behind would have to periodically close up and 'beat the drum' with a nudge – a particularly tricky procedure in rough seas.

This was a tense time for Sir Roger Keyes who was following the slow progress of the convoy from his office in Whitehall. He knew the planned route ran parallel to the French coast where the Germans were establishing harbours for their own use. By operating from ports including Saint-Nazaire and Brest, their fleet was able to operate further out into the Atlantic. Then a series of events began on 17 October which gave Keyes even greater concern.

Whilst the convoy from Gibraltar was struggling through the gale, U-boats from Brest began to wreak havoc on two transatlantic convoys sailing to the United Kingdom from Nova Scotia in Canada. Between 17 and 19 October,

---

[*] The troopship *Neuralia* left at the same time with a convoy of 1093 Gibraltar civilians. Once clear of the coast she detached herself to proceed unescorted to Kingston, Jamaica.

as convoys SC7 then HX79 entered the Western Approaches to the northwest of Ireland, they were attacked by two U-boat wolf packs co-ordinated by Admiral Donitz. Thirty-seven out of seventy-eight ships were torpedoed, with sixteen ships lost in just six hours.*

Elsewhere, early on the morning of the 17th, a *Blenheim* surveillance aircraft spotted four German destroyers leaving Brest heading for the Bristol Channel, with six torpedo boats from Cherbourg heading in the same direction. Three convoys were in immediate danger, OG44 which was going to Gibraltar, SL50 heading for the UK out of Sierra Leone and HG45 which was some way ahead of SL50 off the Bay of Biscay. A force of seven light cruisers and destroyers was sent from Plymouth to intercept the Germans.[16] HG45 was particularly vulnerable having just the one escort. All three convoys were ordered to steer west until the threat was dealt with and the armed merchant cruiser *Pretoria Castle* was detached from SL50 to join HG45.[17] The *British Coast*, being the last boat in the middle section of the convoy and consistently the slowest, found herself separated from the rest. She was shepherded back to the fleet encouraged by colourful language over the megaphone from one of the escorts whose crew would have been aware of the dangers they were heading toward.

---

* Convoy SC7 had left Sydney, Nova Scotia on 5 October with thirty-five merchant ships and one naval escort, the sloop HMS *Scarborough*. Four more naval vessels would meet them in the Western Approaches to the west of Ireland. This was a slow moving convoy as many of the vessels could not make the planned eight knots, not helped by running into a gale a few days out. Three days later on 8 October the fifty boats and two armed merchant cruisers that made up convoy HX79 sailed from Halifax.

Two stragglers from SC7 had already been spotted and sunk by separate U-boats. As the convoy entered the Western Approaches on 17 October it was spotted by a third U-boat which attacked and sunk two more ships. HMS *Scarborough* made a lengthy counter-attack but in so doing was separated from the convoy which, with two recently joined escorts, then moved so far ahead *Scarborough* was unable to rejoin it. On 18 October the next two escorts arrived. The convoy was again sighted and attacked damaging the British ship *Carsbreck* so badly she needed a personal escort to the UK. On the night of 18/19 October, with a weakened escort, the convoy was attacked by five U-boats. Sixteen of the twenty ships sunk on that convoy were lost in six hours.

By 19 October HX79, which was unescorted at this point, had caught up with convoy SC7 and the Admiralty were rushing reinforcements to the area. HX79 was spotted by yet another U-boat which shadowed the convoy until a new wolf pack had assembled. Undeterred by the reinforcements and using the cover of darkness five U-boats penetrated the circle of escorting naval vessels, surfaced and mounted their attack from within the convoy. Twelve of the forty-nine ships were sunk.

To Churchill's despair this was to be the most successful U-boat attack of the Atlantic campaign. In addition to the ships, around 220 merchant seamen lost their lives. The tactics used to escort convoys had proved ineffective at this early stage of the war and led to changes in policy and the way future escorts were defended.

The Admiralty now issued orders to further strengthen the escort of HG45. On 20 October the sloop *Fleetwood* joined the convoy. The following day, having safely escorted convoy OB230 south, the destroyer *Antelope* and corvette *Mallow* were transferred to HG45. Finally the destroyers *Havelock*, *Hesperus* and *Skeena* joined on 22 October. These escorts remained with the convoy until it reached Liverpool.[18]

There was one final piece of drama. They were three days from Barrow off the north-west coast of Ireland when, in the early hours of the morning, the detonation of depth charges was heard and felt. Everyone grabbed their life jackets and ran on deck. A Steward told the passengers he thought a large liner had been torpedoed and damaged and one of her escorts was now attacking the U-boat with depth charges. To Montie it felt as if someone was belting their steel plates with a giant sledgehammer. At the time they were being passed by convoy SL50. With its larger and faster ships, some of which were tankers or liners carrying benzine and oil, it was further out to sea and therefore could have been the source of the explosions.

It was early in the morning of 27 October. Convoy HG45 had got through without loss and the *British Coast* had arrived at its destination of Barrow-in-Furness. The escapees were nearly home.* Unfortunately the bad weather had persisted which meant they were met by snow. In a comic note they were also met by military authorities who wanted to know what they had done with their uniforms as it came to a question of paying for a new one. It was hardly surprising then that orders were ignored in favour of a mad rush to the nearest telephone to call their families before catching a train for their MI9 debrief in London. Diana was already at Barrow – possibly her father had facilitated this. Montie's call to his wife, whom he had left so soon after their wedding, resulted in her managing to board the train at Stafford. The ladies were introduced to each other when Jimmy brought Diana down to the carriage containing Chris, Montie and the others.

The final delay was the train being brought to a standstill at Stony Stratford. Due to a very big air raid on London, all trains en route for the

---

* Although this convoy was successful, few of the cargo ships that made up its number were to survive to the end of the war. The first casualty was the Dutch vessel *Santa Lucia* which had carried on to Belfast with her load of railway sleepers. On 1 November, under instructions of Naval Command, she was heading up the channel of Belfast Lough to anchor in the area off North Brigg Buoy when she struck a mine. She immediately began to sink with the loss of four lives.

capital were being halted. Jimmy and Diana suddenly realised they were only about twenty miles from the family home at Tingewick. Diana went in search of a telephone and rang her mother. Lady Keyes drove over to meet them and somehow managed to cram Jimmy, Diana, Chris, Dennis, Montie and his wife into the car and take them back to Tingewick for the night. They managed to be up at 6 the next morning to catch the train at 8am and continue their journey to London for the debriefing at MI9 whose offices were on the second floor of the Grand Central Hotel Marylebone, now the Landmark.

The men were among the earliest escapees and in consequence MI9 was interested in the routes that each had taken, as well as details of those who had helped them; each man had very carefully concealed any names of people he had met in the event of further capture. Even though they had got through before the Nazi German occupiers and the new Vichy French government were fully organised, it was hoped they could provide some information that would be instrumental in ensuring successful home runs for future escapees and evaders, of which there were to be many.

At the time of the debriefing four months had elapsed since the Fall of France. During the mens' absence the war took to the skies and the survivors of the bombing of Lamorna returned to England as the Battle of Britain was drawing to an end. Hitler's plans for the invasion of England, Operation *Sealion*, are postponed indefinitely. After a period of home leave the four soldiers are given new postings. They have fought, escaped and survived life on the run. They would now return to the fight that would lead to the eventual defeat of Hitler and his Nazi Germany.

CHAPTER TWENTY FOUR

DAKAR

THE EVENTS THAT LED TO
THE BOMBING OF GIBRALTAR

There was much concern amongst the Allies regarding the allegiance of French colonies following the armistice between France and Nazi Germany in June 1940. Although Tchad [as Chad was spelt during the French colonial era] had set off a chain reaction which resulted in Equatorial Africa and Gabon, amongst others, overthrowing the Vichy regime in favour of the Free French, others, including some in North Africa remained under Vichy control. The attack at Mers-el-Kébir (see Chapter Nine) had contributed to colonies choosing not to join the Free French and Allies.

Senegal in West Africa had been a French colony since the mid-19th century after the French expanded from their port on the island of Gorée next to Dakar. On 8 August Churchill wrote to his chief of staff, General 'Pug' Ismay: 'Unless we act with celerity and vigour, we may find effective U-boat bases, supported by German aviation, all down this (West Africa) coast, and it will become barred to us but available for the Germans in the same way as the western coast of Europe.'[19]

The Allies had faced a great deal of hostility from the French locals at Casablanca. However it was strongly believed that General de Gaulle could persuade those at Dakar to join them. Plans were drawn up under the code name *'Menace'*. A task force including HMS *Ark Royal* and 8,000 troops including men of the French Foreign Legion was sent with orders to negotiate a peaceful occupation. If this proved unsuccessful they were to take the city by force. An Allied naval force was also despatched. The original assault date of 8 September was postponed because the force had first to go to Freetown to refuel and the accompanying French troopships could only make eight to nine knots as opposed to the anticipated twelve knots.

The British aircraft carrier HMS *Hermes* had been operating with the French forces in Dakar prior to the establishment of the Vichy Government as the nearby Allied naval base at Freetown in British Sierra Leone was considered to be an inferior port. [In fact it is not a port at all, but an anchorage. Although one of the busiest in the world, it relied on ships anchoring offshore and being loaded or unloaded by wherries.] The French forces included three submarines and several lighter ships. In addition one of the most advanced warships in the French Fleet, *Richelieu*, was being finished off having left Brest in France just before the Germans reached the port: she had been launched just before the outbreak of war and only commissioned in April 1940. She was also undergoing repairs for damage that had been inflicted by a torpedo launched by aircraft from *Hermes* on 8 July in support of the attack on the French Fleet at Mers. *Hermes* had remained on watch outside the port after the attack on *Richelieu*.

Despite attempts at great secrecy, word of the intended expedition became common talk among French troops exiled in England. Now Vichy forces were gathering at Dakar with the intention of imposing Free French authority. A force of three cruisers and three destroyers was also en route, passing unchallenged through the Straits of Gibraltar at full speed. Based on previous intelligence it was thought these French ships were taking advantage of improved relations with the Allies to leave Toulon for Casablanca in order to escape from German and Italian control liable to be imposed at Toulon. Aircraft shadowing the ships confirmed this initial destination, but the cruisers and destroyers quickly slipped out of Casablanca undetected and continued south. It was now believed these ships were carrying reinforcements to man the batteries at Dakar.

By the time the French fleet had left Casablanca the British fleet was south of Dakar. The cruisers *Devonshire, Australia* and *Cumberland* and the *Ark Royal* turned back but did not reach Dakar before the French squadron was at anchor with awnings spread.

Churchill wanted to call off Operation *Menace* but Admiral John Cunningham and Major-General Irwin who were commanding the operation thought otherwise, backed by de Gaulle. A further meeting of the War Cabinet in London agreed to proceed.

On 23 September the Fleet Air Arm dropped propaganda leaflets on Dakar. Free French aircraft flew off *Ark Royal* heading for the airport, but their crews were taken prisoner on landing. A boat with representatives of de Gaulle was fired upon as it entered the port. Vichy coastal batteries opened fire on the Australian heavy cruiser HMAS *Australia*. An engagement between the Allied fleet and the Vichy batteries continued for several hours, during which a Vichy destroyer, *L'Audacieux*, was set on fire and beached. Fog and heavy fire hampered an attempt to land Free French troops on a beach to the south-east. Calling off the assault General de Gaulle said he did not want to 'shed the blood of Frenchmen for Frenchmen'.

The Allies continued to attack the coastal defences over the next two days but the Vichy forces did not back down in spite of losing two submarines and seeing the warship *Richelieu* sustaining further damage.

The Allied fleet suffered heavy damage too. As a result, *Resolution* had to be towed back to Cape Town for repairs while an armed trawler was sunk. Concerned that 'protracted fighting might provide a French declaration of war from Vichy' the War Cabinet decided that Operation *Menace* should be abandoned. The battle of Dakar had not been successful for the Allies. Indeed it could be considered a total humiliation, especially for de Gaulle.

The Vichy government had already ordered one bombing of Gibraltar following the attack on the French Fleet at Mers-el-Kébir in July. Now they ordered a second. During most of the Dakar conflict, bombers of the Vichy French Air Force Armée de l'Air de Vichy, based in North Africa, bombed the British base at Gibraltar.

The British naval formation Force H had been formed to replace the French naval power in the Western Mediterranean. Arriving in Gibraltar a few days earlier were the battlecruiser HMS *Renown* along with destroyers HMS *Gallant* – which had since left – and HMS *Firedrake*. On hearing of the attack on Dakar, *Renown* had been prepared for action stations since 1am on the 24th. At 12.50pm, taking advantage of the broken cloud cover and escorted by fighter planes, sixty Vichy Lioré-et-Olivier 45 bombers flew overhead in waves, dropping their loads. By 2.40pm the attack was over and the all clear sounded. Because of a lack of Allied fighter aircraft and the cloud cover there had been little opposition, although two planes were hit resulting in one of them crashing on landing back at base. British casualties included two members of the Royal Artillery.

The following day an even larger raid was carried out with eighty-one Vichy French planes dropping over 100 bombs on the Rock, harbour and dockyards. This time there were no accompanying fighter aircraft. Most of the bombs missed. However once again some damage was caused, and twenty-one members of the British armed services lost their lives, including fifteen sailors on board the British armed trawler HMT *Stella Sirius* which was sunk. Anti-aircraft defences had been more accurate and managed to shoot down one Vichy plane and damage a second.

Events in West Africa reached the press. Correspondents from the United Press Association filed reports on 24 September that covered almost two columns of newsprint the following day. The most ominous report was received from Vichy following a meeting of the Cabinet when the Foreign Minister, M. Baudouin, read a statement to the press which ended by saying 'It is officially stated that the reported bombing of Gibraltar is not true. No reprisals have thus far been taken, but French reprisals are imminent and will be vigorous.'[20]

Chris and Dennis had noticed the first stirrings of anti-British propaganda when in Paris. It was now in full swing. On 25 and 26 September French national and regional newspapers from *Le Figaro* to *Le Petit Journal* and *Echo d'Alger* gave their version of the events to their readers. Many of the reports use the same wording suggesting there was only one source. De Gaulle was described as a traitor and condemned for his betrayal. *L'Oeuvre* called him the 'French ex-General' 'an adventurer who was in the pay of England solely to fight for our old enemies'. A man who 'claims to stand for Honour and Fatherland, and believes honour consists in making war on his compatriots'. The English 'have already shown their disloyalty in the attack on Mers-el-Kébir. Now this poor excuse is no longer valid; this is a direct attack on a French port on French territory.'

Finally on 27 September Radio Lyons made a statement saying the French Admiralty had announced that as the English Squadron had ceased to attack Dakar, French reprisals on Gibraltar had been suspended.

CHAPTER TWENTY FIVE
THE NOT SO LONELY ROADS

As the four principal escapees headed south they met a number of other ex-PoWs also trying to find a way home. Not all were recorded in their notes. For example Chris and Dennis made no reference to Tom Rennie whom they met twice. We only know of this from Rennie's extended correspondence with Dennis's father. Perhaps fearful of the manuscript being confiscated names were deliberately omitted, with Potts and Besley being just vaguely referenced. The only named escapees were those held in Spain with them and therefore already known to the authorities and the British Embassy.

Fortunately my father had added names in the margins of his journal at a later date. By piecing together MI9 reports with additional information provided by family members it has been possible to retrace some of the steps of these other men.

MAJOR POTTS AND CAPTAIN BESLEY

The 7th Battalion Royal Northumberland Fusiliers were members of the Territorial Army mobilised in 1939, made up of men from the county. However fifty percent of the battalion were pitmen who had to be sent back when mining was classified a reserved occupation. They were replaced by reservists from the Duke of Wellington's Regiment in Yorkshire and militiamen from the Rifle Brigade in London which entailed a great deal of reorganisation. Initially billeted at Gosforth Park Racecourse where they camped in the Tote stands, many friendships were forged during the following weeks of training. A machine gun battalion, they were moved to Alton in Hampshire in the New Year. There, their live firing training with the Vickers machine gun was limited to one belt of ten rounds. They were despatched to France on 4 April 1940 initially under the command of III Corps. However they were quickly attached as Support Group to the 51st Highland Division which was under French command on the Maginot Line, the line of defensive fortifications that had been built to defend the eastern border of France.

When the Germans made their advance through the Ardennes Forest thereby avoiding the Maginot Line but threatening to encircle those defending it, the 51st were faced with a chaotic night-time withdrawal to a line south of Abbeville. Despite putting up stout resistance they were pushed further back to a defensive line along the river Bresle and finally back to St-Valéry.

Major William Charles Wilkinson Potts, 7th Battalion Royal Northumberland Fusiliers, a farmer in civilian life, was captured on 12 June at St-Valéry. He managed to escape from the line of march the same evening, but was recaptured the following day. On the second march he met Captain Besley. That night the two men decided it would not be easy to escape from the motorised transport being laid on for the officers and so they hid among the other ranks, marching out of camp with them. On reaching Hornoy towards the end of the day they hid in a hedge for three hours until the column was well out of sight before heading for the coast at Ault. They spent three days walking up and down the coast but the only boat they could find was a lifeboat too big to be handled by two so they headed south. Skirting to the east of Paris they were arrested again. This time it was by a German Corporal who searched and fed them, ordered them to clean out the yard of a house being used as an HQ, then sent them on their way the following morning. They crossed the border unchallenged by walking in the company of a woman who had been visiting her son in the occupied territory, taking advantage of the large number of pedestrians crossing at the same time. They reached free France on 9 July when they were stopped by police and escorted to Vichy. There they met Chris Waters and Dennis Lennon, travelling to Marseilles with them on 19 July. It was the American Consul in Marseilles who told them they would receive £5 a month, being the allowance that was paid to British officers.

On 24 July the French police visited the Seamen's Mission and demanded to see the Senior British Officer who just then was Major Potts. He was told the police had orders to intern all British soldiers in Fort St-Jean. Captain Besley, Major Potts and four or five other ranks were taken away and interned, while the rest got away.

Whilst at the Fort the Major heard that French and Colonial troops were being sent to Morocco for demobilisation. These could have been Moroccan nationals that the Vichy Government wanted to return to Southern Morocco which had been a French Protectorate since 1912.* Acquiring two French uniforms and withdrawing their parole Potts and Besley climbed down the Fort wall and hid on the Africa bound boat with the French troops. Captain Besley was discovered and offloaded, but although the Major's absence had been discovered some hours before sailing, no attempt was made to find him.

Arriving in Oran on 13 August Potts received a great deal of assistance from the French Foreign Legion soldiers and was able to travel to Fez and then Casablanca. He tried to join in an escape organised by Moroccan Jews. The plan was to board a Spanish fishing boat which would head for Gibraltar with the intention of being intercepted by a British warship, but whilst waiting for three of their party to board, Police came across the sands and arrested everyone. He was eventually sent to a native camp guarded by Arab sentries and a Camp Commandant who seemed very pro German as the Dakar affair had just occurred *(see Chapter Twenty Four)*.

However Potts and other prisoners were able to win the Arab guards round and, in a party of seventeen, able to escape once more, finding a boat that would take them to Gibraltar. Major Potts finally returned to England 15 December 1940.[21]

Captain Charles Robert Ingram Besley, 7th Battalion Royal Northumberland Fusiliers, a solicitor in civilian life, was captured 13 June. He had been sheltering in a wood with the remaining members of his platoon when his CO gave him permission to try and escape. He first entered St-Valéry, hiding in a shed when he saw some Germans approaching. He later attempted to

---

* The French Army contained colonial regiments from Algeria, Morocco, Senegal, Tchad, Niger, Mali and Guinea. These regiments were distinct from the foreign legion but were officered by native Frenchmen. Many were brought to Europe in the Great War and in 1939 the French again brought numbers of them to help defend the Maginot Line. After the armistice they were either returned to their colonies and protectorates – which remained under Vichy rule – or were sent to Lebanon, Syria and Madagascar where they later fought, and were defeated by, the British.

reach the harbour but found the lock gates closed so made his way along the cliffs to the north. He was shot at by machine guns just as dusk was falling and hid in a cornfield. From this vantage point he could see a merchant ship being fired upon and set on fire by German tanks. At about 11.30am the following day he was captured by two German airmen and treated with courtesy under later questioning. He was moved by truck to a camp near Rouen and continued to travel by truck until meeting Major Potts four days later.

Crossing the border into Unoccupied France, he reports them walking down the main route bleue through Moulins. This is the main trunk road between Paris and the French border with Italy and therefore a busy crossing point. Besley pushed the Frenchwoman's pram while she spoke to the German sentries who let them through, as her papers were in order.

Having been discovered on the Africa bound boat, Besley was confined to his room in Fort St-Jean for four days. Here he learnt of a scheme being planned at an English hospital run by the Polish authorities. With the aid of a Polish passport he was able to board a ship the Poles had acquired posing as a crew member, with the intention of picking up other escapees further along the coast. They stayed on board for nine days but the boat was not given permission to sail so he returned to Marseilles. It was now late September and through an American contact he learnt that Sir Samuel Hoare had managed to repatriate all British soldiers who had gone into Spain.

Using his Polish passport, and in company with three Poles, he made his way along the coast and over the frontier where they parted company. Two kilometres further on he walked into a Spanish frontier post. He was first imprisoned in Espolla and then the Castillo at Figueras, with other British prisoners, for eight days. Whilst there he was visited by the British Vice Consul from Gerona who told him the last party had got out by an arrangement made with the Spanish Government against the import of petrol. The prisoners were transferred to Cervera where relations with the guards were strained and brutal, staying for around nine days before being sent to Miranda de Ebro. The treatment of British prisoners was much better at Miranda and there was ample food, except that it consisted entirely of potato stew of which the prisoners tired.

He and the others were eventually released on 12 November, leaving Gibraltar on the 19th, and arriving in Liverpool on 4 December 1940.[22]

FLYING OFFICER HAWKINS

No 103 Squadron (RAF) was a bomber squadron equipped with the monoplane Fairey Battle, deployed to France at the outbreak of war. Having sustained many losses in the Battle for France in the face of a numerically superior and more experienced and better equipped enemy, the squadron was ordered to return to England on 15 June, the day after Ron Hawkins was shot down.

Flying Officer Ron Hawkins, 103 (B) Squadron, BEF, learnt to fly in 1936 when the Air Ministry advertised for vacancies in the Royal Air Force Reserve. Having been awarded his pilot's brevet he applied for a commission in the Reserve of Air Force Officers (RAFO) the following year. The successful application led to one year's training which included ten weeks' experience with No 51 (B) Squadron, after which Hawkins went into Reserve being confirmed in his appointment as a Pilot Officer in the RAFO. Recalled for active service in October 1939, he was sent to France in April 1940 with No 98 Squadron, a reserve and training unit sited far from the front line on the Bay of Biscay.

At the end of May Hawkins was transferred to 103 (B) Squadron, a front line unit equipped with the single engined light bomber Fairey Battle. At that time they were based at Rhèges, ninety miles south-east of Paris. Ten days later they moved to Ouzouer-le-Doyen west of Orléans and on 14 June were ordered to move to Sougé forty miles further west *(see Map 2)*. When Hawkins first joined the Squadron they had thirty-one Battles; this number was now reduced to sixteen. Within minutes of landing at Sougé at 5pm the aerodrome was attacked by nine low-flying enemy aircraft destroying another two Battles.

Within two hours of arriving at the new base four crew were taking to the air again. Hawkins had had difficulty starting his machine, which meant he was the last

Ron Hawkins [Hawkins family]

of his flight to leave and was operating alone on a bombing raid against troops concentrated in a forest south-west of Évreux *(see Map 1)*. He was intercepted by a Messerschmitt 109 squadron of eleven aircraft but managed to release two bombs before his control column was shot away by cannon fire. Ordering his rear gunner to abandon the aircraft he quickly followed, but immediately regretted pulling his ripcord so quickly when given a few short bursts of fire. Hanging limp to sham being hit he landed safely. His aircraft, and one of the ME109s, crashed near the target – the latter presumably shot down by his rear gunner who was captured and taken as a PoW. Hawkins hid his parachute and left the forest as quickly as he could. He lay in a cornfield watching the Germans searching the wood for him. Once darkness arrived he started marching south hoping to reach the Allied lines. He hid the next day and continued his march that night. However he had had nothing to eat since lunchtime two days before and while looking for water in a farmyard was captured by seven German soldiers at about 2am on 16 June.

He spent two days at a prison near Vernon where he was interrogated but managed to pick up the piece of paper on which the interrogator had written his name, rank and number as he left the office. The prison was a former French barracks with about 300 French prisoners. The captors allowed the prisoners to enter the stores to help themselves to French kit, enabling Hawkins to acquire a haversack and water bottle, plus chisel, pliers and a file when no-one was looking. He was then moved to a camp west of Évreux surrounded by barbed wire with a river to the south. Having taken details of the next of kin of three other British officers who were reluctant to join him, he made his escape in the early hours of the 19th by crawling along the sewage trench before swimming the river. On the swim he lost his trousers [and money] which he had removed thinking the water was shallow enough to wade so had to put his shirt on his legs through the arm holes.

Marching by night and hiding by day he reached the coast at Trouville on the 22nd, a day when a friendly farmer gave him civilian clothes and some bread and sugar. He had previously lived on biscuits saved from prison, supplemented by potatoes from the fields and milk when he could find willing cows.

Now in civilian clothes travelling was much easier and he even felt bold enough to acknowledge German soldiers he met on main roads. He crossed the Seine with some refugees and continued searching the coast for suitable boats. The soles of his shoes became worn through leaving him with blistered feet. Having resorted to packing the shoes with canvas from abandoned motor cars then later stealing a bicycle, he arrived at Carteret, the nearest point on the French coast for Jersey. Here he acquired a canvas canoe and paddled to Jersey, landing on 1 July. He was given food and drink and told that the enemy had occupied the island that day so Hawkins returned to France, another fifteen mile paddle. Fortunately he had been brought up in Suffolk where he had learnt to handle small boats sailing on the River Orwell and along the local coastline.

Hawkins now also headed for Vichy with a second stolen bicycle where he met Major Potts, Captain Besley, Captain Waters and 2nd Lieutenant Lennon who invited him to have some food with them in the local internment camp. However when the Officer in Charge started to show an interest Hawkins decided to depart very quickly and reached Marseilles on 16 July.

Hoping to contact a neutral ship he found Marseilles a closed dock. Around this time he met Sous-Officier Mayoux *[Mayhew as known by Chris]*, a French Liaison Officer to the RAF at Coulommiers. They overcame the difficulty of getting past the gendarmes guarding the gates leading to the wharves by pretending to be fishermen. Armed with a piece of bamboo, string and a fish hook, the two managed to creep into the dock yard. However Captains of neutral ships, although friendly, were unable to give sailing dates, and it was noticed that German agents were on board ships that were likely to sail.[23]

Hawkins and Mayoux then teamed up with Chris and Dennis.

LIEUTENANT HOGG AND CAPTAIN RAIKES

The 26th Field Company RE* served with the 1st Infantry Division between 3 September 1939 and 28 February 1940 when it joined the 51st Highland Division, replacing 238 Field Company.[24] Around Christmas 1939 the company had a fifteen day attachment to the French Army in front of the Maginot Line 'to introduce the men to the sensation of being shot over'. German patrols were continually active in the Saar valley and it had been decided that attaching British formations for periods of fifteen days to the French would offer useful

---

* A Royal Engineer field company supports an infantry division whilst a Royal Engineer field squadron is its equivalent supporting an armoured division. A field park company provides a workshop and stores.

experience and acclimatise British battalions to battle. In April the 51st Division took over a divisional sector on the Saar front.

On 7 May 1940 Lieutenant Montie Hogg was granted home leave so that he could wed his fiancée two days later. He left his new wife on 12 May and was back with the Field Company in France on the 18th in time for the battle of Abbeville and river Bresle and the subsequent withdrawal to St-Valéry. An account of the withdrawal was written in History of the Corps of the Royal Engineers Vol VIII:

'*...The British Government pressed immediately that General Fortune's force should at once be withdrawn to Rouen where it could cross the Seine into Normandy. Too late the French Higher Command on 6th June ordered the withdrawal of their IX Corps and General Fortune's Force to Le Havre. Meanwhile the German thrust had cut off their retreat to the south and the greater part of the combined force was hemmed in near St-Valéry. The majority of the RE who had been preparing demolition on the line of retreat got away with a brigade of 51st Division which had been sent to prepare defences at Le Havre, being evacuated from that port and Fécamp. Some of 1st Field Squadron, 26th Field Company with its Officer in Charge and Headquarters 51st Division RE with the Commander RE were in the force encircled. During all these operations, besides their work on demolition and defences the RE units took their share in fighting as infantry, one section of 26th Field Company, under Lieutenant H S M Hogg, defending a bridgehead over the Bresle for a considerable time until relieved by infantry.*'[25]

Lieutenant Hardinge Stephen Monteith Hogg RE, 26th Field Company was awaiting embarkation at St-Valéry on the morning of 12 June when the order to surrender came. Discarding arms and ammunition whilst gathering as much clothing as possible, he and the rest of the 51st Division were marched to a temporary collecting centre for prisoners at the south cliff. After a rough search the 4,000 odd French and British prisoners were marched to a large farm. They were fed on captured rations but there was a shortage of drinking water.

The next day they were transferred by a combination of lorry and marching to a camp near Rouen, possibly Quincanpoix. Lorries were scarce so they would drive to and fro picking up men on the march. Conditions at the camp are described in Chapter Four.

It was here that Hogg met **Temporary Captain Peter Patrick Raikes** RE, Captain Waters and 2nd Lieutenant Lennon and they discussed the possibilities of escape. Only Raikes was in agreement with him to leave immediately.

The following morning at around 11am a riot broke out when the water lorry appeared. The sentries, including the man behind the machine gun trained on the outer wire, left their posts. Hogg and Raikes stepped over the wire and entered the nearby wood.

Hogg did not mention in his report to MI9 that it was he who had instigated the riot. On arrival at the camp he had stepped over the low dividing wire that separated officers from the other ranks to check the welfare of the men in their more crowded section of the camp. He asked one last favour of his men, which was to create as much noise as possible when jostling for position in the queue with the French when the water cart arrived the following morning. He had already decided he was going to try to get away the following day even though he was yet to discuss his plan with Raikes.

After breakfast the two agreed to get away at the earliest opportunity. Immediately the water lorry arrived the wild rush and jostling amongst the men had the desired effect with the sentry and machine-gunner in the shed leaving their posts. That left one machine-gunner at his post but Hogg didn't think he had a good view of the section of fence he wanted to use. There were several French officers near the wire. Hogg crossed first and then the French blocked the view of the machine-gunner so that Raikes could follow.

They marched for eleven nights, finding food and shelter from farms each day, and hiding from German motorcycle patrols which would occasionally search French homes. They swam the Seine at night, but acquiring civilian clothes on the twelfth morning managed to cross other rivers by unguarded bridges.

On the 27 June they were recaptured whilst crossing the river Orne at Ménil–Hermei. It appeared to be an unguarded bridge, but they were taken by sentries from a post hidden behind a house on the far side. Notes they had made during their first few days of escape betrayed them as British Officers. They spent a pleasant night with the Oberleutnant who was in command of the company holding the village, before being transferred to a collecting centre at Falaise where they were held for four days. To their surprise the Oberleutnant gave them a good meal accompanied by music played on the gramophone. He complimented the British on their skilled withdrawal to St-Valéry, but also told them Germany had virtually already won the war, a tale embellished with exaggerated claims of German superiority. He was kindly and never threatening, but they were on their guard lest he was seeking information. They reckoned he was actually just lonely, so let him talk whilst they got on with their meal. On the morning of 3 July they were marched, together with 200 French prisoners to a large camp at Ecouché. As the camp was full Hogg and Raikes, together with eight French officers, were put in a small farm building adjoining the main camp where a Company of German Infantry was billeted. The Company provided the guards.

The following day the Company was moved out to Brest leaving one sentry to guard the gate into the farm as no replacements were available. Informing the French officers of their plans, Hogg and Raikes left the camp via the latrine at the back and marched south. On 17 July they crossed the frontier into unoccupied France in open country near Ciran.

Advised by a farmer that the Military Authorities at Loches would doubtless help, they duly reported the following day and were taken to Bélâbre under Surveillance Libérés *[parole]*. Here they met Captain Bradford[26] of the 1st Black Watch who had been there several days along with two other ranks from the 52nd Lowland Division. Two days later they were joined by Captain Ian Garrow[27] of the Highland Light Infantry and on the 27th A/Captain Fitch of the Norfolk Regiment and Lieutenant Sillar of the RAMC.

The French unit looking after them was due to be relieved the following day, so they decided this would be a suitable time to escape. After reporting as required at the Mairie *[N.B. Town Hall]* at 9.30am, Bradford, Raikes, Sillar, Fitch and Hogg walked out of the town at 9.35 with Garrow and the other ranks leaving after the troops' meal at 12.30pm. Having acquired bicycles during their stay at Bélâbre, and it being easier and safer to travel in small groups, Hogg and Raikes set off on their own. They cycled down the main roads heading roughly in the direction of Perpignan, detouring each time they saw a gendarme to avoid being stopped.

On 5 August they crossed the frontier from the French commune of Osséja into Spain *(see Map 4)* having carried their bicycles over the mountains just south of the border between Bourg-Madame and Puigcerdà. They had travelled forty kilometres along the main road to Ribas when they were stopped by Carabinieros at Planolas. Questioned by a French speaking Spaniard they made no effort to hide the fact that they were escaped British officers.

After spending the night at Planolas, they were taken on foot to Ribas and interviewed by the Guardia Civil. Their French maps and dictionaries were taken away. In the afternoon they were taken by train to Ripoll to be interviewed by the Military Authorities then the Police, always being asked exactly the same questions.

They spent that night in a Military Prison with twelve captured Reds, Spanish Republicans. Conditions were disgusting. Next day they were taken by bus to Figueras and interviewed at the HQ of the Frontier Guard. They demanded the British Consul in Barcelona be informed of their presence not knowing there was an agent in town. After the same questioning and searching they were taken to the Prision Cellular where they were again searched and thumb prints were taken. Conditions were very bad and their treatment no different to that of the other prisoners.[28]

It was a relief to be released from the gaol on 22 August and be taken to Gerona joining Chris, Dennis and the others.

SAPPER RICHARDS

In addition to 26th Field Company, the Royal Engineer element of the 51st Highland Division comprised 236th and 237th Field Companies and 239th Field Park Company with Lieutenant Colonel H M Smail, TD, as CRE.

Sapper Joseph J Richards, 237th Field Company RE Dundee TA, a commercial traveller from Dundee in civilian life, had been captured on 9 June. Two days previously, 237 Field Company had been laying land mines north of Neufchâtel. On 8 June they were ordered to withdraw to Abbeville when Richards and seven others were asked to pick up some broken down lorries. Having done so and returned to Abbeville the men were unable to find any trace of their company so they carried on to Buchy spending the night in a farm. They awoke in the morning to find themselves surrounded by Germans.

From Buchy they were taken by lorry to a large field somewhere south of Amiens where they joined a column of mostly French PoWs.

The following day the British were separated from the French and marched via Doullens, St Pol, Béthune, La Bassée Canal to Lille, about seven days of marching at the rate of thirty-five kilometres a day. From Lille they were taken to Belgium via Tournai, Renaix *[Ronse]*, and Aalst which they reached on 22 June.

On leaving Aalst with the British PoWs in front as usual and the French behind, Richards determined to make his escape. About two kilometres beyond the town he deliberately dawdled in the column until he was right at the end of it, with just one German sentry between himself and liberty.

At a moment when the attention of the sentry was distracted Richards jumped into a ditch at the side of the road unobserved. He waited until the column had wound round the corner of the road and disappeared before rising and scrambling through a high hedge into the grounds of a private house. Crawling through the garden and adjoining woods he found himself in the garden of a smaller house. He nervously approached the front door. The owners were very good and provided him with food as well as a jacket, cap and scarf.

It was his intention to make for the coast, and that night reached Ghent. He went right through the town which was full of German soldiers, making for the open fields beyond where he hid for the night. The following day he kept on in a north-westerly direction. The next three weeks were spent in the neighbourhood of Deinze, and Kruishoutem.

By now he had managed to get a French passport from a grocer. It had been taken off a dead Frenchman. With no idea how to leave Belgium as the whole region was occupied by Germans, farmers advised him to make for the Walloon district to the south. The grocer had also provided civilian clothes and a suitcase so the disguise was perfect.

Richards made his way to Mourcourt spending a week working on a farm. From there he travelled mainly on foot to Tourcoing, Lille, Lens, Arras, Amiens and Beauvais. Leaving Beauvais he was given a lift by a German officer in a lorry who dropped him ten kilometres short of Paris. By now Paris was closed to road traffic with only pedestrians being allowed to enter and leave.

From Paris he continued by way of Rambouillet to Chartres and Orléans. South of Orléans he came across a farm run by a Belgian lady who spoke perfect English and gave him a map showing the route south and the demarcation line. He managed to get a lift from a lorry heading south and was driven through the border at Vierzon on 1 August.

At a small station south of Vierzon he boarded a train to Limoges which was the main point of traffic for evacuees heading north or south. At the station he approached the Commissionnaire Militaire [a Belgian Liaison Officer] for assistance. Richards was given thirty Francs and advised to make for Toulouse where he would find a British Consul. He was also given a train pass and ration tickets with which he could draw food from Red Cross canteens located on every station. Finally he was presented with a letter of introduction to every Commissionnaire Militaire on his route. The Commissionnaire at Toulouse sent him by train to Port-Vendres where he was sent to the military barracks. Two days later, on 8 August, he was escorted by two gendarmes via train to the internment camp at St-Cyprien where he met Captains Johnson and Trythall and Sergeant Herring. The latter had only just escaped from Fort St-John where he had met Major Potts, and six other ranks.

That night, being allowed to go down to the beach, he and Herring went in search of a boat. They found a fishing smack which they launched and rowed out to sea. However two miles out they found a bad leak in the boat. By the time they had travelled seven miles down the coast water was up to their waists. They were forced to bring the boat to shore and return to St-Cyprien.

The following day the two men set out to cross the frontier by way of the mountains. This time they got as far as Le Boulou before being stopped by a gendarme who returned them to St-Cyprien under escort.

Richards now decided to rest for a few days while Herring managed to get away with a Czechoslovakian. On 14 August Richards set off alone, making for Argèles-sur-Mer and from there due south over a high peak in the mountains, which a gendarme had advised was the best route. The five mile journey from Argèles took three days on rations of one tin of beef, a German water bottle full of water and a piece of bread. The two tins of sardines he also carried remained untouched.

On entering the first village in Spain he was arrested and taken to Figueras. The British Consul was prevented from seeing him but did manage to send in twenty pesetas. He was transferred to the Castillo where he eventually met Mr Whitfield before being sent on to Cervera.

His release was finally obtained and Richards was returned to England on 28 September.[29]

PSM CLUBBS

The 5th Battalion Gordon Highlanders were a Territorial Infantry Unit deployed to France in September 1939. During the Battle of France they were serving as part of 153 Brigade in the 51st Division.

Platoon Sergeant Major R Clubbs 5th Gordons, a clerk by profession who had been a reservist for nine years, was in position with A Company outside Abbeville under heavy fire on 11 June 1940. The following morning, 12 June, he was approached by his Captain and told to cease fire. Clubbs gathered his men in a small wood. He told them to break up their rifles, bury ammunition and destroy all pay books and papers before joining the rest of the battalion who were surrounded by German tanks.

At about 11.30am the march east towards Germany began. For the first two days they received no food because the Germans did not have any to give to prisoners. Clubbs was told by one of the Germans that they had not expected to take so many PoWs therefore had not provided for them. On the third day they received some brown beans, which was their diet for the next six days. On the tenth day, reaching Flixecourt, they received some white bread which the Germans had commandeered.

Looking for a suitable opportunity to escape, Clubbs had noticed that when the Germans came to a German grave by the roadside, all the guards turned their eyes towards the grave to read the name. Leaving Flixecourt they passed about twenty graves on the left hand side of the road. When all eyes were turned to the left, Clubbs dived into the hedge on the right and lay there till the column had passed.

That night, 21 June, was spent in a nearby wood having begged some food and civilian clothes from a farmhouse. The following morning he set off for the coast. On the previous day's march he had noticed a lot of British ammunition lying on the roadside about ten kilometres back. He decided to return to the spot to see if he could do anything about blowing it up. However the ammunition turned out to be nearly all aerial bombs and there was nothing he could do.

Six days later he arrived at the village of Mariel about three kilometres east of Abbeville. Here he met an Englishman who had lived in France for a number of years and now passed as a Frenchman. The house was on the main Amiens to Abbeville road. Staying here for two days and watching the large amount of German traffic travelling up and down, Clubbs realised he would not be able to make his escape from the coast and that he would have to make for Spain instead.

He walked from Amiens to Abbeville to Beauvais where he saw a lot of troop activity gathering in the fields. In one of the villages the local Mayor gave him food and lodgings and a letter of introduction to the Mayor of Sailly, a town forty kilometres away. He lodged in Sailly for three days. The Mayor gave him advice on crossing the Seine and a warning to avoid Versailles where the German Police had their headquarters. Unfortunately the suggested river crossing was heavily guarded so Clubbs had to head west before finding a spot where he could swim across at night.

Immediately after crossing the Seine, Clubbs came into contact with large bodies of German troops and found this state of affairs the same as far as the line of demarcation. Heading south to avoid the heavily occupied Chartres, in favour of Châteaudun, he stayed there for two days; the town was full of Germans and guards were walking the streets.

Continuing south, two miles from the Loire he passed a large German flying field. A farmer told him that the aerodrome had been bombed by the RAF the previous Sunday, badly damaging three hangars, but now the Germans were busy filling in holes and moving their flak. Before crossing the Loire he was able to question a French evacuee heading north as to whether the Germans were stopping everyone and asking for 'Laissez passer.' The Frenchman said no, so Clubbs walked across.

At the village of Vernou he met a Frenchman who put him up for three days and gave some information about crossing the line of demarcation. He was then introduced to the Baron at the château of Vernou who gave him a letter to the curé at Mennetou-sur-Cher. This priest showed Clubbs a good place to cross over. That night, the curé arranged with a boy to throw stones into the river Cher at one spot to attract the German sentry's attention, while Clubbs swam across at another.

He continued south via Châteauroux, Limoges and Nexon, where again he was given help at the château, noting all German activity including a recently constructed but well camouflaged aerodrome near Toulouse.

His next stop was Perpignan where he got in touch with the American Vice Consul. Although he was given information about crossing the Spanish frontier, Clubbs was not provided with any money so decided to go to Marseilles. He got as far as Narbonne where he was arrested by the French and sent to the internment camp at St-Cyprien where he met Jimmy and Tommy.

PSM Clubbs was awarded the Military Medal for 'an escape which exemplified the highest powers of observation. Further he was alone.'[30]

LIEUTENANT THE EARL OF CARDIGAN

A motor ambulance convoy is used to clear the sick and wounded soldier from the field ambulance to a casualty clearing station. The 6th Motor Ambulance Convoy (MAC) was deployed to France with the General Headquarters, BEF Headquarters Troops.

Lieutenant The Earl of Cardigan, RAMC, was a writer by profession and member of the TA, but had joined the active list in April 1939. On 28 May Cardigan was commanding the workshop section of the 6th MAC which was working in conjunction with 10th Casualty Clearing Station (CCS) when they were ordered to remain and be captured at Krombeke in Belgium as the Commanding Officer wanted to retain as many ambulances as possible. Taken prisoner the following day the wounded were transferred out by the Germans and on the 30th the British medical officers were driven to Ypres. They spent two days lodged in a schoolhouse tending to British wounded, kept strictly apart from the adjoining buildings housing the French wounded and medical staff. Anyone not a member of the RAMC was then transferred to Boulogne where they stayed another ten days. Cardigan was keen to escape. Around 28 June there was another move by lorry to Lille, but due to insufficient accommodation the prisoners were moved on to Tournai. By now the guard comprised just one lorry driver and one armed guard sitting in the front with the driver. On approaching Tournai the lorry stopped for a moment and Cardigan took his opportunity. He jumped off the tail, stood still in the road until the lorry had continued on its way, then dived into some bushes for cover.

He lay there for about six hours waiting for darkness. At dusk a local café proprietor who had witnessed the escape came for him and took Cardigan back to his house. He was given food, a change of clothes and advice on travelling by day due to the night-time curfew. Following the sun, Cardigan walked about ten miles a day due south, entering unoccupied France near Buxy to the west of Chalon-sur-Saône.

Having walked such a long distance he now caught a train to Lyon where the American Consul advised him to continue to Marseilles, which he did. He bluffed his way out of the need to produce a Carte d'Indentite on the journey by claiming to be American. Arriving at the American Consul in Marseilles he met the British representative, Major Dodds. Due to the difficulty of getting into Spain, Dodds suggested he go into Fort St-Jean and join other escapees there. This course of action did not suit Cardigan so he hid up in a small hotel. Whilst there he met several of the officers interned at Fort St-Jean as they had liberty to go out in the town during the day, as well as Rev Caskie at the Seamen's Mission and an English dentist.

After a week's rest he bought a bicycle. Having heard of a British officer in the fort who had been caught by the police for not displaying a bicycle plaque, he paid the appropriate tax to obtain his before cycling along the coast to Spain, leaving France at Céret and carrying his bicycle over the Pyrenees at Las Illas. Like others before him, he was picked up by the Guardia Civil and taken to Figueras. He spent a few days at the Castillo before being transferred to Cervera and then Miranda de Ebro. After about a fortnight, along with three other British prisoners, he was escorted by train to Madrid where they were all received at the Embassy. Cardigan and the other three joined the group containing Chris and Jimmy.[31]

Lieutenant The Earl of Cardigan was Mentioned in Despatches for his escape.

THE NOT SO LONELY ROADS | 187

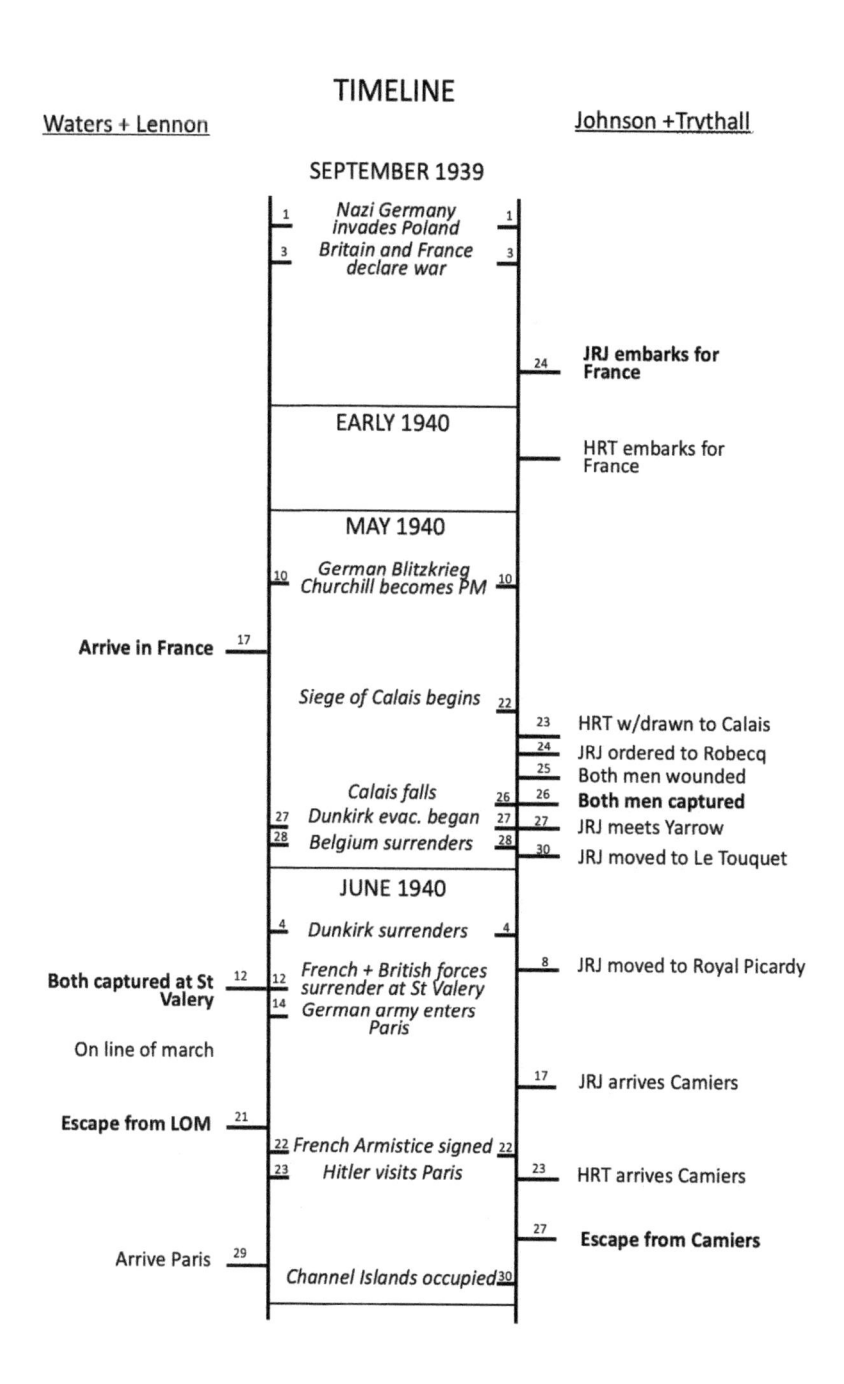

TIMELINE

Waters + Lennon | **Johnson + Trythall**

SEPTEMBER 1939

- 1 — Nazi Germany invades Poland — 1
- 3 — Britain and France declare war — 3
- 24 — **JRJ embarks for France**

EARLY 1940

- HRT embarks for France

MAY 1940

- 10 — German Blitzkrieg / Churchill becomes PM — 10
- **Arrive in France** 17
- Siege of Calais begins — 22
- 23 — HRT w/drawn to Calais
- 24 — JRJ ordered to Robecq
- 25 — Both men wounded
- Calais falls — 26 / 26 — **Both men captured**
- 27 — Dunkirk evac. began — 27 / 27 — JRJ meets Yarrow
- 28 — Belgium surrenders — 28
- 30 — JRJ moved to Le Touquet

JUNE 1940

- 4 — Dunkirk surrenders — 4
- 8 — JRJ moved to Royal Picardy
- **Both captured at St Valery** 12 / 12 — French + British forces surrender at St Valery
- 14 — German army enters Paris
- On line of march
- 17 — JRJ arrives Camiers
- **Escape from LOM** 21
- 22 — French Armistice signed — 22
- 23 — Hitler visits Paris / 23 — HRT arrives Camiers
- 27 — **Escape from Camiers**
- **Arrive Paris** 29
- Channel Islands occupied — 30

188 | FROM A HARD PLACE TO A ROCK

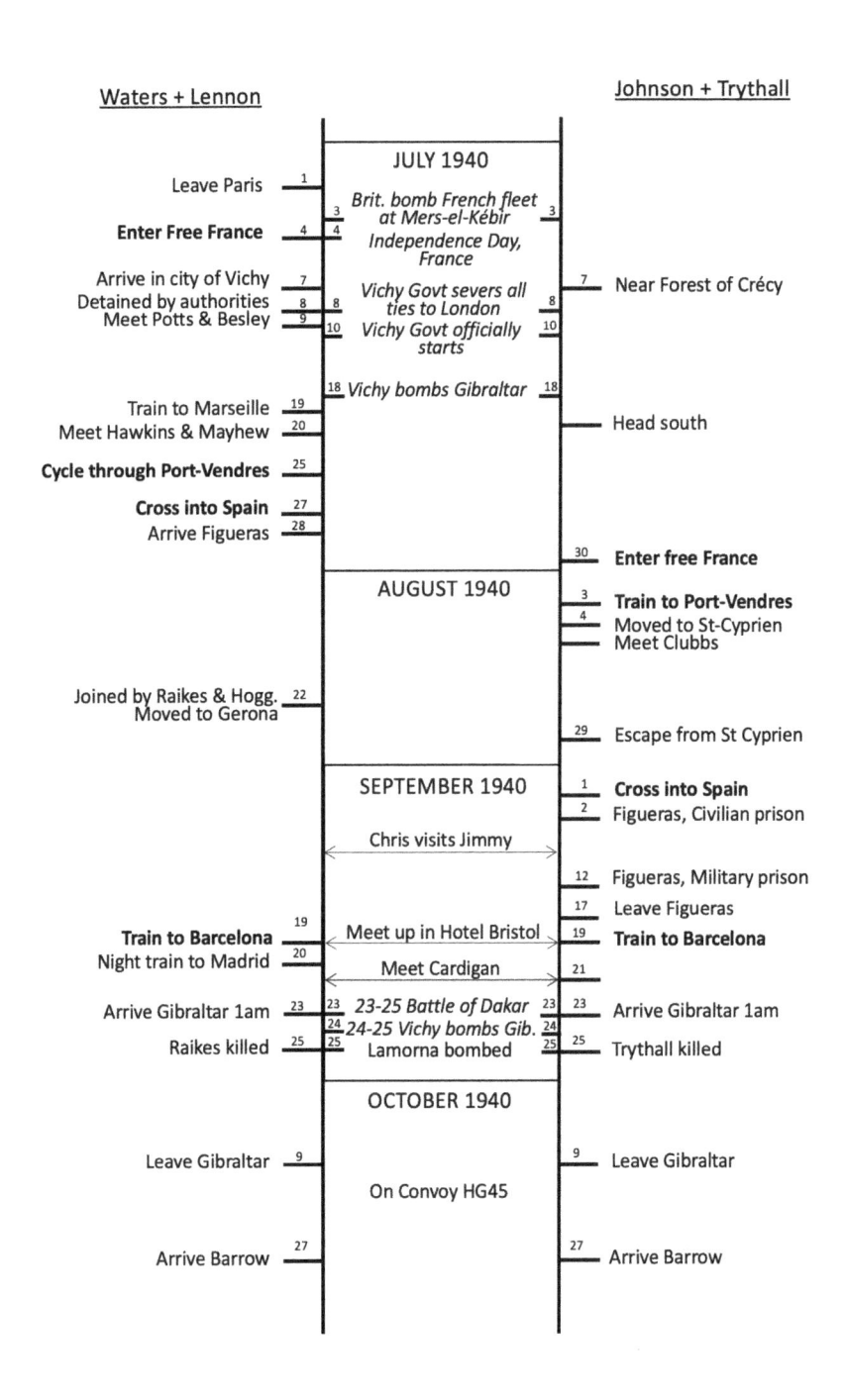

Waters + Lennon | Johnson + Trythall

JULY 1940

- 1 — Leave Paris
- 3 — Brit. bomb French fleet at Mers-el-Kébir
- 4 — **Enter Free France** / Independence Day, France
- 7 — Arrive in city of Vichy | 7 — Near Forest of Crécy
- 8 — Detained by authorities | 8 — Vichy Govt severs all ties to London
- 9 — Meet Potts & Besley
- 10 — Vichy Govt officially starts
- 18 — Vichy bombs Gibraltar
- 19 — Train to Marseille
- 20 — Meet Hawkins & Mayhew | — Head south
- 25 — **Cycle through Port-Vendres**
- 27 — **Cross into Spain**
- 28 — Arrive Figueras
- 30 — **Enter free France**

AUGUST 1940

- 3 — **Train to Port-Vendres**
- 4 — Moved to St-Cyprien / Meet Clubbs
- 22 — Joined by Raikes & Hogg. Moved to Gerona
- 29 — Escape from St Cyprien

SEPTEMBER 1940

- 1 — **Cross into Spain**
- 2 — Figueras, Civilian prison
- Chris visits Jimmy
- 12 — Figueras, Military prison
- 17 — Leave Figueras
- 19 — **Train to Barcelona** | Meet up in Hotel Bristol | 19 — **Train to Barcelona**
- 20 — Night train to Madrid | Meet Cardigan
- 21
- 23 — Arrive Gibraltar 1am | 23-25 Battle of Dakar | 23 — Arrive Gibraltar 1am
- 24 — 24-25 Vichy bombs Gib.
- 25 — Raikes killed | Lamorna bombed | 25 — Trythall killed

OCTOBER 1940

- 9 — Leave Gibraltar | 9 — Leave Gibraltar
- On Convoy HG45
- 27 — Arrive Barrow | 27 — Arrive Barrow

POSTSCRIPT

TOMMY TRYTHALL AND PETER RAIKES

Captain Harold Reuben 'Tommy' Trythall was posthumously awarded the Military Cross for bravery in the defence of Dunkirk. His two children, David and John, received the medal in 1945 from King George VI. John recalled later that the King stuttered something to him, but he could not hear a thing. Captain Trythall's name is written on the Memorial at the Gibraltar Cross of Sacrifice.

Captain Peter Patrick Raikes was posthumously Mentioned in Despatches in January 1941 and awarded the Military Cross in November 1945. His remains are buried in Gibraltar North Front Cemetery.

Tommy Trythall [Trythall family]

CHRIS WATERS

Captain Christopher Dalmahoy Waters was Mentioned in Despatches for his escape. Returning to England he was appointed RE Instructor at the Combined Operations Training Unit at Loch Fyne in Scotland. After a subsequent period at the School of Military Engineering, and then time at the War Office, he assumed command of 77th Assault Squadron RE, equipped with engineer variants of tanks and armoured vehicles known as 'funnies'. These included bridgelayers, mine ploughs, flails, bombards and tracklayers all developed by the 79th Armoured Division. In 1943 he was appointed an instructor at the Army Staff College. In July 1944 Chris took over 26 Squadron RE after its commander Major Tony Younger had to return to England following an injury he sustained on D-Day. With the beaches secured and the advance through France proceeding well, Chris was tasked with retraining the Squadron; its heavy Churchill Armoured Vehicle Royal Engineers, or AVREs, replaced by the much lighter amphibious Landing Vehicle, Tracked, or LVT, for operations on the Dutch and Belgian coast. This was necessary to clear the Germans from the Scheldt estuary and open the vital port of Antwerp for Allied supplies.

The LVTs' first action was Operation *Infatuate*, to drive the Germans from the Dutch island of Walcheren, carrying Canadian troops and Royal Marine commandos in each assault across the Scheldt and onto the island. Chris personally led the first wave of his squadron in the attack. As a result of his outstanding work in reconnaissance and leadership he was selected for the appointment of Brigade Major 1st Armoured Engineer Brigade, organising running the Brigade HQ's two echelons over a 200 mile front for which he was awarded the MBE.

In 1946 he was appointed an Instructor at the School of Combined Operations, followed by a tour in GHQ Middle East as Deputy Assistant Military Secretary. He then joined the British Military Mission to Greece as advisor to the Greek Engineers in the war against the communists, before returning as Chief Instructor of 1 Training Regiment, RE and later instructing at the Senior Officers School. Now a Lieutenant Colonel he was appointed Assistant Adjutant General in the War Office, where he was largely concerned

The arrow is pointing to Chris's LVT at Walcheren [Author's collection]

with manpower planning for the army preparing the way for ending National Service and rebalancing the size of the army for peacetime. His work was recognised with the award of an OBE.

After a final posting as Commander RE Colchester, where, with a £1 Million budget, he was in charge of construction and maintenance of military buildings and installations in Essex, Chris retired voluntarily in February 1959. He had met and later married one of his nurses following a stay in hospital in the early 1950s. With an Australian mother it seemed only natural to emigrate (by boat!) to Australia with his wife Jenny and daughter Timandra on retirement. After a year spent teaching maths and boxing at Scotch College, Perth, he moved to the University of Western Australia as Building and Property Officer where he was responsible to the

Chris dinghy sailing at Instow, Devon [Author's collection]

Vice Chancellor for the administration of an extensive building programme and maintenance of buildings and grounds.

The war had taken its toll both mentally and physically. A return to the UK seemed advisable, although it was taken via a lengthy overland trip through South East Asia, India, Iran, Lebanon and Europe, catching up with a number of ex-army colleagues on the way. This was followed by a six month caravan tour of Europe and Morocco with Jenny, retracing his escape route and a return to Fontmell Magna. Prior to taking up a role similar to the one he had in Perth with London University, Chris had another short stay in hospital where he was diagnosed with a recurrence of cancer and heart problems. Unable to face yet another battle he took his own life at the end of summer 1969.

DENNIS LENNON

Second Lieutenant John Dennis Lennon was also Mentioned in Despatches for his escape. On his return to England he was attached to the 7th Field Squadron who were sent to Africa to join up with the 8th Army. After El-Alamein, the 7th Armoured Division were sent to Italy and saw active service until the end of the war. Having been called up as a Private in 1939, Dennis reached the rank of Major and was awarded the Military Cross at El-Alamein for his part in leading his Troop to destroy twenty-four disabled German tanks in the face of the enemy who were trying to recover them.

Post-war, Dennis returned to life as an architect, initially with Maxwell Fry and then as director of the Rayon Design Centre where, with Terence Conran on his staff, his task was to persuade people to use rayon fibres. Seeing some of Conran's textiles at an end of term show halfway through his design course, Dennis immediately offered him a job. Some of the Conran designed fabrics were featured in the 1951 Festival of Britain.

During the 1950s Dennis started his own practice in London redesigning shops for Jaeger and London Steak Houses. He was ultimately appointed as Interior Design Co-ordinator of the *QE2* in 1968 and was made a CBE for his work. Other contracts included designing the Chalcots Estate in Swiss Cottage, London, on land which had been severely damaged during the war, work at Harrow School, gala nights at Covent Garden and designing sets at Glyndebourne. He was also commissioned to oversee the refurbishment of the Ritz in 1976 and later Reid's Hotel in Madeira. A piece of furniture designed by him is held by the V&A.

Dennis showing HM The Queen a model of the QE2 [Lennon family]

Hamper Mill c1968 [Lennon family]

Described as 'the complete architect designer' Dennis was also an extremely talented water colourist – two of his sketches are included in his escape story. When a teenager at school, one of the cross country running routes passed a derelict mill on the River Colne near Watford. Marrying his Norwegian wife Else in 1947 they purchased this mill and turned it into a family home for their three sons, the eldest of whom was named Chris after his escape partner. Dennis died in April 1991.

Dennis Lennon [Lennon family]

JIMMY JOHNSON

Captain James Robert Johnson was awarded the Military Cross for his efforts in escaping. For a while after his return to the UK Jimmy was able to live at Tingewick House from which he organised the defence of the Bicester Central Ordnance Depot against the expected invasion by Hitler's forces. He was then posted first to the 8th and then to the 9th Battalions of the Royal Welch Fusiliers. This was followed by promotion and appointment as Brigade Major 115 (Royal Welch) Infantry Brigade. In November 1942 he was on the staff of 1st Army when it landed at Algiers. There being no vacancies in his own regiment, he was posted to the Durham Light Infantry who were fighting in Tunisia. He landed with them at Salerno on 9 September 1943. In February 1944 he was appointed Commanding Officer of the 2/4th King's Own Yorkshire Light Infantry when all the senior officers and the Intelligence Officer of the battalion were either in hospital or evacuated and the men almost exhausted and near breaking point. Under Jimmy's energetic and courageous command the men soon became an effective fighting unit once more. He made a point of personally visiting every fox-hole twice a day at huge risk to himself, to ensure his men knew they had not been forgotten. They fought northwards through Italy, breaking through the Gothic Line and eventually defeating the Germans there. For personal courage and leadership in this crucial phase of the war he was awarded the Distinguished Service Order.

After a period in Austria and Staff College Camberley he took over the command of 1st Battalion RWF and sailed with them to the Caribbean. Diana and their three children were able to accompany him. During his tour of command Jimmy, now Lieutenant Colonel, had his unit engaged in a variety of roles including internal security duties on Grenada and Antigua, hurricane relief in Jamaica and the 1953 Coronation celebrations during which a military tattoo was staged for the visit of HM The Queen. [He assigned a newly commissioned officer, Second Lieutenant William Roache, to B Company putting him in charge of the tattoo's firework display.] This was followed immediately by ceremonial and guard duties at the three-power talks in Bermuda between President Eisenhower, Prime Minister Churchill and the French Premier, M. Laniel. As a keen horseman and polo player, Jimmy even managed to provide mounts from the regimental polo stables for the Governor and senior officers for the Queen's Birthday Parade. Jimmy was appointed an OBE in recognition of his leadership and organisational skills, but had handed over command before the great parade at Wroughton in Wiltshire, where The Queen presented Colours to the three battalions of his regiment. Jimmy moved on to Washington as General Staff Officer Grade One (GSO1) Operations and Intelligence with the British Joint Services Mission. His

Jimmy and Diana, with Robin at their daughter Sara's christening 1941 [Johnson family]

final appointment was as Military Attaché in Athens, Greece, where he was promoted to Colonel, local Brigadier.

> William 'Bill' Roache, OBE came to the awareness of the viewing public when he was cast as Ken Barlow in *Coronation Street*. Appearing in the first episode in December 1960, the *Guinness Book of Records* lists him as the longest running actor in a continuing role in the history of television serials.
>
> Bill has fond memories of his time in Jamaica. Jimmy, keen to get everyone on horseback, immediately invited him to join the polo club but the offer of playing on a team had to be withdrawn when it was discovered Bill was left handed. The temporary post-war relaxation of rules forbidding left-handed players [to avoid head-on collisions] did not extend to the island. However Bill was able to spend many evenings in the mess playing bridge with his CO and fellow officers.

Jimmy on set wearing a representation of the British Sudan Expeditionary Force RWF uniform. The medals left-right as viewed are – Egypt Medal 1882, Khedive's Star 1882, India General Service Medal 1896 [Johnson family]

Jimmy retired from the Army in January 1961. During a chance meeting while on a pre-retirement course Jimmy heard that Hollywood director Darryl F Zanuck needed a British military expert for his film *The Longest Day*. The director was particularly keen to employ a senior officer who had not taken part in the Normandy Invasion and could therefore take a detached view when it came to filming specific events. Jimmy had to check on all military matters such as styles of marching, uniforms, guns, etc, to prevent sharp-eyed viewers spotting errors. This was followed by a similar role on the film *55 Days at Peking* about the relief of the legations at Peking during the Boxer rebellion, at which both his father and father-in-law had been present. In Hollywood style Charlton Heston re-enacted the actions of Keyes, the first of the relief party to squeeze through the barricades, entering the American legation compound through a sewer. Filmed in Spain, the Spanish army and Chinese restaurants across Europe provided the extras. Jimmy had to research the uniforms worn by eight different nations in 1900 and train the Spaniards in the different marching styles of those nations.

By now he had bought Tingewick House from his brother-in-law. Jimmy and Diana settled into retirement converting the stables into a pottery where together they built up a busy and successful specialist business using some of the pottery skills acquired from one of Diana's aunts, Phyllis Keyes, who had been a member of the Bloomsbury Group.* One of the last major events in which he took part was the unveiling and dedication of a memorial to the Royal Welch Fusiliers at St Venant on 11 November 1997. After a full life Colonel Jimmy Johnson died 30 August 2002.

MONTIE HOGG

Montie Hogg and his bride Betty 9 May 1940 [Hogg family]

---

*   The Bloomsbury Group was a loose collection of intellectual friends and relatives, many living in the Bloomsbury area of London, with an interest in the arts and a strong belief in the importance that arts had on society and culture. Many prominent people were members including Virginia Woolf and John Maynard Keynes.

Lieutenant Hardinge Stephen Monteith Hogg was awarded the Military Cross for his escape. He later served in Italy and undertook mountain warfare training. After the war he served overseas in Singapore, Hong Kong and Northern Ireland and reached the rank of Lieutenant Colonel. On leaving the army in 1959 Montie worked at the head office of WHSmith before finally retiring. He died on 2 May 1996.

RON HAWKINS

Flying Officer Ronald Hawkins was awarded the Military Cross for his resourceful escape and evasion. A month after his return he wrote to the Irving parachute company applying for membership of their Caterpillar Club, open to anyone whose life had been saved by using an Irving parachute. A distinctive Caterpillar badge was duly despatched to him. In December

Hawkins two years after his escape modelling the flying overalls with the additional pockets. [Hawkins family]

1940 he qualified as a flying instructor and was posted to Cambridge. The school would receive an influx of seventy-five pupils every three weeks to begin a six week course. The pupils were almost all war time conscripts who had volunteered for flying duties. In April 1941, with his log-book endorsed with the assessment of 'Above Average' he was transferred to Cranwell to teach trainee flying instructors. In May 1942 he was posted with the rank of Acting Squadron Leader to No 16 (Polish) Service Flying Training School near Nottingham. Hawkins continued to train pilots and instructors until February 1943 when an assessment upgraded him to the ultimate standard of A1 instructor. In 1943 he was awarded the Air Force Cross for his work in this role, which was described as 'exceptional' in his log-book.

He was transferred to operational flying. After training in low attack fighters, in July he was given command of the temporary station of Snailwell aerodrome near Newmarket. No 309 (Polish) Squadron was based there, flying reconnaissance flights over the Dutch coast searching for enemy shipping. After a week Hawkins decided that Snailwell could run itself without him and unofficially resumed flying with 56 Squadron from Matlaske near Holt just a few miles from the Norfolk coast. He had been previously posted to Matlaske in preparation for taking command of his own squadron. At that time morale on the Squadron was low because of defects with both the Typhoon's airframe and engine. Restrictions had been imposed on how far out over the sea the Typhoons could venture because of the high rate of engine failure. Most of these problems had been solved but the pilots were still cautious especially as any offensive operation involved long flights across the North Sea to the Dutch coast. Hawkins stayed with 56 Squadron when they moved to Manston at the end of the month. He flew on a number of operations including *Night Rhubarbs* which were sorties on which opportunist attacks against enemy ground targets were made. With his escape from enemy territory in mind, Hawkins had begun wearing flying overalls with additional pockets sewn into them. These were filled with items he considered useful should he have to escape again.

Finally in September he was given command of No 3 Squadron at Manston which was equipped with the rocket-firing fighter-bomber version of the Typhoon. The squadron was mainly concerned with flying operations named *Ramrod* [where the main object was the destruction of a target rather than bringing enemy aircraft into battle] and *Roadstead* [bombing sorties against enemy shipping]. Hawkins led a number of these operations over the Lille area of northern France and the islands in the Scheldt estuary of Holland.

On 5 October 1943 Hawkins led a *Ramrod* when the primary target was the Sinclair Petroleum Company's refinery at Langerbrugge about six miles north of Ghent. Hawkins and his No 2 [Sergeant Pottinger] found themselves on their own as they crossed the Ghent-Terneuzen Canal. As they approached the refinery they came under fire from flak guns mounted on railway wagons, just as the two pilots had to pull over on either side to avoid some tall chimneys. As Pottinger levelled out he saw the refinery disintegrating as the bombs released by both pilots exploded. He then saw Hawkins was still turning with smoke billowing from underneath his Typhoon. The aircraft gradually lost height and Hawkins baled out, but he was too low for his parachute to deploy in time. He was buried at Ghent City Cemetery.[32]

BERLITZ MAYOUX

Sous-Officier Mayoux, nicknamed 'Berlitz' because of his tendency to walk about with a copy of the *Berlitz Guide to Europe* in his pocket, was last mentioned when the train was boarded from Gerona to Barcelona. It has not been possible to obtain any further information on him.

BILL POTTS AND BOBBIE BESLEY

Major William Charles Wilkinson Potts was awarded the Military Cross for his escape. He later commanded the Vickers MG training depot at The Dale, Chester followed by an attachment to 14th Battalion Durham Light Infantry but did not have any further overseas postings. He served until 1948 helping to resettle some of those displaced by the war. Bill Potts returned to his farm but died three years later from a sudden acute illness. He was aged 48.

Major Bill Potts
[Major Ret'd C Potts TD]

Captain Charles Robert Ingram Besley was awarded the MBE for his escape and Military Cross for actions with 7RNF prior to capture. Joining 9th Battalion of the Northumberlands he was promoted and deployed to Singapore a few days before its surrender. On 14 February 1942 his party ran into a Japanese machine gun post whilst conducting a recce of new gun positions. Major Besley was killed.

Captain Bobbie Besley
[Major Ret'd C Potts TD]

ED RALDIRIS

On his return to England, Chris wrote to the brother-in-law of **Mr Raldiris** who lived in Pelham, New York. He replied:

December 10th 1940

Dear Mr Waters:-

Your favor of November 8th 1940 was received at my office yesterday and I hasten to answer and assure you that the communication to my brother-in-law will be forwarded at first opportunity. Just when that will be I can't hardly say, as much that you would like to have him know would hardly pass the French or German Censor. I will however advise him that I have had an interesting letter from you saying that both you and Mr Lennon are well, have arrived home and extend thanks for many favors etc. etc. Ed will I am sure fully understand.

I had heard in a vague reference in my Sister's letters that Ed was able to be of help to some friends but of course no names or details were mentioned.

Ed and Hattie left Vichy at the end of July and returned to Paris. In as much as Paris is in the occupied zone and no letters are permitted to enter or leave it is practically impossible to write them. But you may be sure whenever a means of communication is opened I will advise them of your thanks etc.

Even though you are in the midst of a war torn land and of necessity there can be none of the usual happiness of Christmastide may I, nevertheless, express to you my best wishes for as much happiness as can be expected and also the hope that the coming year may bring a victorious peace to you and your brave countrymen and women.

Very sincerely yours,
Henry A. Jackson

MARCELLE DUMAS

Marcelle Dumas had not forgotten the two escapees either. On 5 December she sent a telegram to Chris's father in St Albans, Hertfordshire.

> WHERE ARE CHRIS AND DENNIS LENNON STOP ANXIOUS ABOUT THEM STOP PLEASE WIRE DUMAS CECIL HOTEL VICHY

Despite the difficulties with postal communications between Vichy France and Britain, letters could get through. Chris kept a letter he received from Marcelle dated 10 May 1941: written in French, the translation is as follows.

> Dear Friends,
>
> This letter is an attempt to let you know first of all that about two months ago I received a letter from Dennis dated 28 November, but I am afraid I never received the letter mentioned in your telegram.
>
> I also did indeed receive from Casablanca the repayment of my small loan to two charming vagabonds, but I am not happy about this and am now in your debt. There will never be an end to this. All the same, many thanks but there really was no hurry.
>
> I would love to hear from you. Please will you try writing by airmail via Lisbon. I have had several letters from your country in this way, and my address is still the same.
>
> We will not be going home yet; I now have a good job and would rather stay here to wait for better times.

Dennis's letter was cut up *[i.e. censored]* so much that I still know nothing of your adventures in Spain. That is all a long time ago now.

I wrote to you two or three times at Dennis's address but don't expect you got those letters. Maybe this one will have better luck.

I received a letter from Jimmy too, also very cut up, especially his military address; I am sorry about this as I had something to tell him. He told me he was going to the Indies.

What else can I tell you, apart from the fact that time would pass very slowly if I were not so very busy.

Good luck; I hope you are both in excellent health, and send you my very best wishes.

Marcelle

Marcelle's Jimmy was Second Lieutenant J L Mainprize, Royal Corps of Signals 1st Infantry Division Signal Company, at the time Chris and Dennis were in Vichy. It is unknown if Marcelle was able to get her message to him. He was later promoted to Captain and died on the 12 December 1941 during the Japanese invasion of Malaya.

COLIN YARROW

Lieutenant Colin Drake Yarrow, Queen's Own Royal West Kent Regiment was captured at La Motte Aux Bois on the edge of the Forêt de Nieppe, approximately ten kilometres north of Robecq where Jimmy and the RWF were fighting. The 4th Battalion RWK which was in 132 Infantry Brigade, 44th Home Counties Division, had also been tasked with trying to slow the advancing enemy. The brigade had been defending and counter attacking positions along the Hazebrouck Canal from La Motte to Hazebrouck, before being forced to retreat. During the action Colin was shot. The bullet passed down his back, through his shoulder, buttock and heel.

Other members of his Battalion were less fortunate. Seven men from 'B' Company became separated from their line, finding overnight shelter in a deserted farmhouse on the eastern edge of the forest. Early the following morning they were compelled to surrender to a party of fifteen members of the German SS. On the German officer's command a rear gunner opened fire

Winners of the 1941 Football Cup with Colin in middle of back row and the tall Mike Edwards on his left. [Sir Alan Yarrow]

killing six men. The seventh survived by dropping to the ground at the sound of the first gunshot, feigning death.[33]

Colin was born in Pinner, Middlesex in 1913. He attended Harrow School, followed by Trinity College, Cambridge. In June 1934 he travelled on a tramp ship to Brazil and Latin America. Having gained a First in Engineering in 1935 he joined Selection Trust and then Metal Box in 1938. At the outbreak of war, with his parents now living near Hever in Kent, he joined the Royal West Kent Regiment. He was captured, having been wounded, on 29 May and taken to Hazebrouck for interrogation.

Having helped to conceal the disappearance of Jimmy and Tommy from Camiers for nearly twenty-four hours, Colin remained there for a while longer before being transferred to Oflag VII-D, a PoW camp for officers located in Tittmoning Castle in south-eastern Bavaria. Here he met Lieutenant Mike Edwards *(see Chapter Two)*. In February 1942 the prisoners were transferred to Oflag VII-B in Eichstatt; Tittmoning Castle became an internment camp for men from the Channel Islands of Jersey and Guernsey.

The occupants of the camp kept themselves fit and busy throughout their imprisonment. Football tournaments were held, plays and sketches

Oflag VII-D [Sir Alan Yarrow]

performed including Shakespeare's *Hamlet*, and classes were undertaken in a variety of subjects. Colin studied Law and Accountancy.

As the US Army swept through Germany in the spring of 1945, the prisoners were moved out of camp on 14 April with the intention of moving them beyond the Americans' reach. Determined to show that their spirit was undefeated the officers insisted on marching out of camp. Mistaken for a column of German troops, the PoW column was attacked by American aircraft. Fourteen British officers were killed and forty-six wounded. The camp was liberated two days later, though it was some time before transport met the men who had already started their march home.

After the war Colin returned to civilian life running the offices of Metal Box in the Far East. He first married in 1948 and two of his three children were born in Malaysia. In 1998, with his third wife, he went to Klosters in Switzerland, where his family used to ski before the war, to visit the hotel where the family had stayed. His mother had used the hotel as a forwarding address to send him food parcels during the war. Being neutral they could post them on. Arriving at the hotel, Colin asked if Herr Smidt was still alive and the old man behind reception said 'Ja, I am Smidt'. Colin introduced himself and said he had called in to say thank you for sending on the parcels some fifty years ago.

Smidt looked at him with a smile, bent down to rustle in a drawer and standing up said "I knew we would meet again. By the way here is the outstanding bill for postage which was never paid".

Colin died aged 89 in 2003.

LAMORNA

Lamorna was rebuilt as a private residence. As can be seen from these photographs taken in 2020 the balcony offers commanding views of the harbour.

[Patsy de Soisa]

HISTORICAL REPORT

OF

1ST FIELD SQUADRON RE
SEPT 1939 - JUN 1940

*Gates presented to the village church of Fontmell Magna
by the 1st Field Squadron RE [Author's collection]*

During the summer of 1939 the 1st Field Squadron RE was carrying out its customary manoeuvres with 1st Cavalry Division on Salisbury Plain, and was in camp at Tidworth when war was declared. Officers and NCO's who were with the squadron at this time are shown at Appendix A. On mobilisation the 1st Armoured Division, as it then became, concentrated in South West England, in preparation for embarkation from the southern ports. The 1st Field Squadron RE which together with the 1st Field Park Troop RE (formed on mobilisation) provided the RE element of the Division, moved its HQ, with 2 Troop (Tp) to Fontmell Magna in Dorset on 13 September. The majority of reservists had by then arrived, together with Lieutenants Fenney, Ryder and Woodcraft. 1 Tp and 3 Tp were despatched at the same time to Southampton Docks to assist in the construction of air-raid shelters. On 13 October they returned to HQ. Here the billets required much attention and between spells of what training could be carried out, had only just been made habitable when

1st Armoured Division was ordered to move to Suffolk for a concentrated divisional training programme. 1st Field Squadron with 3 Tp (Lieutenants Ryder and Fenney) and the Fd Pk Tp (Captain Barter) moved to Halstead on 2/3 November, whilst 1 Tp (Lieutenants Waters and Woodcraft) were at Newmarket and 2 Tp (Lieutenants Constant and Shepherd) at Stevenage.

Much time was again taken up in improving the billets of 1st Armoured Division rather than in collective training, and after a spell of Christmas leave the squadron moved back, on 10 January, to the Dorset area; HQ and 1 Tp returning to Fontmell Magna, 2 Tp to St Leonards, near Ringwood and 3 Tp to Wimborne. After an extremely cold spell the whole squadron went to Pangbourne on 3 March for 3 weeks wet bridging training, and from there moved south again to Corfe Mullen near Wimborne. During this period Lieutenant Rix-Trott of the New Zealand Engineers was attached.

Training at Pangbourne [Author's collection]

At last it seemed as if the Division would be joining the BEF across the channel, but it was not until 1 May that the Warning Order was received. In the meantime the squadron had been reinforced with five new officers – Lt McGrath and 2nd Lieutenants Tricker, Harley, Pratt-Johnson and Lennon, whilst Major Williams had become Commander RE 1st Armoured Division *[N.B. and was promoted to Lieutenant Colonel]* (vice Lieutenant Colonel Broomhall became General Staff Officer I) and Major Cleeve had assumed duties as Officer Commanding.

Now followed feverish activity in the quartermaster store, drawing stores and a completely new set of vehicles, loading, painting of divisional and embarkation signs, and inoculations.

On 10 May Germany invaded Holland and Belgium and the "phoney war" came to an abrupt end. On 11 May the advance party under Lieutenant McGrath left Southampton for Le Havre, and the vehicles, under Lieutenants Ryder and Harley, followed on 13 May. On 14 May *[N.B. as the Germans were crossing the Meuse]* the squadron was inspected by HM the King, accompanied by HM the Queen, who spoke to several of the men and bade the unit God Speed. Two days later the main body embarked at Portsmouth. Officers who were with the unit on embarkation were:

O.C.	Major D.W.A. Cleeve
2 i/c	Captain C.D. Waters
Subalterns	Lieutenants McGrath, Ryder, Fenney
	2nd Lieutenants Pratt-Johnson,
	Harley, Tricker, Lennon
1st Field Park Tp	Captain R.H.P. Barter. Lieutenant Clarke.

The squadron arrived at Le Havre in the early hours of 17 May, by which time the advance party had moved some 150 miles north-east to Arras. They were very soon ordered to move back and on 18 May joined the squadron at Bolbec, see sketch map, where the unit was awaiting orders under command of the Support Group, 1st Armoured Division.

On 20 May *[N.B. the day the Germans from the Meuse had reached Abbeville and the coast]*, the squadron was ordered to move at once to Mantes *[-la-Jolie?]* 85 miles south-east. No reason is recorded for this move. The roads were blocked with refugees and half the squadron became lost in the confusion. However it finally assembled at La Belle Côte *[?]* near Mantes, only to move north-west again two days later to St Saëns, some 20 miles south of Dieppe. Meanwhile German tanks were reported at St Quentin and it became only too clear what role the squadron was to fulfil from now on, and for which it had been ordered to St Saëns. This was to prepare the first of several demolition lines – on this occasion the river Béthune from Neufchâtel to Dieppe a front of some 20 miles. All three troops were employed, the dividing lines being through Osnoy and Dampierre. After all night work on 22/23 May, all the bridges were prepared for demolition. This was the squadron's first real task in France. All charges were successfully in position, when orders were received to move at 1700 hours on the same day to the river Somme, to come under command of 2 Armoured Brigade. A difficult night move of some 40 miles, with no lights, followed, and with the men already tired after the previous night's work. Four lorries came to grief.

The next day, the 24th, was the squadron's first under fire. It was now at Airaines, and 1 and 3 Tp furnished protection to AFV Armoured Fighting Vehicle recces of the river Somme in the early morning. 2 Armoured Brigade (Queens Bays and 9th Lancers) tried to seize and hold three crossings over the river, without success, and fighting took place on the river line. The squadron however suffered no casualties. The following day the units were ordered to withdraw to Hornoy, which was heavily bombed. Meanwhile three officers were sent to reconnoitre the river Bresle from Senarpont to Le Treport, in preparation for bridge demolition. They returned to Hornoy late on 26 May to find the squadron leaving for Blangy, and another difficult night move followed. Here they again came under command of the Support Group, and the same evening moved on to the Forêt du Helle.

In these pleasant surroundings, which lent an air of unreality to the war, the squadron heard the depressing news of the capitulation of the Belgians *[N.B. on the 28 May]*, and of the plight of the main body of the BEF, now cut off from the French Army. *[N.B. The BEF started evacuating from Dunkirk on 27 May and by 4 June the Germans were free to concentrate on areas of resistance elsewhere.]* What much needed rest could be taken was marred by a day of pouring rain, which ended with orders to prepare the line of the river Bresle from Haudricourt to Senarpont for demolition. This was not the sector which had previously been reconnoitred, and a difficult day followed on 29 May. All bridges were however ready for demolition by 1100 hours on the 30th and were later handed over to the Sappers of 51st Division (236 Field Company). Meanwhile a reconnaissance of the railway line from Aumale to Formerie was made, with a view to its continuation as a demolition line. Exactly how much of this was carried out is not recorded, but at least some bridges were prepared for demolition, some blown, and at least one minefield and some booby-traps laid.

So far, where casualties were concerned, the squadron had been lucky, but now our own booby-traps took the first toll, and one NCO and two other ranks were killed in an accident.

On 6 June, Sergeant Redfern and 14 men, who were carrying out work in the same area, were caught in a German attack and disappeared. The enemy were in fact now very close, and on the same day 1 Tp blew a demolition in the face of their advance. The whole unit took up a defensive position. Home-made bombs, which had previously been made of jam tins and gelignite, were handed out, and the squadron prepared to defend itself. However, no attack materialised, and late that night the squadron withdrew to the Basse Forêt D'Eu. That evening a move back to Les Grandes Ventes began, but during the move a German attack developed and the squadron became split up. A night of confusion followed. The only bridge over the river Béthune which was not blown was that at Bures. All traffic, military and civilian, including two French Divisions, poured across this bridge all night, determined to reach the south side before dawn. Somehow the squadron managed to get across and to concentrate at Les Grandes Ventes early on June 8th.

The 1st Armoured Division had meanwhile withdrawn to the south of the river Seine. What few tanks were left were in need of refit. But the Support group, including 1st Field Squadron, were attached to 51st Highland Division, and remained in the battle area. The Germans were driving westwards fast, and the way was now cut off. Rumours of evacuation were heard, and soon it was only a question of where, and when.

On 22 April, the 51st Highland Division had been detached from the rest of the BEF to come under the command of the French Third Army and was stationed by the Maginot Line. It had therefore escaped encirclement with the rest of the BEF. It was pulled back to a new line roughly along the river Somme and had to hold a line four times longer than would normally be expected. It was attacked very heavily over 5-6 June.

51st Highland Division was now working with the 4th French Division and orders were given to fall back on Le Havre, with the object of embarking there and, possibly, re-landing further down the coast.

A night move followed to the south-west, and on 9 June the squadron was concentrated at Beaunay.

The situation was fast becoming desperate. It was known that the Germans had reached Yvetot and were certain to try and cut off the British and French troops in the Le Havre peninsula. The next day 1 and 2 Tps were defending Biville in conjunction, with two troops of 237 Battery, 101st Light Anti-Aircraft and Anti-Tank Regiment RA *[which had been formed from 5th Royal Welch Fusiliers]*. Squadron HQ were still at Beaunay. In the afternoon 2 Tp were shelled resulting in several casualties.

At 1700 hours the order was received to withdraw towards St-Valéry-en-Caux. It was obvious that in the growing confusion there was no hope of getting the squadron through as a unit. Written orders were therefore given to each troop to move independently, if necessary by half troops, with each party under an officer.

That night was the worst of all. Officers peered at maps with torches heavily screened, following unfamiliar roads and trying to keep their parties under control. A party under 2nd Lieutenant Tricker were caught in a German attack and only one NCO and six men got through. The HQ party were heavily shelled and sustained several casualties. Traffic jams held up each convoy at every cross-roads, and each party of vehicles got through as best it could.

The following day, the 10th, about half the squadron arrived at St Genevieve, outside St-Valéry, where they were intermittently shelled throughout the day, and at 1800 hours moved to a wood north-east of the town, where they spent the night. The task of 51st Highland Division was now, with the French, to defend St-Valéry until ships arrived for evacuation. The Germans had reached Fécamp.

The 11th June began ominously quietly, with an occasional German reconnaissance plane overhead. The morning was spent putting what vehicles were left out of action. The expected shelling started at 1200 hours and was followed by bombing. The town of St-Valéry was soon on fire. It was said that ships would arrive that night, and those who were not detailed for the defence of the town moved down to the beach. The enemy soon commenced firing at the cliff faces from the opposite side of the bay, and several were buried in the falls of rock.

During this time squadron HQ remained in St-Valéry, and troop leaders were ordered to take as many men as possible along the beach in preparation for embarkation. Night fell, but firing and shelling continued and the town, many parts of which were ablaze, was stoutly defended. In particular all who were there will remember the courage of those who occupied the lighthouse at the end of the pier, and with machine gun fire helped to repel attacks from the West.

But no ships came into the harbour, and hopes began to fade. Those who had moved eastwards along the beach were more fortunate. At least one ship succeeded in getting close in to Veules-les-Roses, and on this Lieutenants Ryder, McGrath, Fenney and Pratt-Johnson with some fifty NCOs and men, embarked. *[N.B. In total, 2,230 men were evacuated from the Veules-les-Roses beaches during 12 June.]* Lieutenant McGrath in particular performed feats of valour during the embarkation and received the DSO. Lieutenant Fenney was awarded the Military Cross. Both these fine officers were subsequently killed in North Africa.

The following morning, the 12 June, saw the Germans in St-Valéry itself and on the cliffs above the beaches. The odds were hopelessly against the Allies caught in the town and on the beaches, and no ships could get near in daylight. Those who had got away in small boats but were still in sight of the shore were targets for German artillery, and many were sunk. At about 1100 hours Major-General Fortune, Commander of 51st Division, was compelled to surrender formally and firing ceased.

Thus, after only a month of Active Service, almost the whole of 1st Field Squadron became prisoners of war. Heart-break was dulled by reaction, and the deadly tiredness brought on by many nights without sleep. Men lay down exhausted and slept until roughly stirred by their guards, and the long trail to Germany began. The details of this dismal march need not be recorded. Of the 290 Officers and men who embarked a month previously, only four Officers and some sixty-five men returned to England. The casualties had amounted to about twenty-five killed and wounded. The remaining 200 becoming prisoners of war included Major Cleeve, the O.C., and Captain Barter O.C. of the 1st Field Park Tp. These two officers felt it their duty to stand by their NCOs and men in this hour of adversity and, with them, suffered five years of captivity, returning safely in 1945. Captain Waters and 2nd Lieutenant Lennon, two of the remaining five officers, escaped and after a five month journey through France, Spain and Gibraltar, returned to England in November.

This brings to an end the record of 1st Field Squadron in the first campaign in France; a record which, considering their inexperience and the short time in which they had to learn the arts of war, against overwhelming odds, was a fine one.

Major-General Fortune was one of the most senior British officers taken prisoner in the Second World War. He was knighted by King George VI after the war 'for his continued resistance to the Germans and services to his fellow PoWs'.

As well as the 200 REs taken prisoner, more than 10,000 members of the 51st Highland Division were captured and marched to Germany, via Belgium, following the route the Germans had advanced against them. Their destination was Stalag XX-A at Toruń, about 120 miles north-west of Warsaw. Some were loaded into canal barges for part of their journey, but all eventually travelled by train in cattle wagons. There were a number of escapes, mostly in the early stages of the march. Of the 290 British Army PoW escapees who returned to Britain by the end of June 1941, 134 were members of the 51st Highland Division.

Those still in captivity in 1945 had to endure 'the Long March' of around 450 miles to Germany in the depths of winter as the Soviets advanced.

APPENDIX A

1st Field Squadron RE
Officers and NCOs with Unit on Mobilization

Majors	H. Williams OC, D.W.A. Cleeve 2 i/c
Lieutenants	C.D. Waters 1 Tp, J. Constant 2 Tp, R.H.P. Barter 3 Tp
SSM	G.W. Bond
SQMS	Mallett, Cloke
Sergeants	Briggs, Simon, Ough, Tilsey, Jeffries, Tubb
Lance-Sergeants	Cullen, Clow, Wilkinson, Moorhead, Johnson, Chant, Ferraro, Cumper, Miles
Corporals	Kent, Harding, Templeman, Sansom, Cunliffe, French, Woods, Brockett, Plummer, Blackmore, Unthank, Rimmer
Lance-Corporals	Dick, Bray, Hardie, Chadwick, Jenkinson, Watson, Elsemore, Young, King, Leech, Harness, Baillie, Stewart, Stothart, Gale, Redfern, Barnes, Butcher, Harris, Boyes, Wolstenholme, Hall, Lee, Mayhew, Syers, Perry, Jones, Morton, Beecham, Markham, Payne, Wariner, McNairn.

APPENDIX B: *SKETCH MAP*

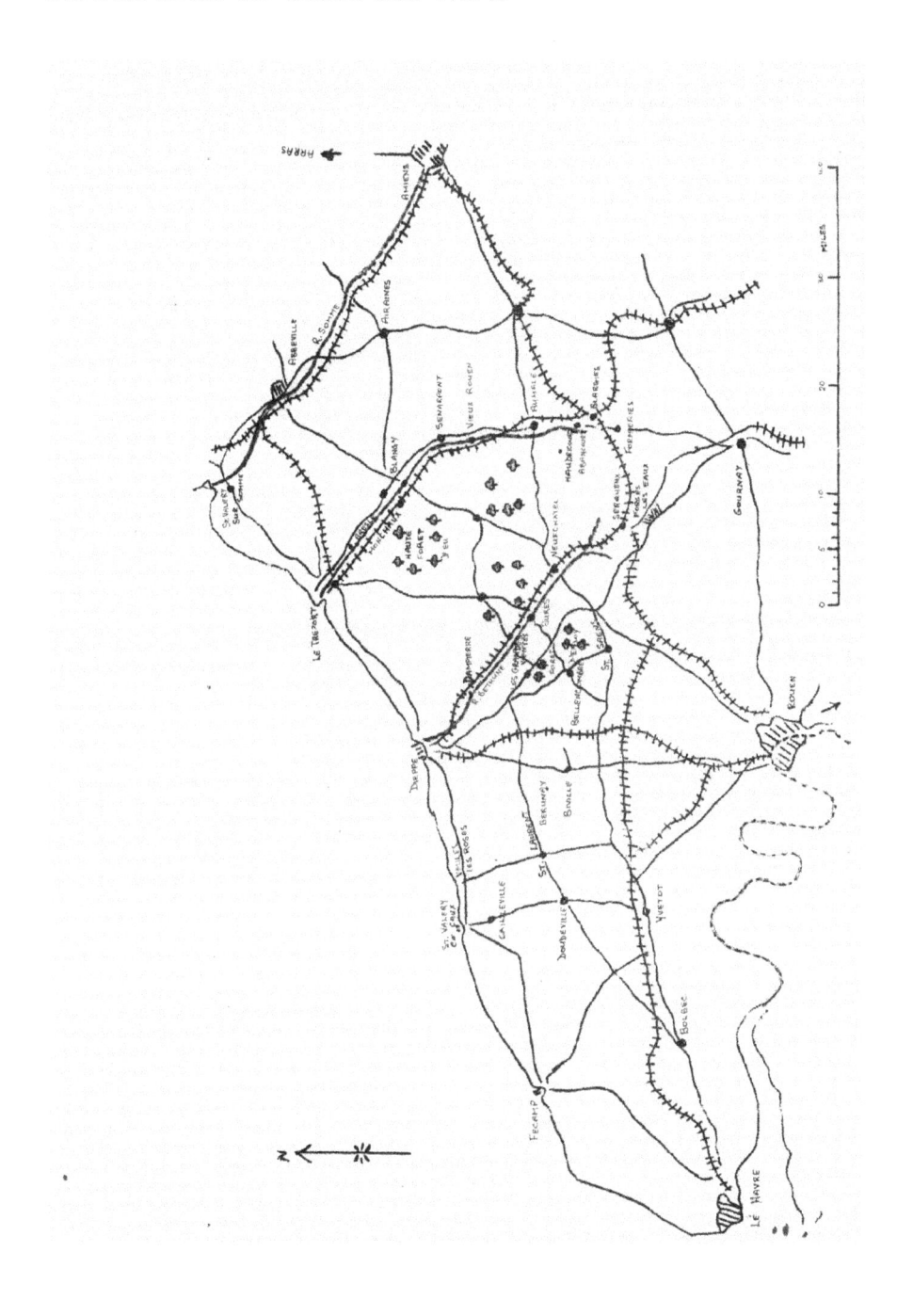

FINAL THOUGHTS AND ACKNOWLEDGEMENTS

I have long felt this is a story deserving of a wider audience. I hope you have enjoyed reading this book as much as I have enjoyed researching and compiling it.

A number of points stand out for me. Chris and Dennis met some fascinating people during their escape and by writing a journal whilst the details were fresh in their minds they have managed to bring everyone to life. Likewise their first-hand experience of the German propaganda machine starting up in a newly occupied country, the bureaucratic difficulties of Vichy France and life in Spain which was treading a thin line of neutrality between the Allies and the Axis power.

It is of note that they 'acquired' bicycles on their first day on the run and remembered not to give themselves away by cycling on the wrong side of the road. Other escapees were unable to take advantage of the opportunity so quickly and many walked or hitched all the way to the Free Zone.

The elation of every border crossing was so quickly dashed by having to face new dangers. At times it must have felt like a game of snakes and ladders without the ladders. However they were right to keep moving on. Shortly after they left Marseilles the Vichy police, accompanied by a Gestapo officer from the Harbour Commission, took to visiting the Seamen's Mission twice a week in the early hours of the morning in order to round up all the military men and escort them to Fort St-Jean. Identification papers were checked more frequently and more often at railway stations and on the trains. The American identity certificates may not have stood up to repeated scrutiny by both Vichy police and Gestapo and many escapees ended up in the prison at Toulouse.[34]

It was fortunate too that the Germans did not learn of Jimmy's family connections. If his captors had known he was the son-in-law of Admiral of the Fleet Lord Keyes who had inflicted so much damage on them in World War One, they would have kept a much closer guard on their prisoner.

To my knowledge Chris, Dennis, Hawkins and Mayhew seem to be the only men caught after crossing the Pyrenees to have avoided internment in a Spanish prison. This could have been down to their American papers declaring them as stranded seafarers, or because the Jefe in Figueras was persuaded to contact the British representative, Mr Rapley, so quickly. Most likely it was down to Mayhew declaring at such an early stage they were 'British Officers escaped from France' *(see Chapter Twelve)*. The Third Geneva Convention which replaced the 1929 Convention on Prisoners of War, allows for anyone who has escaped to be repatriated should they subsequently be caught in a neutral country, whereas evaders could be detained for the duration of a war. As a neutral country Spain was therefore obliged to release at an early date anyone declaring themselves to have escaped from captivity. The four men were very fortunate as by all accounts conditions in Spanish prisons in those days were extremely unpleasant, particularly Miranda de Ebro where so many ended up whilst the British Consul pleaded their case. Being vouched for by Chris and Dennis could also have speeded up the release of Hogg, Raikes, Jimmy and Tommy.

Having only recently come across the photograph showing the destruction of Lamorna, I find it remarkable that the manuscript survived. It is doubtful they would have remembered and recorded so many details at a later date. This would have been a loss to some of the families of those mentioned in these pages. So many were unable or unwilling to record their experiences. According to his brother, Chris was also able to return with a number of German newspapers acquired in Spain, including one with the photograph of the German soldier giving orders to the English bobby.

The kindness of the French people cannot be overlooked. So many helped to clothe, feed and shelter escaping prisoners at great personal risk. This kindness must have posed even more difficulties and dangers once the German occupation became firmly established.

Strangely I did come across a copy of Chris and Dennis's escape on the internet. My father had met a Red Cross volunteer in early 1941 and given her a copy of his manuscript. She had hung on to it, met and married an American and took it with her to America. On her death her son came across the manuscript and, not wanting it to be lost forever, uploaded it to his Oregon USA Hikers website before sending the original papers to the Imperial War Museum, where they now reside.

Many years ago, Uncle Jimmy gave me the first few pages of an unfinished manuscript he was writing. Although no more than four pages were written, it did at least give me a starting point. I must thank my cousins, Robin and Andrew, for generously allowing me to reproduce the letters Jimmy had written to Diana as well as providing additional anecdotes. Jimmy's grandson James was also very helpful searching the family albums for suitable photographs.

Finding Nigel Hogg, the son of Montie who had been with Dad and Dennis at the start and end of their escape, was most fortuitous. Nigel was able to provide additional details of the events in Gibraltar along with the boat trip back to England.

I would like to thank and acknowledge the families of all the other men mentioned in these pages who have provided so much material. Peter and Chris Lennon have been very encouraging giving me full access to their grandfather's scrapbook. Sir Alan Yarrow forwarded copies of his father's photographs taken within Oflag VII-D. A failed search for photographs of Jimmy playing rackets led me to the Royal Welch Fusiliers archives which are held at Wrexham Museum. Here Lieutenant-General J P Riley CB DSO late RWF and Chairman of the RWF Trust was enormously helpful providing details of actions relating to the RWF and other theatres of war mentioned within these pages, as well as producing photographs and drawings held by the Museum. Having a number of published books to his name he offered a wealth of experience in getting my manuscript to a presentable shape. In addition he introduced me to Rob Goodfellow who in turn put me in touch with William 'Bill' Roache. This resulted in a lovely telephone conversation with somebody who had actually served with my uncle. Meanwhile Al Poole, a former 1RWF Warrant Officer and a Trustee of the Museum Collection Trust helped me to find the Trythall family. Tommy's grandchildren, Andrew, Robert and Joanna provided photographs and family stories which enabled me to complete Tommy's story. Ipswich Memorial Society kindly put me in touch with John and Peggy Hawkins. With the help of his family, John, nephew of Flying Officer Hawkins, kindly forwarded a biography of his uncle together with photographs. Finally a telephone conversation with Major (Ret'd) Chester Potts provided me with background information on his grandfather and Captain Besley. Chester had contacted Peter Lennon some years ago. He now helped me to prepare the notes on the actions of 7RNF prior to the surrender of the 51st.

Chris Bellers of Fontmell Magna Historical Society must be mentioned for typing up Dad's manuscript, and providing dates and notes about events happening elsewhere that had an impact on both escape stories. My cartographical skills are poor so I was very grateful when Fergus Davidson offered to prepare the maps of both escape routes, whilst Erica Dutton introduced me to Powerpoint and helped produce the Timeline. Pauline Buchanan was a constant and invaluable help with the French translations, Daphne Newton kindly produced a sketch of the hospital at Camiers from an image my searches had uncovered and Cambridge University came up trumps with a copy of a letter whose original could not be found in the family archives.

Gibraltarians have also been extremely helpful. Phil Smith of the Gibraltar National Museum has been very responsive at answering a number of my questions and put me in touch with Ian Balestrino who gave me access to his article on the sinking of HMT *Stella Sirius*. I must also thank Patsy de Soisa who very kindly provided the photographs of rebuilt Lamorna.

Finally I must thank my proof readers, Kathy Eccles, Sue Lewis and Sarah Chambers, who between them have offered their varied areas of expertise to check this work. And, most importantly, special thanks must go to my husband Barry Slade who has helped to shape this book and patiently waited while I have commandeered the computer.

Timandra with her Uncle 1995

ILLUSTRATIONS

Timandra with her father Chris c1960	Frontispiece
[Author's collection]	
Chris riding Pot Luck at the Aldershot Show 1939	2
[Author's collection]	
Dennis sketching on a river bank 1938	3
[Reproduced by kind permission of the Lennon family]	
2nd Battalion Polo Team	5
[Reproduced by kind permission of the RWF Museum Trust]	
Harold and his bride Lucy in 1922	8
[Reproduced by kind permission of the Trythall family]	
Digging in at Ottenburg	12
[Reproduced by kind permission of the RWF Museum Trust]	
German tank at St Venant	13
[Reproduced by kind permission of the RWF Museum Trust]	
Germans crossing the bridge at St Venant	14
[Reproduced by kind permission of the RWF Museum Trust]	
Captured Aid Station at St Venant	16
[Reproduced by kind permission of the RWF Museum Trust]	
PoW Arrival March – water colour by WSA Clough-Taylor	17
[Reproduced by kind permission of the RWF Museum Trust]	
St-Valéry-en-Caux late 1930s?	26
[Author's collection]	
The map taken from the estaminet	35
The Times 28 June 1940	51
[Author's collection]	

Sketch of Notre Dame de la Garde – by Dennis Lennon | 69
   [Reproduced by kind permission of the Lennon family]
Dennis's Certificate of Identity | 70
   [Reproduced by kind permission of the Lennon family]
The entrance to the train tunnel at Cerbére | 76
Sketch of market day at Figueras – by Dennis Lennon | 89
   [Reproduced by kind permission of the Lennon family]
Gerona rooftop 1 | 99
Gerona rooftop 2 | 100
   [Author's collection]
Sketch of Camiers TB Sanatorium – by Daphne Newton | 108
Port Vendres, 1928 – by Bloomsbury Group member Roger Fry [1866-1934] | 127
   [Reproduced by kind permission of Philip Mould & Company]
Jimmy Johnson in Perpignan | 134
   [Reproduced by kind permission of the Johnson family]
Lamorna September 1940 | 154
   [Reproduced by kind permission of Gibraltar National Museum]
Gibraltar – Catalan Bay 1940 | 158
   [Author's collection]
Flying Office Ron Hawkins | 174
   [Reproduced by kind permission of the Hawkins family]

POSTSCRIPT

Tommy Trythall | 189
   [Reproduced by kind permission of the Trythall family]
Gibraltar Cross of Sacrifice | 189
Lieutenant Peter Raikes's grave | 189
   [Author's collection]
Chris's LVT at Walcheren 1944 | 191
   [Author's collection]
Chris dinghy sailing at Instow, Devon | 191
   [Author's collection]
Chris Waters | 192
   [Author's collection]
Dennis showing HM The Queen a model of the *QE2* | 193
   [Reproduced by kind permission of the Lennon family]
Hamper Mill c1968 | 193
   [Reproduced by kind permission of the Lennon family]

Dennis Lennon — 194
  [Reproduced by kind permission of the Lennon family]
Jimmy and Diana Johnson with Robin at Sara's christening — 195
  [Reproduced by kind permission of the Johnson family]
Jimmy Johnson — 195
  [Reproduced by kind permission of the Johnson family]
Jimmy on the set of 55 Days in Peking — 196
  [Reproduced by kind permission of the Johnson family]
Montie Hogg and his bride Betty — 197
  [Reproduced by kind permission of the Hogg family]
Hawkins two years after his escape — 198
  [Reproduced by kind permission of the Hawkins family]
Major Bill Potts — 200
  [Reproduced by kind permission of Major (Ret'd) Chester Potts TD]
Captain Bobbie Besley — 201
  [Reproduced by kind permission of Major (Ret'd) Chester Potts TD]
Winners of the 1941 Football Cup — 204
  [Reproduced by kind permission of Sir Alan Yarrow]
Oflag VII-D — 205
  [Reproduced by kind permission of Sir Alan Yarrow]
Colin Yarrow in Oflag VII-D — 205
  [Reproduced by kind permission of Sir Alan Yarrow]
Lamorna 2020 — 206
  [Reproduced by kind permission of Patsy de Soisa]

HISTORICAL REPORT

Gates presented to the village church of Fontmell Magna — 209
Training at Pangbourne — 210
Appendix B – Sketch map — 218
  [All Author's collection]

Timandra with her Uncle 1995 — 222
  [Author's collection]

FURTHER READING

Books:

Andrew Bradford, *Escape from St-Valéry-en-Caux – the Adventures of Captain B.C. Bradford* (Stroud, 2009)

Donald Caskie, *The Tartan Pimpernel* (Edinburgh, 1999)

Winston S. Churchill, *The Second World War, Volume II, Their Finest Hour* (London, 1949)

Rob Goodfellow, Jonathan Copeland and Peter O'Neill, *Reflections on The Times and Life of William 'Bill' Roache: Actor for the Ages* (Auckland New Zealand, 2022)

Bill Innes, *St Valery The Impossible Odds* (Edinburgh, 2004)

Gordon Instone, *Freedom is the Spur* (London, 1965)

Elizabeth Keyes, *Geoffrey Keyes VC of the Rommel Raid* (London, 1956)

Sir Roger Keyes, *Adventures Ashore and Afloat* (London, 1939)

J.M. Langley, *Fight Another Day* (London, 1974 reprinted Barnsley, 2013)

Sean Longden, *Dunkirk: The Men They Left Behind* (Stroud, 2009)

Arthur J Marder, *Operation Menace – The Dakar Expedition and the Dudley North Affair* (Oxford 1976)

Airey Neave, *Flames of Calais: A Soldier's Battle 1940* (London, 1974)

P.R. Reid, *The Colditz Story* (reprinted London, 1983)

Lt-General Jonathon Riley, Lt-Colonel Peter Crocker and the late Lt-Colonel Richard Sinnett, *Regimental Records of the Royal Welch Fusiliers, Vol. V, Part One, November 1918 – May 1940* (Solihull, 2019)

Major R.S. Waters, *Simple Tactical Schemes with Solutions* (Forgotten Books, reprinted 2016)

Major R.S. Waters, *History of the 5th Battalion (Pathans) 14th Punjab Regiment formerly 40th Pathans: (The Forty Thieves)* (London, 1936)

Articles in Journals:

Ian Balestrino, 'The Bombing and Sinking of HMT Stella Sirius', *Gibraltar Heritage Journal,* 2019

Major R.S. Waters, 'Ballooning in the French Army during the Revolutionary Wars', *Army Quarterly* Vol. XXIII, No 2

Major R.S. Waters, 'Reminiscences of the Mobile Reserve Detachment, 13 Company and E Company, 15th Battalion Hertfordshire Home Guard by Salwekhtama', *Hertfordshire Archives and Local Studies* D/EYo/4/19

On-line Resources:

www.barrymerchantseamen.org.uk
www.convoyweb.org.uk
www.conscript-heroes.com
www.flamesofwar.com – British 1st Armoured Division, May 1940

ENDNOTES

1. 2nd Searchlight Battery War Diary, T.N.A. WO 167/681
2. http://ww2talk.com/index.php?threads/captain-anthony-donnithorne-taylor-m-c-15-19-the-kings-royal-hussars.19612/ Accessed September 2021
3. T.N.A. WO 208/3299/90
4. Bridge, Carl 'Churchill, Hoare, Derby, and the Committee of Privileges, April to June 1934', *The Historical Journal*, vol. 22, no. 1, 1979, pp. 215–227. www.jstor.org/stable/2639020. Accessed 22 February 2021
5. War History OnLine Sept25, 2016 *Churchill ordered millions of pounds paid in bribes to keep Spain out of World War Two* Accessed December 2020
6. J M Langley, *Fight Another Day*, (London, 1974), p141
7. Matt Nesvisky 'The Allies, Spain and Oil in WWII', *The National Bureau of Economic Research*
8. https://www.europeanmemories.net>memorial-heritage/camp-dinternement-de-saint-cyprien accessed December 2020
9. https://www.Apra.asso.fr/Camps/en/camp-st-cyprien accessed December 2020
10. Papers of Sir Samuel John Gurney Hoare (1880-1959), second Baronet, and first and last Viscount Templewood – Cambridge University Library XIII:2(37)
11. https://www.naval-history.net/WW2CampaignsUboats.htm accessed 10 February 2021
12. Winston S Churchill, *History of the Second World War Volume II, Their Finest Hour* – (London, 1949) p 528-529
13. https://barrymerchantseamen.org.uk/articles/bmsww2part1.html Accessed February 2021
14. https://historicalrfa.org/requisitioned-auxiliaries/160-requisitioned-auxiliaries-a/1462-requisitioned-auxiliary-ardeola Accessed January 2021
15. https://www.naval-history.net/xGM-Chrono-10DD-23F-HMS_Firedrake.htm Accessed December 2020
16. https://ww2aircraft.net/forum/threads/this-day-in-the-war-in-europe-the-beginning.41546/page-64
17. https://www.naval-history.net/xDKWW2-4010-23OCT02.htm Accessed 12 February 2021
18. https://www.naval-history.net/xDKWW2-4010-23OCT01.htm Accessed 12 February 2021
19. Winston S Churchill, *Their Finest Hour* Chapter XXIV

20 https://paperspast.natlib.govt.nz/newspapers/WT19400925.2.53 Accessed 28 July 2021
21 T.N.A. WO 208/3300/134
22 T.N.A. WO 208/3300/121
23 T.N.A. WO 208/3299/43
24 https://www.researching ww2.co.uk/field-company-bef accessed 10 February 2021
25 Major-General R P Pakenham-Walsh *History of the Corps of the Royal Engineers Vol VIII 1938-1948* pps 43-44 'South of the German Break-through', Chatham, 1958
26 Captain Bradford – See further reading Conscript Heroes
27 Captain Garrow, Captain Fitch and Lieutenant Sillar – ditto
28 T.N.A. WO 208/3299/80
29 T.N.A. WO 208/3299/72
30 T.N.A. WO 373/60/325
31 T.N.A. WO 208/3299/88
32 https://www.northlincsweb.net/103Sqn/html/ronald_hawkins_103_squadron.html Accessed December 2020
33 https://www.tracesofwar.com/persons/71763/Bell-Bertie.htm Accessed September 2021
34 Gregor Macdonald, *St Valery The Impossible Odds* Chapters *The Tartan Pimpernel* and *The Work of Rev. Donald Caskie* – see further reading

INDEX

Abbeville, 24, *37*, 171, 177, 180-3, 211
Admiral Beatty, 6
Admiral Jellico, 6
American Consul Marseilles, 71,130, 133-4, 171, 185
American Consul Perpignan, 184
Amiens, *37*, 41, 180, 181, 183
Anderson, 2/Lt, RA, 10
Ardennes, 7, 171
Aubigny, *54*, 55
Aumale, 25, 212
Australia, 1, 4, 132, 191
Auxi-le-Château, *37*, 40
AVRE, 190
Awards and Decorations:
    Air Force Cross, 199
    CBE, 193
    DSO, 10, 194, 215
    MBE, 190, 201
    Mention, 186, 189, 190, 192
    Military Cross, 6, 10, 22n, 189, 192, 194, 198, 200, 201, 215
    Military Medal, 184
    OBE, 1, 10, 191, 195, 196
    TD, 10, 180
    Victoria Cross, 6

Ball, Lt, RAMC, 153-4, 157
Barcelona, *83*, 94, 141-142
Barclays Bank, 8, 124
Barter, Capt R H P, RE, 210-11, 215, 217
Benerville, 116-17, 119, 126
Besley, Capt C R I, 7RNF, 63-4, 68, 103, 170-4, 201

Béthune, 13, 32, *37*, 58, 180
Bloomsbury Group, *127*, 197, 224
Bonella, Pvt, RE, 27
Boxer Rebellion, 4, 196
Boyle, Lt, RWF, 13-14
Bradford, Capt B C, 1st BW, 179, 227
Brest, 25, *101*
British Army Units, Corps and Regiments:
    1 Armoured Brigade, 27
    1st Armoured Division, 24, 51, 209-13
        Support Group, 24-6, 211-12
    1st Army, 194
    1st Infantry Division, 176
    2 Armoured Brigade, 212
    2nd Infantry Division, 7, 14
    6th Infantry Brigade, 124
    6th Motor Ambulance Convoy, 184-5
    7th Armoured Division, 192
    8th Army, 192
    51st Highland Division, 21, 24-7, 46, 95-6, 171, 176-7, 180, 182, 213-16
    79th Armoured Division, 190
    Artists Rifles, 4
    Black Watch, 93, 96, 158,179
    Combined Operations, 6, 190
    Durham Light Infantry, 194
        14th Battalion DLI, 200
    Gordon Highlanders, 27, 137, 182-3
    Mounted Military Police, 7
    Queen's Own Royal West Kent Regiment
        4th Battalion, 18, 203
    Royal Army Medical Corps, 150, 154, 179, 185
    Royal Artillery, 109, 168

Searchlight Regiment, 8-10, 111, 125
Royal Corps of Signals
    1st Infantry Division, 203
Royal Engineers, 1, 2, 4, 10, 234
    1st Armoured Engineer Brigade, 27, 190
    1st Field Park Troop, 24, 209, 211
    1st Field Squadron, 2, 4, 24-7, 49-51, 145, 177, 209-15
    7th Field Squadron, 192
    26th Assault Squadron, 190
    26th Field Company, 31, 176-7
    77th Assault Squadron, 190
    236th Field Company, 180, 212
    237th Field Company, 180
    239th Field Park Company, 180
Royal Northumberland Fusiliers
    7 Battalion, 170-71, 201
    9 Battalion, 201
Royal Scots Greys, 6
Royal Welch Fusiliers, 4, 14, 109n, 194-7, 214, 221, 227
    1st Battalion, 4, 7, 12-15, 195
    2nd Battalion, 4, 5
    5th Battalion, 214
    8th Battalion, 194
    9th Battalion, 194
    115 (Royal Welch) Infantry Brigade, 194
Surrey Yeomanry, 7
Territorial Army, 7-8, 10, 171-2, 180, 182, 185
The Kings Own Yorkshire LI
    2/4th Battalion, 194
The Kings Royal Hussars
    15th/19th Regiment, 21-2
British Consulate:
    Marseilles, 71-3
    Vice Consul Barcelona, 90-8, 140-42, 180
    Vice Consul Figueras, 84, 86-7
    Vice Consul Geneva, 137
    Vice Consul Gerona, 173
    Vice Consul Perpignan, 129
British Embassy Madrid, 92, 95, 142-3, 155-6
British Expeditionary Force, xvii-xviii, 7, 9, 13, 24, 46, 49, 161, 212
British Indian Army, 40th Pathans, 1
Burger, Pvt P, 46-9

Calais, 9-11, 24, 34, *37*, 125, 227
Cambridge University, 2, 141, 143, 204, 222

Camiers, 11, 107-11, *108, 115*, 126, 204
Cardigan, Lt The Earl of, RAMC, 143, 150, 153, *158*, 184-6
Caskie, Rev Donald, 71-2n, 185, 227
Castillo Figueras, 140, 173, 182, 186
Cerbère, 75-8, *77*, 94
Certificate of Identity, *70*, 71-5, 78, 81, 219
Cervera, 173, 182, 186
Chamberlain, Neville, xvii-xviii, 155
Channel Islands, 89, 116-17, 126, 176, 204
Chantilly, *37*, 43
Charterhouse, 2, 4
Châteaudun, 184
Châteauroux, *54, 57*-58, *120*, 122, 126, 184
Cherbourg, 24, 25, 163
Christopher, Capt L de L, 40th Pathans, 2
Churchill, Winston, xviii, 6, 9, 58, 102, 156, 160, 163n, 166-7, 195, 227
Cleeve, Maj David, RE, 26, 32n, 33, 50, 211, 215
Cloke, Sergeant Major, RE, 27, 217
Clough-Taylor, Capt W S A, RWF, *5*, 18, 109
Clubbs, PSM R, GH, 137-141, 143, 182-4
Codd, Corp, RWF, 109
Colditz, 10n, 15, 17, 32n, 227
Conran, Terence, 192
Convoys:
    HG45, 161-4,
    HX79, 163n
    OG44, 163
    SC7, 163n
    SL50, 163-4
Cour-sur-Loire, 119, *120*

Dakar, 166-9, 172, 227
Dalmahoy, Capt J F C, 40th Pathans, 2
Davies 49, CSM G, RWF, 17
Deauville 116, 118n
de Gaulle, Gen Charles, 166-9
Deighton, Maj, RA, 10, 125, 128
Dodds, Maj, 71, 185
Dohem, 34, 36, *37*
Dorchy, Mrs, *99*
Dorchy, Paul, 90, 141
Doullens, 18, 31, *37*, 40, 115, 180
Duke of Windsor, 90
Dumas, Marcelle, 62, 65, 202-3
Dunkerque, 58-61
Dunkirk, 7, 9, 24, 46, 62, *115*, 189, 227

Eden, Anthony, 9

Edwards, Lt Mike, RWF, 15, *204*
Eisenhower, Dwight D, 151, 195
El-Alamein, 96, 192, 215
Espolla, 138, 173
Evans 57, RWF, 109
Evans 74, RWF, 109
Evans, F/Lt A J, RAF, 151
Evans, Major-Gen Roger, 24
Évreux, *37*, 175

Fenney, Lt George, RE, 26, 50, 209-15
Figueras, *77*, 83, 85-9, *138*, 139-40
Films:
    55 Days at Peking, 196
    From Russia with Love, 17
    The Desert Fox, 6
    The Longest Day, 196
Fitch, A/Capt, Norfolk Regiment, 179
Flixecourt, 183
Fonda Mallol, Hotel, 87, 89
Fontainebleau, 52-3, *54*
Fontmell Magna, 4, 192, *209*, 209-10
Force H, 162, 168
Fort St-Jean, 72, 172-3, 182, 185, 219
Fortune, Major-Gen V, 177, 215
Franco, Gen F, 88, 102-3
French Armistice, 22-3, 36, 128, 166, 172
French Army:
    3rd Army, 213
    4th Division, 213
    7th Army, 24
    9th Corps, 25, 177

Gallipoli, 5, 7
Garrow, Capt Ian, HLI, 179
Geneva Convention, 130, 220
Gerona, *77*, 92, 97-100, *99*, 143
Gewurtz, 129, 131-2
Gibraltar, 4, 52, 65, 88-9, 142-4, 149-54, 157-60, 167-9, 172-3, 189, 222
Gibraltar Cross of Sacrifice, *189*
Gilchrist, L Corp, RWF, 17
Gort Line, 7
Gran Hotel, Figueras, 86, 88, 90
Grant, Jacqueline, 20-22
Greece, 150, 190, 196
Guardia Civil, 82, 144, 179, 186

Harness, Sergeant, RE, 27, 217
Harrow School, 204
Hawkins, F/O Ron, RAF, 71n, 73-4, *99*, *100*, 143-4, 151, 160-1, 174-6, 198-200
Hazebrouck, 34, *37*, 203
Heywood, Maj, Royal Artillery, 9
Hitler, Adolf, xvii-xviii, 6, 16, 39, 66, 89, 90, 165
HM King George VI, 4, 189, 211, 215
HM Queen Elizabeth, 4, 211
HM Queen Elizabeth II, *193*, 195
HMAS *Australia*, 167-8
HMS *Firedrake*, 152, 162, 168
HMS *Pretoria Castle*, 163
HMS *Renown*, 150, 152, 168
HMS *Scarborough*, 163n
HMT *Arctic Ranger*, 152
HMT *Stella Sirius*, 152, 157, 169, 228
Hoare, Sir Samuel, 102-3, 143, 155-6, 173
Hogg, Lt H S Montie, RE, 31-2, 91-2, *99*, 142-3, 150-4, 158-9, 162-5, 176-80, 197-8
Holland, xvii, 37-8, 149, 190, 199, 211
Hong Kong, 1, 4, 6, 198
Hotel Bristol, Barcelona, 141, 142
Hotel Peninsular, Gerona, 97-101, 143
Hotel Royal Picardy, 107
Hughes 87, RWF, 109

Jersey – *see Channel Islands*
Johnson, Diana, 4, 6, 21, 135, 140, 152, 164-5, 195, 197
Johnson, Jimmy, 4-7, 12-23, 91, 105-44, 150-65, 194-97
Johnson, Robert, RWF, 4, 7
Johnson, Robin, 7, 118n, 124n, *195*

Kenyon, Capt W P, RWF, *5*
Keyes, Elizabeth, 124, 227
Keyes, Lt Col Geoffrey, RSG, 6, 227
Keyes, Lady, 4, 6, 165
Keyes, Lord, 4-6, 110, 155, 162, 196, 227
Keyes, Phyllis, 197
Krombeke, 185

l'Etoile, 115
La Bassée Canal, 13-14, 180
Lamorna, 150-4, 158-9, 206, *206*
Laniel, M., 195
Le Havre, 24, 25, 27, *37*, 51, 177, 211, 213
Lennon, Dennis, 3-4, 24-7, 29-101, 142-45, 150-54, 157-65, 192-4, 210-15
Lennon, John, 3, 46-9, 51, 93-4
Leopold III, King of the Belgians, 6, 40
Le Touquet, 11, 18-22, 114, *115*, 125

Liomer, 115, 116
Lisieux, 116, *117,* 126
Llewelyn, 2/Lt Desmond, RWF, 16-17n
Lorris, 53, *54*
LVT, 190, *191*

Madrid, 87, 100, 142-3
Maginot Line, xviii, 7, 171-2n, 176, 213
Mainprize, 2/Lt J L, RCS, 62, 203
Marguerite, M., 117-18n
Marles, 115
Marseilles, 1, 45, 67-73, *83,* 94, 171-3, 176, 185, 219
Mayhew, Sous-Officier, 73-5, 81-3, 86-7, 97, *99-100*, 141, 176, 200
McGrath, Lt, RE, 215
McLennan, Joan, 132n
Mennetou-sur-Cher, *120,* 184
Merchant Taylor's School, 3
Mers-el-Kébir, 59, *101,* 152, 166, 168
Méry-sur-Cher, *54, 55, 120*
MI6, 102-3
MI9, 10n, 31n, 95, 103, 151, 165, 170
Miranda de Ebro, 143, 173, 186
Montreuil, 114
Morocco, 143, 151, 166-7, 172, 192, 202
Munich Agreement, 6
MV *British Coast*, 161-4

Narbonne, 75, *83,* 123, 184
Neave, 2/Lt Airey, 10n, 227
Netherlands – see Holland
Neufchâtel, 37, *37,* 180, 212
New Zealand Field Artillery, 7
Nicholson, Brig C, 9
Norway, xviii, 6

Oflag IV-C – *see Colditz*
Oflag VII-B – Eichstatt, 204
Oflag VII-C – Laufen, 17
Oflag VII-D – *see Tittmoning*
Oliver, 2/Lt, RA, 10
Operation *Infatuate*, 190
Operation *Menace*, 166-8, 227
Operation *Plunder*, 96n
Operation *Sealion*, 117, 165
Osséja, *101,* 179

Paris, *37,* 38, 39-45, 72, 95, 171, 181, 201
Parker-Jervis, Lt E C, RWF, *5*, 20n
Parole, 122n, 137, 172, 179

Pathé News, 6
Pat O'Leary Line, 10n
Perpignan, 74-75, *77,* 123, 127, 129, 133-6, 151, 179, 184
Plato Unico, 88
Ponches, 115
Portugal, 65-6, 84, 90n, 93-4, 161
Port-Vendres, 75-6, *77,* 123, *127,* 129, 182
Potts, Maj W C W, 7RNF, 63-4, 68, 170-2, 182, 200
Pourtabourde, M., 44
Pyrenees, 75-80, 83, 98, 136-8, 182, 186

QEII, 193
Quincanpoix, 177

Raikes, Capt Peter P, RE, 27, 31, 91-2, *99-100*, 143, 150-4, 157, 177-80, 189
Raldiris, E, 63, 65, 201-2
Rapley, Mr, 86-7, 90-1, 97
Red Cross, 20, 108, 124, 131, 134, 181, 220
Rennie, Maj Tom, Black Watch, 93-6
RIBA, 3
Richards, Sapper J J, RE, 91, 140, 180-2
Rivers:
    Arnon, *54,* 56
    Authie, 115, 126
    Béthune, 212-3
    Bresle, 25, 171, 177, 212
    Canche, 115, 126
    Cher, *54, 55, 56*, 119-21, 126, 184
    Escaut, 13
    Loire, *54,* 119-20, *120,* 126, 184
    Orne, 178
    Seine, 25, *37,* 44, 51, 116, *117,* 126, 175, 177, 178, 183-4, 213
    Somme, 22, 24, *37,* 115-6, 126, 212-3
    Touques, 117, *120*
Rix-Trott, Lt, NZ Engineers, 210
Roache, William 'Bill', 195, 196n, 221
Robecq, 7, 13-15, *115,* 203
Rocé, 118, *120*
Rommel, Field Marshall E, 6
Ronchois, 116, *117*
Rouen, 31-2, *37,* 116, 173, 177
Royal Air Force:
    No 3 Squadron, 199
    No 56 Squadron, 199
    No 98 Squadron, 174
    No 103 (B) Squadron, 174
    No 202 Squadron, 151, 161

No 309 (Polish) Squadron, 199
Royal Military Academy, 2, 152
Ruyssevelt, F van, 37-8
Ryder, Lt, RE, 209-15

Sailly, 183
Saint-Aubin-lès-Elbeuf, 116, *117*
St-Cyprien, 91, 125, 128-37, *138*, 182, 184
St Pol, 17-18, 31, *115*, 180

St Geneviève, 25, 214
St-Valéry, 4, 21, 25-32, *26*, *37*, 49-50, 75, 83, 93, 114, 116, 171-2, 177, 214-5
St Venant, 7, 13, *14*, *16*, 18, 197
Samer, 37, *37*
Scheldt Estuary, 190, 199
Seamen's Mission, Marseilles, 71-3, 94, 171, 185, 219
Shaw, George Bernard, 66
Shell-Mex, 3, 47
Sillar, Lt, RAMC, 179
Somaliland, 88n
Somme Battle of, WWI, 7
Sommery, 116, *117*
Sougé, *54*, 174
Spain, 34, 45, 52, 80, 93-5, 102-3, 149
Spanish Civil War, 86-8, 98, 102, 128

Tasmania, 6
Taylor, Capt A D, 15th/19th KRH, 21-2
Templewood, Lord – *see Hoare, Sir Samuel*
Thatcher, Margaret, 10n
Thynne, Fsl, RWF, 109
Tingewick, 131, 165, 194, 197
Tittmoning, 15, 204, *205*
Torre-Torr, Brig W W, 95, 98, 100, 143
Tourgéville, 116, *117*
Tournai, 180, 185
Trafalgar Battle of, 149, 151
Tricker, 2/Lt, RE, 210-211, 214
Trythall, Arthur, NZ FA, 7
Trythall, David, 189
Trythall, John, 189
Trythall, Lucy, *8*, 125, 151, 159
Trythall, Tommy 7-11, 109-44, 150-54, 157, 189
Turvey, SM, RWF, 17

Uhlman, Johannes, 66-67, 71

Vendôme, 119, *120*

Vernou, 184
Veules-les-Roses, 26, 215
Vichy, *54*, 60-5, 68, 93, 157, 171, 176, 201-2
Vichy Government, 59, 78, 129-30, 152, 165-72, 202, 219-20
Vierzon, *54*, 55, 181
Vilamaniscle, *77*, 82-5

Waters, Chris, 1-2, 24-27, 29-101, 142-45, 150-54, 157-65, 190-92, 209-217
Waters, Lee, 93
Waters, Maj R S Ret'd, 1-2, 49-51, 93, 221, 222
Whitfield, Mr, 90-2, 97-9, 140, 142, 182
Widehem, 112, *115*
Williams, Col H, RE, 49-51, 211
Williams, L/C, RWF, 109
Wingrove, Sam, RA, 11
Wodehouse, P G, 20n
Woodcraft, Lt, RE, 209-10, 215
Woolwich Military Academy, 2, 152, 158

Yarrow, 2/Lt Colin, QOR WKR, 18, 20-2, 107-11, 203-6
Younger, Maj A, RE, 190
Younghusband, Lt-Col Sir F E, 1
Ypres, 1, 185

Zanuck, Daryl F, 196
Zeebrugge, 6

This book is printed on paper from sustainable sources managed under the Forest Stewardship Council (FSC) scheme.

It has been printed in the UK to reduce transportation miles and their impact upon the environment.

For every new title that Matador publishes, we plant a tree to offset CO_2, partnering with the More Trees scheme.

MORE TREES
LET'S PLANT A BILLION TREES

For more about how Matador offsets its environmental impact, see www.troubador.co.uk/about/

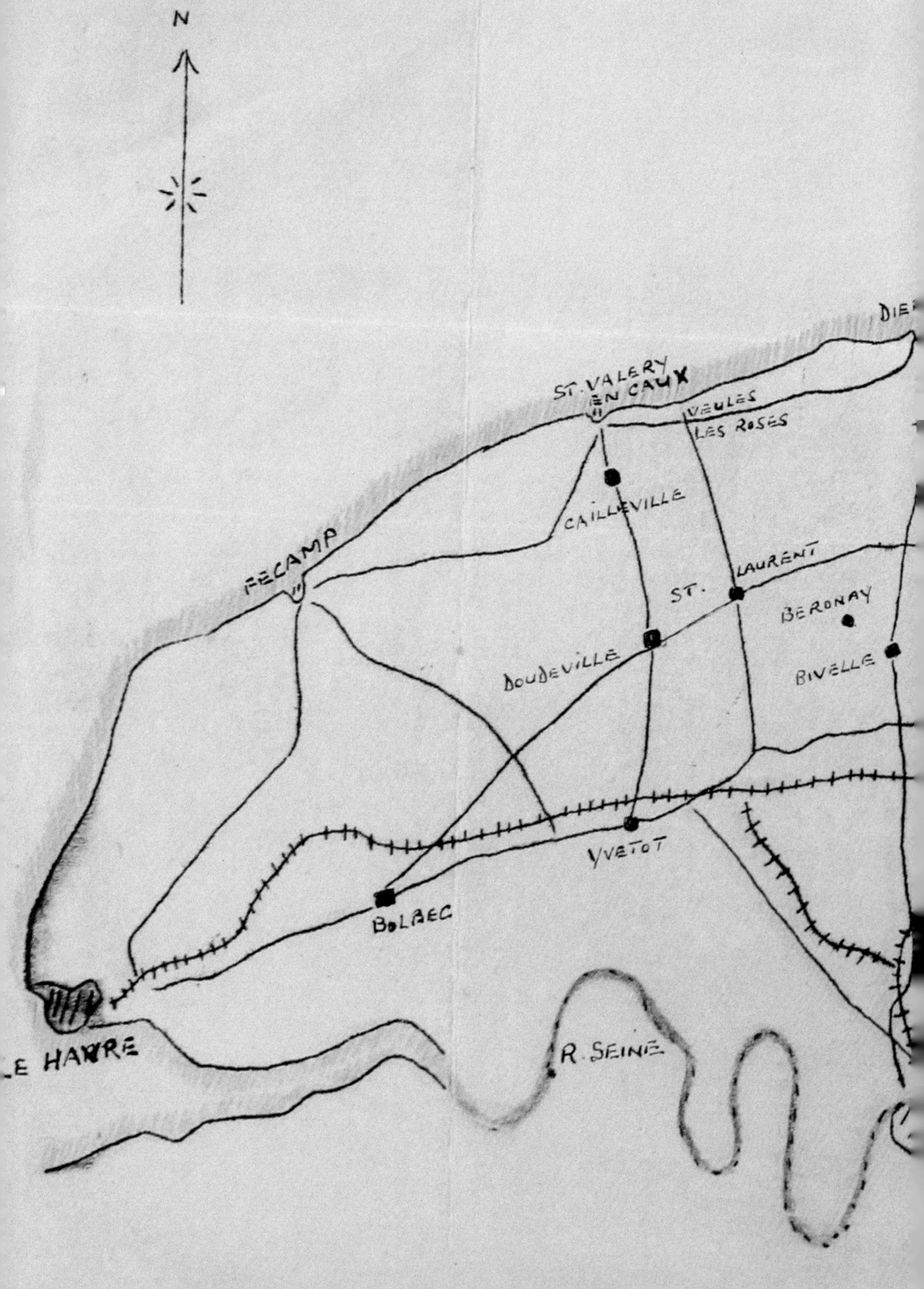

N
DIE
ST. VALERY
EN CAUX
VEULES
LES ROSES
CAILLEVILLE
FECAMP
ST. LAURENT
BERONAY
DOUDEVILLE
BIVELLE
YVETOT
BOLBEC
LE HAVRE
R. SEINE